Planning and Evaluating Computer Education Programs

edited by

Randy Elliot Bennett

Educational Testing Service

Merrill Publishing Company
A Bell & Howell Information Company
Columbus   Toronto   London   Melbourne

Cover Photo: Merrill/Lloyd Lemmerman

Published by Merrill Publishing Company
A Bell & Howell Information Company
Columbus, Ohio 43216

This book was set in Futura Light.

Administrative Editor: Jennifer Knerr
Cover Designer: Cathy Watterson

Library of Congress Catalog Card Number: 86-63010

International Standard Book Number: 0-675-20499-2

Printed in the United States of America

1 2 3 4 5 6 7 8 9—92 91 90 89 88 87

Contributors

Randy Elliot Bennett
Senior Research Scientist and Director, Technology Lab
Educational Testing Service, Princeton, New Jersey

Gary Bitter
Professor of Computer Education, Microcomputer Based Learning and Research Department
Arizona State University, Tempe, Arizona

Lud Braun
Director, Academic Computing Laboratory
New York Institute of Technology, Central Islip, New York

Terence R. Cannings
Associate Professor of Education
Pepperdine University, Los Angeles, California

John F. De Gilio
Lecturer, Education Department
Vassar College, Poughkeepsie, New York

John M. Hanna
Director of Personnel
Fort Knox Community Schools, Fort Knox, Kentucky

Donald C. Holznagel
Director, Computer Technology Program
Northwest Regional Educational Laboratory, Portland, Oregon

Robert J. Illback
Director of Student Services
Fort Knox Community Schools, Fort Knox, Kentucky

Howard Kimmel
Director, Center for Pre-College Programs
New Jersey Institute of Technology, Newark, New Jersey

John F. McManus
Professor of Education
Pepperdine University, Los Angeles, California

Stephen M. Shuller
Computer Studies Department Head
Scarsdale High School, Scarsdale, New York (formerly with Bank Street College of Education)

Stan Silverman
Assistant Director, Academic Computing Laboratory
New York Institute of Technology, Central Islip, New York

Brian Stecher
Professional Associate
Educational Testing Service, Los Angeles, California

Susan Wilson
Senior Research Assistant
Educational Testing Service, Princeton, New Jersey

Preface

In the fall of 1980, the nation's elementary and secondary schools owned some 31,000 microcomputers. By mid-1985, this number had surged to over a million. By 1990 more than three million microcomputers will be housed in the schools.

The phenomenal rate at which schools are purchasing microcomputers has created an urgent need for knowledge about the effective use of computer technology in education. Teacher trainers skilled in the use of microcomputers, as well as computer-literate teachers and school administrators, are badly needed. To meet this demand, colleges and universities are offering courses and specializations in educational computing, and school districts and state education departments are developing in-service courses to give personnel the competencies they need to apply computer technology sensibly.

These various educational programs require information resources, particularly materials that will help teachers, administrators, and teacher trainers understand the substantial amount of planning involved in purchasing microcomputers and incorporating them into the school curriculum. Many educators do not realize, for example, that acquiring microcomputers often entails costs significantly greater than those for hardware alone. Among these additional expenses are software to make the machines perform specific tasks, training programs to help teachers learn to operate the machines and effectively integrate them with the curriculum, and facilities to house and protect the district's hardware and software investment.

These program-planning resources must be reinforced by materials geared to help teachers and administrators learn to evaluate computer education efforts. Without evaluation, teachers and administrators cannot know (1) to what use a district's computers are being put, (2) whether particular groups of students (e.g., females, minority group members, handicapped students) are being unintentionally excluded from computer education programs, (3) whether to use computers in place of traditional methods of instruction, and (4) whether particular computer education programs should be extended to other grade levels and school buildings. *Planning and Evaluating Computer Education Programs* meets this need for information. It provides information for developing and improving computer education programs in elementary and secondary schools.

The text is meant primarily for graduate and undergraduate education students enrolled in educational computing courses. These courses teach prospective teachers and administrators how to plan for, implement, and evaluate the use of microcomputers in the school curriculum.

Administrators and teachers who need innovative ideas and examples of effective programs will also find the book useful, as will state department personnel and others who are responsible for setting policy and providing leadership in computer education.

Each chapter is written by an individual or team with special experience and expertise in that area. The contributors have worked with hundreds of schools and districts to develop and improve computer education efforts. Their broad range of experience encompasses work with different types of schools and programs. They offer perspectives formed on the basis of this range of experience and procedures that have been applied successfully in a variety of local contexts. Besides this great diversity, many of the contributors have also worked closely with individual schools, which has helped them develop an understanding of the intricacies of school functioning and of the problems teachers and administrators regularly face.

We begin with an overview of computer education that introduces a nine-step process for planning and evaluation. Chapters 2 through 10 present an independent perspective on a particular task. Bennett describes the different purposes that computer education can serve and offers a procedure for choosing among them. Holznagel and Braun discuss the problems of software and hardware selection. Each describes a way to organize the selection process so as to collect the most trustworthy information for decision making. In Chapter 5, De Gilio describes the problems with personnel and physical facilities that one can encounter in establishing a computer education program: some of these involve staffing, space, power, furniture, security, and environmental control. Bitter describes a procedure for computer education curriculum planning and offers examples of curricular applications. Training teachers to use computers is the subject of Kimmel's chapter, which considers topics to be covered in training and how training should be conducted. In Chapter 8, Stecher shows how to estimate costs of computer education so as to plan resource requirements. Perspectives on facilitating and monitoring are the focus of Cannings and McManus in Chapter 9. They highlight the importance of involving teachers in the planning process and gaining the support of school administrators. Finally, Stecher discusses the thorny problem of evaluating the effects of computer education by listing common evaluation questions, describing workable research designs, and offering examples of evaluation efforts.

Chapters 11 through 13 present three case studies, each of which describes the specific procedures, issues, and problems associated with planning and evaluating a computer education program. Chapter 11 describes the evolution of a computer education program in one school; Chapter 12 relates the issues involved in planning and evaluating a district-level program; Chapter 13 describes the IBM Model Schools Program, a nationwide computer education effort involving many of America's largest school districts.

Contents

1 Planning and Evaluating Computer Education Programs: An Overview   1

Perspectives on Planning and Evaluation   2
Perspectives on Computer Education Programs   7
A Framework for Planning and Evaluating Computer Education Programs   9
Summary   11
References   12

2 Identifying a Purpose for Computer Education Programs   13

Computer Education Programs: Goals, Rationales, and Approaches   13
Choosing a Purpose for Computer Education   19
Summary   22
References   23

3 Selecting Software   25

Educational Roles and Software   26
The Software Selection Process   31
Summary   38
References   39
Appendix   40

4 Choosing Hardware   **43**

How Can You Use This Machine? 44
Choosing—Preliminary Considerations   45
An Approach to Decision Making   47
Comparing and Rating Computers   49
Peripherals   54
Making the Purchase   56
Summary   59
References   59
Appendix   61

5 Planning a Computer Center   **63**

Basic Considerations in Establishing a Computer Education Center   63
Summary   77
References   78

6 Planning a Computer Education Curriculum   **79**

Computer Education: A Brief Overview   80
Microcomputer Infusion   81
Establishing a Computer-Infused Curriculum   82
Microcomputer Infusion Examples   85
Summary   92
References   92
Appendixes   94

**7 Training Teachers to Incorporate Computers
into the School Curriculum**   **103**

The "Computer-Literate" Teacher   104
The In-Service Training of Teachers   105
Summary   118
References   120
Appendixes   122

8 Estimating the Cost of Computer Education   **127**

Introduction to Costs   128
Cost Analysis Procedures   129
Cost Analysis Examples   133
Using Cost Information   140
Meeting the Costs of Computer Education   142

Summary 144
References 144

**9 Facilitating and Monitoring a Computer
Education Program**   145

Promoting a Building-site Concept of Implementation 145
Involving Appropriate Individuals in the Implementation Process 147
Defining the Role of the Principal 149
Defining the Roles of the School-site and District-level Coordinators 151
Facilitating Equal Access 152
Monitoring Program Implementation 154
Summary 161
References 161

**10 Evaluating the Outcomes of Computer
Education Programs**   163

Why Evaluate Computer Education? 163
The Relationship Between Program Activities and Outcomes 167
Measuring the Outcomes of Computer Education 170
Designing an Outcome Evaluation 178
Using Evaluation Results to Improve Computer Education 184
Summary 185
References 185
Appendixes 187

**11 Planning and Evaluation: A School
Perspective**   195

Program Organization and Structure 196
The Planning Process 197
Implementation 198
Evaluation 203
Critical Success Factors 204
Summary 206
References 206

**12 Planning and Evaluation: A Districtwide
Perspective**   207

History and Organization of the Microcomputer Program 208
Planning and Implementing the Microcomputer Program 211
Future Perspectives: The Five-Year Plan 220
Summary 222
References 222

**13 Planning and Evaluation: A National
Perspective**   **223**

Planning   225
Implementation   234
Evaluation   246
Summary   250
References   250

Index   **255**

1
Planning and Evaluating Computer Education Programs: An Overview

Randy Elliot Bennett

Computers are being incorporated into America's educational institutions at an unprecedented rate. The volume of computer purchases being made in education is second only to those in business, with large school districts and state departments making bulk purchases in the thousands (THE Report, 1985). State education departments are issuing computer literacy guidelines, providing technical assistance, and revising teacher certification requirements to include computer competencies (Reinhold & Corkett, 1985). Schools and districts are offering adult-education courses in computing, loaning machines and programs to students and their families, and arranging hardware and software purchase discounts for them (McGinty, 1985). Mastery of computer skills is being included in the National Assessment of Educational Progress (NAEP), universities are requiring undergraduate education majors to take computer courses ("Colleges Pave Different Routes," 1985), and a growing number of higher-education institutions are asking that entering freshmen buy machines as a condition of admission.

This tidal wave of interest in educational computing has been stimulated by a complex set of influences. These influences include the belief, buttressed by a series of national commission reports, that American education is wanting and that this deficiency puts us at a serious disadvantage in competing economically and in remaining strong militarily (National Commission on Excellence in Education, 1983; The National Science Board Commission on Precollege Education in Mathematics, Science, and Technology, 1983; Twentieth Century Fund Task Force on Federal Elementary and Secondary Education Policy, 1983). The educational potential of the technol-

1

ogy also is impelling its rapid adoption. Computers and associated devices (e.g., videodiscs, digitizing tablets, environmental probes) make possible educational experiences that were previously too costly, dangerous, or otherwise impractical to provide. These and other influences have coalesced into a grass-roots movement that, in the form of school boards, parents, government officials, and students, is forcing educators to establish computer-education programs.

In comparison with other educational programs, computer education is unusually costly to implement. Not only must computers be purchased—a nontrivial capital investment in itself—but funds must be expended for equipment repair and maintenance, facilities modification, furniture, software, supplementary materials, teacher training, and supplies, among other things. The total cost of establishing and operating a computer-education program can be daunting, and hardware is clearly only one element of that cost (Stecher, 1986).

The high cost of computer education demands that careful planning and systematic evaluation go into the development of any new program. Without careful planning and evaluation, some very expensive mistakes can be —and have been—made. This chapter introduces planning and evaluation as processes that can be used to develop and improve computer-education programs. It first offers a perspective on planning and evaluation and then defines computer education in terms of its place in the system of services that compose the school district. Finally, it describes a framework for planning and evaluating computer-education programs.

PERSPECTIVES ON PLANNING AND EVALUATION

The successful application of planning and evaluation to computer education requires, among other things, some understanding of what planning and evaluation are, what characteristics make for quality in them, how they have traditionally been applied in the schools, and what a workable planning and evaluation process might entail.

Planning is the process employed in developing a new program or improving an existing one (Maher & Bennett, 1984). Determined in the planning process are the purpose of the program; the staff, objectives, materials, activities, schedule and other elements that should compose the program; the methods for its evaluation; and the ways it should be changed for the better (including its possible termination). Planning is based on the results of evaluation; a continuous process, it goes on before, during, and after a program's implementation.

Evaluation is also a process employed in designing or modifying a program; it involves gathering information about the various aspects of a program so that judgments about it can be made. Evaluation provides information about the need for the program, the appropriateness of program goals, the strengths and weaknesses of different development options, the manner in which the program is carried out, and the ultimate success of the effort. This information becomes the basis for program improvement. Evaluation supplies the information from which planning decisions are made.

Good planning and evaluation have four major characteristics. These characteristics are derived from the work of the Joint Committee on Standards for Educational Evaluation (1981) and are adapted to apply to planning as well as evaluation.

First, planning and evaluation must be useful. That is, planning and evaluation should serve the program development and improvement needs of those responsible for managing and carrying out the program. Providers and managers must therefore be involved closely in the planning and evaluation process if it is to respond to their needs.

Second, planning and evaluation should be accurate. Planning and evaluation activities should be conducted in thoughtful, systematic, and technically defensible ways. Information gathered in a hurry, through a disorganized set of procedures, or with instruments of questionable validity is likely to be inaccurate.

Third, planning and evaluation must be practical. Projected planning and evaluation activities must be capable of being carried out. They must take reasonable amounts of staff time and disrupt other school activities as little as possible. Finally, and most importantly, they must be worth the effort required to conduct them. There is little point in developing intricate curricular plans, training an entire faculty, and evaluating a long list of software packages when only a few computers are slated for purchase!

Last, planning and evaluation should be conducted with concern for propriety. The informed consent of evaluation subjects should be obtained and their right to needed programs preserved even if participation in those programs makes impossible the use of rigorous evaluation designs (for instance, true experimental designs call for the random assignment of pupils to programs, a situation that may not always be acceptable). Planning and evaluation results should be documented and be readily available so that all interested parties can examine and review them critically.

With various levels of sophistication, planning and evaluation have been practiced in schools for a long time. Good teachers, for example, have constantly made judgments about the effectiveness of their teaching and have adjusted methods and content accordingly. Administrators similarly make judgments based on their own perceptions and on the opinions of others about the need for new programs and the effectiveness of existing ones. These judgments often are based on information gathered through informal and unsystematic means.

While this type of informal planning and evaluation is sometimes appropriate, it has important limitations. First, planning and evaluation efforts of this kind lack documentation. Lack of documentation reduces utility in that program staff have no explicit plan to guide their service delivery efforts. It raises questions of propriety because the bases on which program modifications are made cannot be traced, nor can the procedures of evaluation be inspected and critiqued by others.

Informal approaches also call into question the accuracy of planning and evaluation efforts. Such approaches are frequently characterized by minimal forethought and poor organization, resulting in program designs and evaluations that are often low in technical quality. In addition, informal approaches imply reliance on technically inadequate data-gathering procedures (e.g., unstructured observations) that may allow the results of evaluation to be contaminated by irrelevant influences (e.g., subjective biases) and the existence and effects of those influences to remain undetected.

The consequences of faulty, informal planning and evaluation activities are especially serious for computer education. Computer-education programs require unusually large commitments of capital, personnel, and facilities (see Stecher, 1986; see also Chapter 8). A wrong decision can be both costly and difficult to reverse. For example, school officials may decide that they want to start a business computing program that will prepare students for work in regional industries. Lacking a systematic approach to planning and evaluation, they decide on a computer brand because it is the most popularly used in education, and buy a variety of business-type programs because they are offered by a well-known publisher of educational materials. Soon after, they learn that the machine and software are seldom used in local industry. While the computers and the software may be put to good use by other district programs, getting the correct machine and software for the business computing program will cost many more thousands of dollars than the district currently can afford.

While the large majority of planning and evaluation efforts traditionally undertaken in the schools have been informal and unsystematic, more thoughtful approaches—especially toward evaluation—have been used. These efforts often have been connected with large federal programs, such as Title I, which required formal studies of program effects. At other times, formal planning and evaluation activities have been associated with the work of research and evaluation units in big city school districts, with the activities of state education agencies, or with research organizations.

Despite these praiseworthy efforts, many of the formal evaluations conducted in schools have been of little direct use for developing and improving educational programs (David, 1981; vanderPloeg, 1982). Because they need to serve the requirements of federal programs or of upper-level administrators in large districts, these evaluations generally have focused on accountability and compliance-monitoring issues (e.g., Was the program carried out according to federal requirements? Was the program effective overall?). Although these issues are important, they are less central to the business of program development and improvement than are other questions.

The approach to planning and evaluation suggested in this book is built around a generic planning and evaluation process. This process is meant to encourage greater organization and systematicity than that associated with traditional methods. At the same time, it focuses planning and evaluation efforts on the critical educational concerns of program development and improvement, thereby providing increased utility. Finally, it is meant to be practical and to be capable of being implemented in an ethical way. The nine tasks composing this process are listed in Table 1-1.

The first task, identifying the program's purpose, involves determining the overall goal the program will attempt to achieve, the general approach to achieving it, the population to be served, and a rationale for wanting such a program in the first place. Once these basic requirements are known, the following six tasks are carried out: materials and equipment are selected, facilities and staffing arranged, guidelines (e.g., policies, procedures, specific curricular objectives and activities) established, training for staff members designed and delivered, and the costs of the program estimated so that a budget can be developed and monitored. When the program finally is launched, it must be nurtured and watched to identify potential problem areas. Last, the effects of the program should be evaluated to determine if it is worth extending to other district schools or to other student populations.

Several comments should be made about the relationship of these tasks to one another and to planning and evaluation in general. First, planning and evaluation tasks interact. For example, materials and equipment will help determine the requirements for physical facilities. At the same time, the facilities that are available may restrict the materials and equipment that

TABLE 1-1   A generic planning and evaluation process

Planning and Evaluation Tasks

Identify a purpose for the program
Select materials
Choose equipment
Arrange facilities and staffing
Establish program guidelines
Train program staff
Estimate costs
Facilitate & monitor program activities
Evaluate program outcomes

can be accommodated. Scientific laboratory equipment may require a particular type of facility with substantial space and with specialized power, security, and environmental characteristics. Modifications in the facility may be feasible, allowing the electrical, security, and environmental requirements of the equipment to be met. The available space, however, may be too small, necessitating the purchase of fewer units than originally planned.

While the tasks interact, they do not necessarily have to occur in a strict sequence. Once the program's purpose is established, tasks related to materials, equipment, facilities, guidelines, training, and costs may be undertaken in tandem. In other situations, guidelines may already exist in state or federal legislation. These guidelines may dictate the purpose, as well as other program characteristics.

Tasks also need not be viewed as discrete entities undertaken for a fixed period and considered no more. Curricular guidelines, for example, rarely are developed completely before the new program begins. Rather, curricula evolve over time. A curriculum may be very general initially and may become more specific as activities and materials are created. As time goes by, some activities, materials, and objectives may be dropped while others are added. In a sense, the curriculum may never be completed. Teacher training also may operate in this way. Staff development usually will be provided before the program begins in order to familiarize teachers with program goals, methods, equipment, and activities, but such training will likely continue to be offered on a regular basis as new problems are encountered and new training needs discovered.

Fourth, in one form or another, planning and evaluation come into play in every task. The selection of materials and of equipment both constitute planning tasks. Each, however, involves the evaluation of materials and equipment with respect to program requirements and with respect to competing products. Similarly, the assessment of program outcomes is primarily an evaluation task. Yet the evaluation itself must be carefully planned.

Finally, as a group the tasks composing the planning and evaluation process provide a structure for defining the critical elements of most educational programs. This structure can be used to develop a written set of specifications, or program plan: a statement of the purpose, materials, equipment, facilities and staffing, guidelines, training design, estimated costs, facilitating and monitoring activities, and evaluation scheme that will compose the program. The program plan serves as a document for discussion and critical review. It provides a means for communicating the substance of a proposed program to others and for getting their suggestions on its educational soundness and feasibility. The plan also serves as a guide to staff in carrying out the program, letting them know what goals they should strive to achieve, and what materials, equipment, and activities they should use in achieving those goals. Last, the program plan is an evaluation tool. It sets standards for assessing the operation and effects of the program.

How is the planning and evaluation process applied to computer-education programs? An answer to this question requires some discussion of what a computer-education program is.

PERSPECTIVES ON COMPUTER EDUCATION PROGRAMS

Because computer education programs exist within the context of the various other programs that compose the larger school district, they are defined in part by the place they occupy in this larger structure and the relationships they share with the other programs in it.

One useful conceptual scheme for organizing the services offered by school districts is offered by Maher and Bennett (1984). This scheme divides the school district into five service-delivery areas: assessment, instruction, related services, personnel development, and administration. Assessment, instruction, and related services are delivered directly to children; personnel development and administration constitute support services.

Each service area is composed of a series of related programs. A program is an organized configuration of resources—people, materials, and facilities—designed to assist an individual, group, or organization in meeting a specific need. The assessment service area is intended to provide information for making educational decisions about individual children. Examples of programs within the assessment services area are school health screening and comprehensive special-education evaluation. Instruction is intended to facilitate academic and social development and includes subject-matter programs—such as language arts, foreign languages, mathematics, science, social studies—and programs for special populations—such as economically disadvantaged, handicapped, gifted, or limited English-speaking students. Related services are meant to provide students the ancillary support they need to benefit from instruction, and include such programs as counseling; speech, occupational, and physical therapy; transportation; and lunch. The goal of personnel development is to ensure that staff members possess the competencies necessary to perform their jobs adequately. In-service workshops, organized consultation and supervision, and support for taking graduate courses or attending professional conferences all constitute examples of personnel development efforts. Finally, administration is the management function that coordinates the delivery of all services in the system. Administration includes staff supervision, fiscal management, plant maintenance, program-compliance monitoring and reporting, and planning and evaluation. Administrative services set the organizational conditions needed for all other services to function.

The various programs that compose the school system constantly interact. At the service level a clear set of interrelationships exists: assessment provides information for identifying the areas in which students need instruction and for locating students needing special programs; related services supplement instruction; personnel development assists staff in gaining and maintaining the competencies needed to deliver services in all areas; and administration coordinates the activities of the entire system.

In addition to interacting among themselves, school programs influence and are influenced by the community at large. Students may be placed with local businesses for work-study, teachers may work in local industry during the summer or after school, and school buildings may be employed for community activities when not in regular use. Similarly, community members sit on the school board, volunteers assist in the delivery of various district programs, and parent-teacher organizations raise money for and otherwise support school activities.

How do computers fit into this complex system that we call the school district? The answer is, "almost everywhere!" Computers are being used in assessment for everything from presenting tests, to scoring them, to summarizing the results. In the related services area, computers plan bus routes, assist in the provision of career and college counseling, and help disabled students speak, move, and perceive sensation (Bennett & Maher, 1984). Though computers are not used frequently to instruct school staff members, programs have been—and likely will continue to be—developed to train educators in selected job-related skills (e.g., administering and scoring tests). Finally, in administration computers keep student records, track school expenditures, and produce payrolls.

So what are computer-education programs? They are not focused on any of the above school-district computer applications; rather, they are concerned with instructional applications of computers. In this book, we define a computer-education program as an instructional program—that is, an organized configuration of resources—that teaches with or about computers.

This definition implies several things. First, a computer-education program is not a piece of software, a computer laboratory, or a class that regularly visits the lab. It is an organized collection of resources—teachers, administrators, facilities, materials, equipment, etc.—intended to achieve specific goals. Second, the goals of the computer education program may focus on learning about the computer or they may center upon more traditional school subjects such as English, mathematics, social studies, or the sciences. Programs intending to impart general computer literacy skills or competence in the BASIC programming language are examples of the former type of computer-education program. The latter type of program is illustrated by organized, school-wide efforts to encourage subject-matter teachers to incorporate the computer into their instructional routines (see Chapters 11 and 13).

A FRAMEWORK FOR PLANNING AND EVALUATING COMPUTER-EDUCATION PROGRAMS

How can computer-education programs be planned and evaluated? This question can be answered best by first proposing a framework for planning and evaluating educational programs generally. This framework is presented in Figure 1-1.

The framework presented in Figure 1-1 is composed of two dimensions: the planning and evaluation process and district service-delivery areas. The planning and evaluation process consists of the nine tasks described earlier. The service delivery areas are the five basic components of any school district—assessment, instruction, related services, personnel development, and administration.

This framework implies several fundamental characteristics about the nature of planning and evaluating educational programs. First, planning and evaluation are applicable to all programs and services that comprise the school district. The common perception that only instructional programs need to be planned carefully and evaluated is inaccurate and unfortunate.

Second, the planning and evaluation process is generic: its general form can be applied to planning and evaluating any area of service delivery.

Third, the framework implies that school programs exist within a system of interrelated components (which, in turn, exists within a similar, though ever more complex system—the community). Programs may influence one an-

FIGURE 1-1   A framework for planning and evaluating educational programs

Planning and Evaluation Process	School District Service-Delivery Areas				
	Assessment	Instruction	Related Services	Personnel Development	Administration
Identify a purpose					
Select materials					
Choose equipment					
Arrange facilities and staffing					
Establish guidelines					
Train staff					
Estimate costs					
Facilitate & monitor activities					
Evaluate outcomes					

other, influence organizations outside the school, or be influenced by such entities. These mutual influences need to be considered in planning and evaluation efforts.

Fourth, the framework implies that planning and evaluation is a team effort. Why? The process must be shared equally by individuals with two types of competencies: those versed in the planning and evaluation process and those intimately familiar with the substance of the program. This type of collaboration brings both methodological and programmatic expertise to the planning and evaluation effort. In addition, it encourages a sense of ownership in the program as well as a greater willingness to accept and use evaluation results.

Finally, while the general process of planning and evaluating is the same regardless of service area, the specific methods used in applying any one planning or evaluation task to any one service may differ from that used in another part of the process or for another service. The content of planning and evaluation—the methods, staff, and activities—will, therefore, frequently differ as the focus or stage of the planning and evaluation process changes.

What relevance does this general framework have for computer education? Planning and evaluating computer education is just one specific case of planning and evaluation in education generally. This perspective allows the many useful approaches and procedures developed for educational planning and evaluation to be applied to computer education. Figure 1-2

FIGURE 1–2   A framework for planning and evaluating computer-education programs

Planning and Evaluation Process	Instructional Services Computer Education Programs
Identify a purpose	
Select software	
Choose hardware	
Plan the computer center	
Plan a curriculum	
Train teachers	
Estimate costs	
Facilitate & monitor activities	
Evaluate outcomes	

presents an adaptation of the general planning and evaluation process to computer education.

This computer-education planning and evaluation framework differs in only minor ways from the more general one. Instead of spanning the five service-delivery areas, the horizontal dimension now is focused on only one area: instructional services. Within this area, one particular type of instructional program—computer education—is of interest. The vertical dimension —the Planning and Evaluation Process—remains the same except for the specification of four tasks. The tasks of selecting materials and equipment are narrowed to selecting software and hardware, respectively. Similarly, the general process of arranging for facilities and staffing becomes one of planning a computer center. Finally, the task of establishing guidelines now centers on planning a curriculum.

The body of Figure 1-2—the intersection of the process and service dimensions—represents planning and evaluation content. Content is the substance of planning and evaluation in computer education—the methods, activities, and results that make up a particular planning and evaluation effort. In the following chapters independent readings on these methods, activities, and results are presented: one reading for each of the nine tasks composing the planning and evaluation process and three illustrating the application of planning and evaluation content in field settings.

SUMMARY

This chapter has introduced several concepts central to planning and evaluating computer-education programs. Planning and evaluation were seen as complementary processes meant to facilitate program development and improvement. Characteristics of good planning and evaluation include utility, accuracy, practicality, and propriety. A generic, nine-step process intended to incorporate these characteristics was proposed.

Computer education was viewed as one class of program existing within the larger school district. The school district was conceptualized as being composed of five general service-delivery areas: assessment, instruction, related services, personnel development, and administration. Each service is composed of a group of related programs. Computer-education programs were seen as instructional programs—that is, organized configurations of resources—that teach with or about computers.

The process of planning and evaluating computer education programs was embedded in a framework for planning and evaluating educational programs in general. This framework suggested that planning and evaluation exhibit several important characteristics; among the more important of these were that school programs interact with one another and influence and are influenced by outside forces, that planning and evaluation is a team effort, and that the specific methods and activities that compose any given planning or evaluation effort will vary.

The framework for planning and evaluating computer-education programs was viewed as a specific case of planning and evaluating educational programs in general. The framework included nine tasks based on the generic planning and evaluation process. The application of these tasks to specific computer-education programs constitutes the content of computer-education planning and evaluation.

REFERENCES

Bennett, R. E., & Maher, C. A. (1984). *Microcomputers and exceptional children.* New York: Haworth Press.

Colleges pave different routes to computer literacy for teachers. (1985, July 17). *Education Computer News,* pp. 1–3.

David, J. L. (1981). Local uses of Title I evaluations. *Educational Evaluation and Policy Analysis, 3,* 27–39.

The Joint Committee on Standards for Educational Evaluation. (1981). *Standards for evaluations of educational programs, projects, and materials.* New York: McGraw-Hill.

Maher, C. A., & Bennett, R. E. (1984). *Planning and evaluating special education services.* Englewood Cliffs, NJ: Prentice-Hall.

McGinty, T. (1985, November/December). Making the home-school connection: Six programs that encourage educational computing at home. *Electronic Learning, 5*(3), 31–36.

National Commission on Excellence in Education. (1983, April). *A nation at risk: The imperative for educational reform.* Washington, D.C.: U.S. Department of Education.

The National Science Board Commission on Precollege Education in Mathematics, Science, and Technology. (1983). *Educating Americans for the 21st century.* Washington, D.C.: National Science Board.

Reinhold, F., & Corkett, K. (1985, October). Mandates: EL's fifth annual survey of the states. *Electronic Learning, 5*(2), 25–31.

Stecher, B. (1986). The cost of implementing computer-based education. In H. F. Cline, R. E. Bennett, R. C. Kershaw, M. B. Schneiderman, B. Stecher, & S. Wilson, *The electronic schoolhouse.* Hillsdale, NJ: Lawrence Erlbaum Associates.

THE Report. (1985, April). Education: A big ticket market. *THE Report,* p. 2.

Twentieth Century Fund Task Force on Federal Elementary and Secondary Education Policy. (1983). *Making the grade.* New York: Twentieth Century Fund.

vanderPloeg, A. J. (1982). ESEA Title I evaluation: The service of two masters. *Educational Evaluation and Policy Analysis, 4,* 521–526.

2

Identifying a Purpose for Computer Education Programs

Randy Elliot Bennett

"Cheshire Puss, would you tell me, please, which way I ought to go from here?
  "That depends a good deal on where you want to get to," said the Cat.
  "I don't much care where—" said Alice.
  "Then it doesn't matter which way you go," said the Cat.
  "—so long as I get **somewhere**," Alice added as an explanation.
  "Oh, you're sure to do that," said the Cat, "if only you walk long enough."
                            Lewis Carroll, Alice's Adventures in Wonderland

Like all educational endeavors, computer-education programs should be aimed at reaching some particular endpoint, at achieving some general purpose. Without a purpose, they, like Alice, are apt to wander aimlessly.

What is a purpose? A purpose is a general description of the overall goal a program is meant to achieve, the general approach or major activity used to achieve that goal, the target population with which it will be achieved, and the rationale for achieving it. This chapter discusses the various purposes to which computer-education programs can be put, and offers an approach for choosing among them.

COMPUTER-EDUCATION PROGRAMS: GOALS, RATIONALES AND APPROACHES

Computer-education programs generally serve one of two general goals. Programs of the first type attempt to achieve traditional content goals with the aid of computers. Programs of the second type teach students about computers. Students can be taught with or about computers in various ways. What rationale supports each goal and the various approaches to achieving each goal?

Teaching Students with Computers

Students should be taught with computers only if such teaching provides some advantage over conventional methods. The case for such teaching is made in part by the perceived failure of current educational methods and practices. Much evidence supports the argument that American education is not preparing the country's youth as it should. Since the early 1970s, studies have documented a decreased emphasis on basic skills, fewer homework assignments, and rising disciplinary problems. Especially at the secondary level, school textbooks have become easier, nonessential elective courses have proliferated, and test scores of many kinds—from college admissions scores to those from the National Assessment of Educational Progress—have declined (Turnbull, 1985). In combination, these results present a bleak picture, one that threatens the continued economic, political, and military strength of our nation.

If American education is failing to teach traditional content, then the practice of teaching students with computers can be offered as one potential solution to this problem. This argument has some degree of theoretical and empirical validity. From a theoretical perspective, the computer can individualize instruction to a greater degree than traditional methods, is eminently patient, can provide immediate reinforcement, and can offer experiences that might be otherwise impractical to provide.

A substantial amount of research has been conducted on teaching traditional content with computers. This research has focused on using computers to present instruction. Large and small-scale studies have been undertaken at the elementary, secondary, and college levels. Main-frame, minicomputer, and microcomputer-based programs have been investigated, and a variety of subject-matter areas have been considered. The studies have found that students learn more, require less time for learning, and show more positive attitudes toward coursework using computers (Kulik, Bangert, & Williams, 1983; Kulik, Kulik, & Cohen, 1980; Murphy & Appel, 1984; Ragosta, 1983). This does not suggest that computer-based instruction can—or should—replace traditional methods, or that it is more cost-effective (i.e., that it produces more learning for the same cost or the same learning for a lower cost). It does, however, suggest that computer-delivered instruction can be an effective supplement to traditional techniques (Education Turnkey Systems, undated, 1985; Roblyer, 1985).

Computers can be used in other ways to teach traditional content. One such way is through the use of applications programs. In many schools, word processing programs are being used to help students develop writing skills (Solomon, 1985). The computer serves as a motivational device—many students seem to like writing with it—but also as a device that makes the concept of revision practical; most good writers painstakingly go through several drafts of a piece before they are satisfied that it says clearly what they want to say. Getting students to appreciate the value of this approach to writing is difficult unless the process of revision can be made a little less cumbersome, and word processors do just that.

A second type of applications program that might be used to achieve traditional goals is the database management system. These programs help store, manipulate, and retrieve information. Students may learn a great deal about the organization of a body of knowledge, the relationship among facts composing that body, and how to ask and answer research questions by working with a database manager. For example, using a database composed of information about the U.S. Presidents, students might be asked to find out whether there are relationships between such factors as being president and being male, being president and being of a particular religious affiliation, and being president and holding a particular occupation. The nature of and reasons for any discovered relationships might then be discussed.

The argument for teaching traditional content by using applications programs appears theoretically sound. As with some other types of computer-based instruction (particularly simulations), applications programs have the potential to allow students to play a more intellectually active role in the learning process. Students take on this role when they are challenged, placed face to face with a problem that needs to be solved. Such a role is thought by most educational psychologists to enhance motivation and facilitate learning. With database management programs, for example, the potential for an active role is clear: students' discovery of relationships within a data set may lead to their formulating hypotheses, which they may test through further data analyses.

In comparison with the amount of information available about programs that present instruction, little data exist on the use of applications programs in education. The most comprehensive attempts to encourage the use of applications programs for achieving traditional curricular goals were made by two projects supported by IBM (see Chapter 13 and also Cline, Bennett, Kershaw, Schneiderman, Stecher, & Wilson, 1986). Although innovative uses of applications programs were observed in these projects, several problems were encountered (Bennett, 1984), not the least of which was the enormous amount of time required to integrate these software packages into traditional curricular areas. Integration required teachers to develop lessons, activities, and data files for students to use with the applications packages. Since the conclusion of the IBM programs, however, several publishers have released applications packages, data files, and activities made for elementary and secondary school populations. These products should make it easier to integrate applications packages in traditional curricular areas.

A third way in which computers can be used to support traditional content is through programming. Many educators have argued that programming can enhance the development of mathematics and of various higher-order thinking skills. It has been widely argued that programming in mathematics can be used to teach a variety of concepts and processes (The College Board, 1985; Papert, 1980a). For example, the concepts and mechanics underlying many basic formulae might be more completely understood if taught through a few paper-and-pencil solutions followed by a programming exercise. Programming a computer to solve an equation requires a thorough conceptual and mechanical understanding of the formula. One must know the equation well enough to state it in the incremental step-by-step terms required for electronic processing, and this thorough knowledge of the equation might develop best as a result of attempts to program it.

Some researchers argue that the development of such higher-order thinking skills as creativity, logic, and problem solving can also be enhanced by programming (see Papert, 1980b). For example, the algorithmic thinking required for writing computer programs—that is, the process of specifying a problem and breaking its solution up into a series of decision rules—demands and encourages the development of logic and organizational skills.

Though a good theoretical argument can be made for using programming to teach certain types of traditional content, relatively little research on the effectiveness of programming for these purposes has been conducted. The studies that do exist have produced equivocal results, some finding programming to be associated with gains in such areas as problem-solving and some not (e.g., Clements & Gullo, 1984; Linn, 1985).

Teaching Students about Computers

Why teach students about computers? Some of the more frequently offered reasons are that such training provides preparation for a technological society, for a vocation, and for further academic study. Each of these rationales for computer education bears some examination.

There can be no argument that our society is rapidly becoming a technological one. Microprocessors control the television, video-cassette recorder, and the stereo hi-fi system. They run the microwave oven, the thermostat, and our digital watches and clocks. They control numerous sytems in our automobiles, and help operate gasoline pumps, cash registers and hundreds of other machines.

The role that computers play in our society is enormous and still growing rapidly. Whether we realize it or not, most of us interact with computers many times each day. It is sensible on this basis alone to want to teach students something about these devices.

A second reason for teaching students about computers—vocation preparation—is equally compelling. In industry, computers are almost everywhere, and those businesses that do not now use computers soon will. Computers keep the payroll, personnel records, inventory, and sales orders. Secretaries use them to type letters, memoranda, and reports. Executives use them to store, manipulate, and retrieve data; to exchange information with field offices and sales staff; to build budgets and track expenses; and to create graphics for reports and presentations. The number of jobs requiring employees to use computers is growing rapidly, with some estimates suggesting that 30% of the work force already uses these machines in some way (Goldstein & Fraser, 1985).

A third rationale for teaching students about computers is to prepare them for further academic study. Several influential reports have suggested that technological knowledge be considered a new prerequisite for college study (e.g., The College Board, 1983). A growing number of institutions appear to have embraced this view: these schools require freshmen to purchase computers as a condition of admission.

It seems, then, that a defensible rationale for teaching students about computers can be constructed. However, as is true for teaching students *with* computers, various approaches can be taken, each encompassing a different level of computer skill and each based on a different rationale. For example, one very common approach to teaching students about computers is to familiarize them with computer fundamentals: the computer's history, its role in society, how the computer works, and what it can do. This approach can be justified easily on the basis of preparation for society, vocation, and further academic study.

A second popular approach to teaching students about computers is programming instruction. Some educators feel that this approach is more difficult to justify than other instructional uses of computers. While computers are inside almost everything, these educators correctly note that they have not really made most products that much more difficult to operate. The directions may be confusing at first, but no one needs a programming course to learn to operate the microwave, set a digital watch, program the video-cassette recorder, or use the bank's money access machine. Yet each of these represents an interaction with a computer or with a computer-controlled device.

With respect to vocational preparation, it is true that computer use in business is widespread and growing rapidly. However, most workers appear to use computers in ways that do not require extensive training. It is estimated, for example, that only about 5% of the current work force requires extensive computer-related training (Goldstein & Fraser, 1985). These individuals include engineers and scientists who design computers, teachers of computer science, computer programmers, systems analysts, and repair personnel. Although these occupations are growing rapidly, they are expected to constitute no more than 1% of the work force by 1995.

A similar argument is made regarding teaching students about computers in preparation for further academic study. Relatively few students will enter academic programs in which intimate knowledge of the computer is required. While more institutions are requiring entering students to purchase computers, many of these institutions are engineering schools which, as a whole, cater to a small proportion of the college-bound population. At the other institutions, computers will be used primarily for word processing and, to a lesser extent, for information retrieval, both of which require relatively little formal preparation.

There is, of course, another side to these arguments. With regard to preparation for a technological society, it is correct that we can interact with a wide range of microcomputer-based machines without knowing a thing about computer programming. On the other hand, all of these machines—everything from the microwave oven to the video-cassette recorder to the compact disk player—were programmed to do certain things at the factory and can be programmed further by us to do others. In fact, almost every electronic device from a 35mm camera to the space shuttle's control systems must be programmed at some level in order to function effectively. Programming has become a fundamental means of getting things done in our society. Not everyone can program computers—very few people, in fact, actually program to any degree of complexity. However, its pervasiveness provides a reasonable argument for wanting students to be aware and to have some basic understanding of programming.

As to vocational and academic preparation, one can offer additional arguments to support the teaching of programming. Clearly, some students may wish to go into academic programs or careers that require programming knowledge. These students will have difficulty deciding if such programs and careers are right for them if they have had no exposure to programming. Also, most of those who use computers in business learn through on-the-job training ranging from a few hours to a few months (Goldstein & Fraser, 1985). A good deal of this training appears to focus on teaching employees to use applications packages, particularly spreadsheet and database management programs. These packages typically use mini programming languages to implement their advanced functions. To the extent that students can acquire this kind of programming knowledge, they may become more attractive to some employers. On-the-job training takes time, and time is money. The applicant who comes to the job already trained has a decided advantage over the computer-illiterate but otherwise equally qualified competitor.

So, is it justifiable to teach about computers through programming? One probably would be hard-pressed to offer a convincing rationale for providing all students with intensive programming experiences. Such experiences, however, may be reasonable for the relatively small number interested in pursuing computer studies more seriously. At the same time, it is easy to justify teaching all students at least something about computers, and hard to imagine that this does not include some minimal exposure to programming.

CHOOSING A PURPOSE FOR COMPUTER EDUCATION

Given the two basic goals for computer education and the various approaches to achieving each, how does one go about choosing a purpose for a given program? Before this question can be answered, some comments on the relationship between programs and purposes are in order.

First, a school or district may have several computer-education programs, each serving a different purpose. These programs may fall within the purview of a comprehensive, integrated computer-education effort or they may operate in isolation from one another. One program may be oriented toward teaching basic skills with computers to remedial students, while a second may focus on the development of advanced computer programming skills for college-bound students. The programs may use some of the same resources—they may share the same computer lab—or they may have separate resources.

Second, a single program may serve two purposes. In a sense, many computer-education programs attempt to do this; they often teach both with and about computers. For example, a program may use the Logo computer language primarily to help introduce children to geometric concepts, but also to teach them something of computing fundamentals. Similarly, secondary-school students may learn some aspects of American history by using applications programs, but also may learn a bit about how to use these programs generally. Achieving both ends successfully sometimes can be difficult and may in some cases be inappropriate. For example, in a program that uses computer presentation to help remedial students improve their basic mathematics skills, instruction about computers beyond that required to run math lessons may distract students from the main focus of the program.

What purpose underlies most computer-education programs? Research suggests that at the elementary level, most computing activity revolves around teaching *with* computers—in particular, using computers to present basic skills instruction ("Third of Students," 1985). In contrast, at the secondary level learning *about* computers is currently the dominant activity. However, a major trend noted in this research is toward the use of applications programs as an aid in teaching traditional content ("Third of Students," 1985; Barbour, 1984).

With these comments as preface we suggest a four-step process for identifying a purpose for computer education. This process will clarify what the computer-education program is intended to achieve, how the program will achieve it, whom the program will serve, and why the program makes sense.

1. Gather input from all interested parties.   To succeed, innovative programs like computer education require much in the way of human, financial, and physical resources. Such resources presume broad-based support in the school and community. It is important to begin building support early in the life of the program. Therefore, a first step in establishing a program purpose is to gather input about school needs and directions for computer education from all those who are likely to have some stake in it: teachers, parents, administrators of other affected programs, students, and community members. These individuals can act as a computer-education planning and evaluation committee, or as an informal advisory group to the program director. They should represent their constituencies well and be made to recognize that their contributions will be taken seriously.

2. Consider the issues raised by various alternative purposes.   It is the committee's job to determine whether the program will primarily teach about or with computers, what general approach the program will take, whom it will serve, and what justifies it all. Many different programs are possible, each raising a different set of questions that will have to be considered.

Primary among the issues to consider in choosing a program purpose is compatibility with local needs. For example, two purposes might be under consideration: teaching college-bound students about computing through programming and teaching vocational students about computing through machine repair and maintenance. Do these purposes serve the needs of the students, the school, and the community? The adequacy of these purposes would need to be questioned, for instance, if there were not enough college-bound or vocation-bound students in the school to support the programs or if the community could not provide jobs for graduates of the vocational program. If both purposes appear compatible with local needs, which is the more compatible? If neither purpose is compatible, what purpose does fit local needs?

A second, related issue in considering program purpose is equity. Research has suggested that certain student groups sometimes are afforded less access to computers than—or different access from—other groups (Education Turnkey Systems, 1985). Females, minority group members, and handicapped students are reported to be among these underrepresented groups. Females may enroll less frequently in computer-education electives because of a lack of confidence in their mathematical abilities and an erroneous assumption that the courses require math background (Education Turnkey Systems, 1985); alternatively, because of social stereotypes they may gravitate to word processing classes while males enroll in programming courses. Some minority members, because of low achievement levels, may be less likely to take part in computer education when those programs require advanced prerequisites (e.g., algebra). Similarly, physically handicapped students may be excluded because of the cost of adaptive devices needed to facilitate their interaction with the computer. Simple solutions to these equity problems do not always exist. However, the potential for such problems and possible solutions to them must be considered when the purpose is being selected.

Third, the resource implications of different purposes should be taken into account. The exact costs of developing a computer-education program cannot be estimated accurately at this stage. However, some very rough ideas might be developed based on the experiences of others. Given these rough ideas, is there a reasonable chance that a program to achieve the purpose can be supported, or is a program aimed at this purpose completely out of the question? As an example of the general effect of purpose on cost, consider just the hardware expenses of two programs: one intended to help teach elementary students mathematical concepts through Logo and another meant to impart word processing skills to vocation-bound high school seniors. Logo will operate on very inexpensive computers. In addition, elementary students can work on Logo in pairs and need not interact with the machines on a daily basis to learn the desired concepts. In contrast, to develop word processing proficiency each student in the vocational program will need frequent, one-to-one access to a machine. Also, the machines used must be similar to those employed in local businesses—that is, high-end, expensive equipment. Hence, the second program can be expected to require more units per student and more expensive units than the first; and hardware is only *one* piece of the total cost of computer education.

3. Finalize the purpose and use it to build the program.   Once the purpose is agreed upon, it should be put into a written statement describing the overall goal, the population to be served, the general approach to be taken, and a rationale for the program. Because the statement represents the basic building block around which the computer-education program will be constructed, it should be clearly worded, well-conceived, and educationally sound.

The purpose should be used by program designers at every planning and evaluation stage. To the extent feasible, all elements of the program should be developed to be consistent with the program purpose. Departures from the purpose in designing the program can limit—even fatally damage—chances for success. Buying inexpensive, grade-school-quality computers for a program intended to teach college-bound high school students computer science is foolish. If the computers are not capable of running the advanced programming languages needed for computer science instruction, the purpose of the program will be defeated. The implications of any such departures from the program purpose should be carefully considered, justified, and documented.

4. Evaluate the purpose and adapt it as necessary.   Computer education is in its infancy, and like an infant it is rapidly developing. The conditions that prevailed two years ago no longer do today. As a program is being built, and over its operational life, it is sensible to periodically reconsider its purpose and adapt this purpose as necessary. Times change—and so should educational programs.

Does the purpose of a particular program still make good educational sense? In a few years we likely will know much more about the value of using programming as a means of teaching traditional content. We may have better insight into the effectiveness of teaching math concepts using Logo. Regardless of the theoretical soundness of any approach, if the weight of the evidence is negative the purposes of such programs—indeed, the programs themselves—will need to be reconsidered.

Is the purpose still responsive to local needs? The purpose of a computer-education program originally may have been to teach college-bound students about computing. School demographics change, however, and sometimes very rapidly. As families with college-bound students move out and those whose interests are more vocationally focused move in, the program may need to be reoriented.

Finally, does the program appear to be capable of achieving the purpose? An advanced computer skills program may prove consistently unsuccessful in preparing college-bound students for subsequent computer science coursework. This situation may be due primarily to the capabilities that the students bring to the program. Their problem-solving abilities may be poorly developed and their logical thinking deficient. Given this situation, it may be advisable to shift the focus of the program to something more readily attained and more appropriate to student needs. Programs, after all, should continue only so long as they can serve a useful purpose.

SUMMARY

All educational programs should have a purpose and computer-education programs are no exception. Without a clear purpose, programs are likely to wander aimlessly, achieving little, if anything, of value.

With respect to planning and evaluation, a purpose can be considered to include the overall goal a program is meant to achieve, the general approach or major activity used to achieve that goal, the intended target population, and a rationale justifying the existence of the program.

Computer-education programs can serve two general goals: teaching traditional content with computers or teaching about computers. Various approaches to each of these goals can be taken and each goal can be applied to a variety of target populations. Rationales for some of the more common approaches to achieving each goal were discussed.

The process of choosing among the various purposes for computer-education programs consists of four steps: gathering input from all interested parties, considering the issues raised by alternative purposes, finalizing the purpose and using it to build the program, and evaluating the purpose and adapting it as necessary. The results of this process will serve as the basis for all further development of the computer-education program.

REFERENCES

Barbour, A. (1984, October). Computing in America's classrooms, 1984: The new computer literacy emerges. *Electronic Learning,* pp. 39–44, 100.

Bennett, R. E. (1984, November). Teachers reach out and touch with PCs. *PC Magazine,* pp. 335–337.

Clements, D. H., & Gullo, D. F. (1984). Effects of computer programming on young children's cognition. *Journal of Educational Psychology, 76,* 1051–1058.

Cline, H. F., Bennett, R. E., Kershaw, R. C., Schneiderman, M. B., Stecher, B., & Wilson, S. (1986). *The electronic schoolhouse.* Hillsdale, NJ: Lawrence Erlbaum Associates.

The College Board. (1983). *Academic preparation for college: What students need to know and be able to do.* New York: Author.

The College Board. (1985). *Academic preparation in mathematics: Teaching for transition from high school to college.* New York: Author.

Education Turnkey Systems, Inc. (1985). *Uses of computers in education* (RR–85–07). Washington, D.C.: National Commission for Employment Policy.

Education Turnkey Systems, Inc. (undated). *Computer-assisted instruction (CAI): The bottom line.* Fairfax, VA: The International Communications Industries Association.

Goldstein, H., & Fraser, B. S. (1985). *Training for work in the computer age: How workers who use computers get their training* (RR–85–09). Washington, D.C.: National Commission for Employment Policy.

Kulik, J. A., Bangert, R. L., & Williams, G. W. (1983). Effects of computer-based teaching on secondary school students. *Journal of Educational Psychology, 75,* 19–26.

Kulik, J. A., Kulik, C. C., & Cohen, P. A. (1980). Effectiveness of computer-based college teaching: A meta-analysis of findings. *Review of Educational Research, 50,* 525–544.

Linn, M. C. (1985). The cognitive consequences of programming instruction in classrooms. *Educational Researcher, 14*(5), 14–29.

Murphy, R. T., & Appel, L. R. (1984). *Evaluation of the Writing to Read instructional system.* Princeton, NJ: Educational Testing Service.

Papert, S. (1980a). Teaching children to be mathematicians vs. teaching about mathematics. In R. P. Taylor (Ed.), *The computer in the school: Tutor, tool, tutee.* New York: Teachers College Press.

Papert, S. (1980b). *Mindstorms.* New York: Basic Books.

Ragosta, M. (1983). Computer assisted instruction and compensatory education: A longitudinal analysis. *Machine mediated learning, 1,* 97–126.

Roblyer, M. D. (1985). *Measuring the impact of computers in instruction: A non-technical review of research for educators.* Washington, D.C.: Association for Educational Data Systems (AEDS).

Solomon, G. (1985, November/December). Writing with computers. *Electronic Learning,* pp. 39–45.

Third of students, fourth of teachers have access to computers. (1985, August 28). *Education Week,* p. 5.

Turnbull, W. W. (1985). *Student change, program change: Why SAT scores kept falling* (College Board Report No. 85–2). New York: College Entrance Examination Board.

3
Selecting Software

Donald C. Holznagel

When purchasing computers, school personnel all too frequently fail to devote sufficient attention to software selection. Yet, it is software that makes a computer more or less useful. Software can turn a computer into a good or bad tutor, word processor, information retrieval device, mailing label generator, or any of a variety of other devices. Thus, the selection of appropriate software is crucial to making an investment in hardware pay off.

The process of selecting instructional materials for schools is often systematic. Films, textbooks, worksheets and other materials, whether chosen by individual teachers or district committees, are typically selected with regard to instructional objectives, student needs, preferred instructional approaches, budgets and other factors. Frequently, during this process criteria are established, outside opinions are obtained, and product samples are examined. Since software can turn a computer into an instructional device, software, too, should be considered instructional material. As such, its purchase should be undertaken with the same care and organization as are purchases of other instructional media.

This chapter is intended to give the reader the basic information needed to develop a workable software selection process. First, some ways in which computers can be used and the software needed to support these uses are discussed. Then, a three-stage approach to software selection is described.

EDUCATIONAL ROLES AND SOFTWARE

Computers can play various roles in education. To make sensible selection decisions, it is necessary to understand these roles and be aware of the types of software that exist for implementing them. Discussed here are two instructional roles—teaching about and teaching with computers—and one administrative one, instructional management.

Teaching about Computers

In this category, the computer serves as the object of instruction; that is, *the computer* is the subject matter. Four major classifications under which students typically study the computer are computer literacy, programming, vocational preparation, and computer science. These classifications provide a reasonable framework for thinking about the computer as the object of instruction. It should be noted, however, that such instruction may be organized differently in different schools and that new areas of instruction may develop.

Computer literacy.   Computer literacy involves the awareness, attitudes, and knowledge necessary to understand the effects of the computer on society. In literacy courses pupils study the computer as an increasingly important technology that contributes to the solution of social and economic problems and that creates new problems as well. Though computer literacy courses vary widely in content, they generally cover such topics as orientation to computers, their present and future roles, their capabilities and limitations, and their implications for society. The "orientation to computers" segment may include the history of computing, an overview of computer parts and how they work, and a general introduction to how people communicate with and control computers. Some hands-on experience with computers usually is included.

In addition to teaching computer literacy through a specific course, literacy may be engendered by embedding computer content in other established courses found throughout the elementary and secondary curriculum. In this alternative approach, the components of literacy are still the same, but are addressed in a variety of contexts and at a variety of times. For example, the associated computer mathematics may be handled in the math curriculum, the electronics in the science curriculum, and the computer's social impact in the social studies curriculum. Content on the applications of computers may be modelled by using the computer regularly for simulation, problem-solving, and other instructional purposes. With respect to timing, simple skills such as keyboarding may be covered early in the grade sequence, while other topics may be introduced later.

In the traditional approach, the software used might include computer languages, operating systems, word processing and database management programs, and other software generally employed in business and in the home. In the embedded approach, the focus more likely is on non-programming software, and probably involves heavy use of simulation, problem-solving, and generic applications packages (e.g., database management and word processing programs).

Computer programming. General-purpose computer languages such as BASIC, Logo or Pascal are the usual focus of programming courses at the elementary and secondary levels. In advanced programming courses, students may have the opportunity to develop software in assembly language, and hence learn how to control a computer at a more fundamental level. Because a variety of languages can be used with a microcomputer, students can be introduced to other, more specialized languages as necessary.

Computer language software generally comes in two forms: interpreters and compilers. As a program is run, interpreters translate it line by line into the elemental language of binary digits understood by the machine. Every time an interpreted program is run, it must be retranslated. In contrast, compilers translate the entire program into this elemental language. The elemental version of the program can then be saved and executed on demand. Compiled programs, therefore, invariably execute faster than interpreted ones. Hence, compilers are used in most serious computer-science and business applications. Interpreters, however, generally are better initial learning tools because programs written with them can be immediately executed. In this way, errors can be quickly found, corrected, and tested without the lengthy time needed to recompile.

Vocational preparation. Courses teaching vocational or computer skills typically have included practical training in data entry, word processing, terminal operation, computer operation and programming for data processing functions (e.g., payroll, personnel records). Traditionally, these skills have been taught using main-frame or minicomputer systems. Microcomputers, however, are proliferating rapidly and expanding enormously in capacity and speed. These machines increasingly will take on many of the data processing requirements of industry and government. As a result, vocational programs will need to place increased emphasis on the operation of microcomputers and their peripherals.

Software used in secondary-school vocational training programs needs to be the same as that employed in business, including the full-capability word processing, database management and spreadsheet systems used on microcomputers. While a simplified word processor, for example, might be useful at an introductory stage, mastery of it is not likely to make the student readily employable.

Computer science. Essential to computer science is the study of the machine and its processing technology. While computer science includes heavy use of computer languages, the focus of the field is far broader than simply teaching students to program. Among other things, it includes the study of algorithms, or procedures for solving particular problems; data strutures, or organizations for storing data; operating systems (i.e., the programs that control the flow of information to, from, and within the computer); compilers and interpreters; and hardware.

Microcomputers are the primary machines available for classroom use. As such, computer science often will focus on the specific technology, operation and programming of these machines, rather than on the larger and more complex components involved in minicomputers or mainframe systems. In pre-college computer science, the content may include just enough programming methodology to understand how the computer can be made to produce certain results, or it may—depending on the discipline(s) with which the course is associated—involve mastery of more complex algorithmic analysis and programming skills.

The software used in the teaching of computer science may include both computer languages and tutorials that teach students fundamental concepts.

Teaching with Computers

During the last decade, the variety of ways in which computers are used to teach traditional content has expanded. Among the instructional uses discussed in this section are drill and practice, tutorial, simulation, problem solving, and generic applications. In one form or another, these uses may be found across grade levels and curricular areas. However, it should be noted that these uses may be distinct only in a conceptual sense: in practice, they may overlap, combine, or deviate from the typical patterns described.

Drill and practice.   Drill and practice focuses on the review or consolidation of an already-acquired knowledge or skill. It is therefore particularly applicable in curricular areas where specific facts need to be learned or skills developed, such as in arithmetic, spelling, history, reading, foreign languages, and the sciences.

The drill-and-practice software format usually consists of a computer-presented problem and a student-entered answer. Within this general design, a great variety of methods is used for indicating correct or incorrect responses, providing hints, branching students to different problems according to the correctness of their answers, and grading performance. Some software of this type is capable of keeping detailed records of an individual student's performance.

Tutorial.   In the tutorial mode the computer provides new information and engages the student in a question-and-answer dialogue about that information. In this role, the computer can help the student discover and integrate information, and route the tutee to new material or to remedial instruction, depending upon the program's evaluation of the student's response. While drill-and-practice software typically discriminates only right answers from wrong, tutorials can be built to deal with a wider variety of response, thereby heightening the instructional experience. The major prerequisite for developing a successful tutorial program is, of course, that the algorithm for teaching a topic be defined clearly so that it can be programmed.

Simulation.   Simulations are built around models of physical or social situations. The model, which necessarily simplifies the situation being presented, can be organized either as a pedagogical scenario or as a game with which the student interacts in order to accomplish certain goals (e.g., successfully land a plane, keep a nuclear power plant from experiencing an accident). This instructional method can produce exceptional motivation and interest, and often provides the only practical, safe, or possible experience with a given situation. For example, simulations can present experiments in genetics or radioactivity which, for reasons of time and/or safety, cannot be conducted by students in the classroom.

Problem solving.   The role of the computer in problem solving may be divided into two categories: using the computer as a complex problem-solving device, and using it as a vehicle for teaching problem solving. In its role as a problem-solving device, the computer is used not simply as is a pocket calculator, for example, but rather is employed as a tool for solving complex, multidimensional problems. In this role, it provides the student with information that would otherwise be very difficult to obtain.

Problem-solving programs do not deliver instruction or correction; they simply allow the student to enter the relevant data and then proceed to perform the manipulations necessary to solve the problem. For example, using a program to solve problems concerning payments on long-term loans, the student might be directed to enter information on the amount borrowed, the interest rate, and the term of the loan. The computer might then perform the necessary manipulations and print out the monthly payment, the outstanding principal remaining after each installment, and an annual summary of interest paid. Such programs typically are designed to solve quickly many problems of the same kind.

The second problem-solving role, using the computer as a vehicle to teach problem solving, has students write programs to solve specific problems. Teaching problem solving in this manner requires that the student understand the concept being programmed and develop skills sufficient to program the steps that compose the solution. It demands logic and precision, and thus encourages the development of these skills.

This use of the computer has been tried successfully as early as grade one, where a few simple flowcharting and programming skills can allow children to develop clear problem solutions. In the upper grades, the approach can involve complex activities encompassing the development of games, data management programs for teachers or for the school, industrial drawing programs using specialized graphics, mathematics problem-solving programs, and musical compositions.

As with the applications described earlier, the computer can be used effectively for problem solving in many different curricular areas. The single most important requirement is that problem solving be relevant to the particular subject matter. Mathematics, the sciences, and business are especially appropriate for this computer application.

Generic applications. Generic applications programs include database managers, word processors, spreadsheets, graphics, and graphing utilities. These programs can be used to help students achieve traditional school goals. For example, using a database management program, students in social studies classes can analyze data they have collected through surveys or questionnaires. Likewise, students can collect from records historical data about a community to create a "picture" or "model" of that locale. Once this information is entered into a database, the students can pose questions about the nature of life in the community and use the database management program to gather the information they need to formulate answers.

Instructional Management

In addition to the two major categories of instructional use described above, the computer can perform services for the teacher. These services are delineated below in three general categories: diagnosis, instructional planning, and student assessment and program evaluation.

Diagnosis. Computers can play an important role in helping the teacher develop a profile of strengths, weaknesses, and other variables needed to set student learning goals. The computer can store and retrieve historical records, normative data, and test information. It can generate, present, and score diagnostic tests, and can produce the summaries and reports needed for effective diagnosis.

Software for educational diagnosis comes in several forms. Some programs score, analyze, and report the results of published tests administered in paper-and-pencil format. Others are more capable, presenting published conventional tests or completely new instruments in computerized form. Some programs are still more general, allowing objective test items written by the teacher to be entered for subsequent presentation and scoring.

Instructional planning. Instructional planning involves specifying the educational goals, experiences and settings necessary to meet the student's diagnosed needs. Setting goals is one of the most important steps in the instructional process. Efficient goal setting requires that considerable quantities of information be organized. General content areas, such as reading and math, need to be broken down into goals, and these goals in turn segmented into measurable objectives. Finally, goals and objectives must be arranged in some meaningful developmental order. Once this organization is achieved, a method must be developed for making goals and objectives readily accessible so that they can be assigned more easily to individual students. The computer can assist this process by providing a means for storing and retrieving descriptions of goals and objectives.

In addition to organizing goals, instructional planning must consider diagnostic information in conjunction with the staff resources, instructional strategies and activities available to meet student needs. The computer can assist in this task by identifying instructional materials appropriate for students with different diagnostic characteristics, by grouping and scheduling students for various remedial services, and by generating individual or group activity prescriptions.

Software for instructional planning can be obtained through commercial publishers or constructed using a database management system. Such systems allow information to be stored, manipulated, and retrieved efficiently.

Student assessment and program evaluation. Assessment describes the student's progress in relation to specified goals. Program evaluation analyzes the effectiveness of instructional procedures and materials. The computer can support these activities by storing, generating, and presenting test items; scoring and analyzing student responses; and generating reports of student test performance, grades, and other evaluative data. As it does for diagnosis, software for assessment and evaluation ranges from programs that score only existing tests to those that allow locally created test items to be entered and administered.

THE SOFTWARE SELECTION PROCESS

The process of selecting instructional software should be organized and systematic. One approach to organizing this process is built around three stages: identification, curricular matching, and evaluation. The process assumes that the school district has identified the subject areas and grade levels in which computers will be employed. Deciding on these subjects and grades is part of the task of establishing a purpose for computer education and of building a computer-education curriculum. More information on these tasks can be found in Chapters 2 and 6.

Identification

The subjects and grade levels of intended computer use provide the basic information from which to begin identifying relevant software. In fact, most software information sources are organized along these dimensions. If hardware requirements already have been established, this information too must be entered into the process. Three software information sources are reference catalogs, databases, and marketing catalogs.

Reference catalogs.   Several catalogs published annually list and sometimes describe the software products issued by various publishers. The fact that these catalogs often focus on one brand of hardware is helpful to schools that already own or have already decided to purchase machines of a particular type. One of the most complete and comprehensive of these catalogs is *The Educational Software Selector* (TESS), produced by EPIE (Education Products Information Exchange).

Databases.   Two major computer databases assist in identifying available software. The first is RICE, Resources in Computer Education, developed and maintained by the Northwest Regional Educational Laboratory. RICE contains descriptive information about educational software and its producers. It can be accessed through the BRS (Bibliographic Retrieval Services), Inc., information system, and can be searched using the ERIC descriptors (Houston, 1984).

The second database is EPIE On-Line, produced and maintained by EPIE. EPIE On-Line is a computerized version of TESS, the print resource noted above. EPIE On-Line, however, is more current because new information is added regularly. The database can be reached through the CompuServe Information Service.

Marketing catalogs.   Every major publisher of software distributes a catalog of its products. These catalogs usually are organized by subject and level. Unlike other sources, vendor catalogs typically present a limited selection of products that fit a particular need. Also, these catalogs sometimes may picture products more favorably than they deserve.

One sensible approach to using these three resource categories is first to search through a database or reference catalog. Such a search is likely to produce the most recent information and the largest number and variety of products. This information then can be supplemented with data gathered from recent marketing catalogs. The result of this search should be a list of software targeted for a particular subject and grade level; for example, math software for grades three through six.

Curricular Matching

Once the software that corresponds to the subjects and grade levels targeted for computer use has been identified, it must be integrated with specific curricular objectives. Many textbook publishers offer descriptive materials which match software with common texts. If one of these texts already has been determined to mesh with curricular objectives, software that supplements the text may, by extension, satisfy these same objectives. However, where such information is not available, district personnel will need to turn to other sources (e.g., colleagues' recommendation, software reviews) to identify the packages that are likely to address each objective. The result of this step should be a list of software that can be used, for example, in grades three through six for achieving specific subtraction, multiplication, division, and fractions objectives.

Evaluation

Once packages that appear to match district objectives have been identified, these packages must be evaluated. Evaluation is the heart of the software selection process: it is the part in which the most effort and time is expended, and the part that produces the information on which final selection decisions likely will be based. Discussed below are a framework, two general evaluation approaches, a combined approach to evaluation, and special factors in evaluating software.

A framework for evaluation.   What is meant by the phrase *software evaluation?* Evaluation can be thought of as the use of objective or subjective procedures to obtain and organize information for appraisal in relation to stated objectives, standards, or criteria (Houston, 1984). One way to organize the phases of the process of software evaluation is by the potential effort required and the type of information produced. In the MicroSIFT project of the Northwest Regional Educational Laboratory, four evaluation levels were identified (NWREL, 1983).

The first, or screening, level provides subjective data of a general nature, and consumes the least amount of evaluator time. At this level, an evaluator makes a cursory examination of a package, noting its completeness, operational readiness, and suitability for its intended use (i.e., with respect to the required hardware configuration and the suggested subject matter). As a general screening stage, this level might take five to fifteen minutes.

The second, or descriptive, level produces more objective data. It includes identifying the product's source, cost, components, and intended grade level, subject matter, purpose and objectives. In this stage, which takes fifteen to thirty minutes, the evaluator may make some subjective judgments when data are not expressly provided. For example, if the purpose or instructional objectives are not clearly stated, these will need to be inferred.

A third level, review, primarily involves the professional judgment of one or more people experienced in using computers in the grade level or subject at which the package is aimed. This level is clearly subjective. Most major evaluation projects, such as MicroSIFT and EPIE, and most periodical reviews, are conducted at this level. The time involved can range from six to thirty-six hours depending on the number of evaluators used, the complexity of the package, and the time available for review. Evaluation at this level cannot be performed adequately without the evaluator actually using the package.

The final level, research, includes any other more extensive evaluation techniques, such as the collection of pretest and posttest data, satisfaction levels, and observational or computer records of students using the software. Data in this category might be objective or subjective, and the procedures typically are time consuming and expensive. Results may shed light on such important characteristics as instructional effectiveness.

The above categorization is arbitrary: certainly evaluation as it is conducted requires a continuum of time expenditure and produces a range of information. Still, the above categorization serves to indicate generally the different levels of potential effort and the different results that are likely to occur. As such, it offers to school districts target levels at which to aim their evaluation efforts.

Approaches to evaluation. Two general approaches for school staff in gathering the evaluative data needed for software selection are to use evaluation results produced by someone else, or to set up an in-district evaluation procedure.

External software evaluations are compiled by two major national projects. Both have developed, tested, and implemented forms and procedures for evaluating instructional software. In the MicroSIFT project at the Northwest Regional Educational Laboratory (NWREL), evaluations are completed according to a standard form that includes predefined criteria but also allows for open-ended comment. Each evaluation report is a composite of the opinion of three professionals: two teachers of the subject and level for which the material is intended, and one computer-education specialist. Reviewers are volunteers selected by a coordinator located at one of over two dozen education agencies participating in the SIFTnet evaluation network. A booklet, *The Evaluator's Guide* (Northwest Regional Educational Laboratory, 1983), describes completely the MicroSIFT evaluation criteria and their interpretation, and is available from the International Council for Computers in Education (ICCE). Sample copies of the MicroSIFT forms are included in an appendix to this chapter.

The second major source of software evaluations is the EPIE Institute. EPIE also uses a standard form that includes predefined criteria and space for comments. The evaluation reports represent the opinions of professionals employed in various educational capacities and are the result of a project involving EPIE, Consumers Union, and a network of large school districts. School district staff are trained by EPIE. The reports are published as *Micro-Courseware PRO/FILES* and may be obtained by subscription. In some locales, statewide subscriptions have been arranged through state departments of education.

Both the EPIE and MicroSIFT projects offer standardized reports based on the reviews of several evaluators, and both use the first three evaluation levels described above. That is, they both employ some sort of screening, description, and professional review.

Other procedures for courseware evaluation have been developed, some as modifications of the aforementioned procedures. The booklet, *Evaluation of Education Software: A Guide to Guides* (Jones, 1983), produced by the Southwest Educational Development Laboratory, is a compendium of ten procedures and forms used in major evaluation efforts, including those of EPIE and MicroSIFT.

Some comment about the various forms is appropriate; first, the forms overlap extensively. Nearly all call for consideration of the subject content of a package, the intended objectives and instructional process characteristics, and the technical implementation and packaging of the product.

Second, forms may be more or less useful depending upon subject-matter area, as the relative importance of instructional process criteria may vary with subject. One exemplary effort to construct criteria for a single subject area was made by the National Science Teachers Association (NSTA) Task Force on Computer-Augmented Science Materials. The resulting form is available from NSTA. A second science-oriented form is a modification of the MicroSIFT form, developed by that project and available from the Northwest Regional Educational Laboratory.

Third, forms may differ in length and detail, a reflection of the compromises any designer faces. These compromises reflect the type of information required by the audience for the evaluation and the time they can devote to reading the information. Also reflected is the amount of time evaluators will have to carry out the process.

Finally, forms vary in the emphasis they place on different criteria. Those involved in a particular evaluation project may place greater weight on a particular criterion (e.g., the use of color and graphics) than would another group. One form from the CONDUIT organization (Jones, 1983), allows the user to indicate the weights assigned to various criteria.

Because these forms often have been extensively tested, many educators find existing forms useful. In some cases, the forms may be used intact. In other cases, they may need to be modified to reflect local conditions, or completely new forms may need to be designed.

The need to adapt an existing form or design a new one is influenced by several factors. One such factor is the audience for the evaluation: the type of information required by decision makers must be represented on the form, and the amount of information and the format in which it is to be presented must fit the audience's requirements.

A second factor is the evaluator's time constraints. The chosen form needs to match the time available for evaluation. A form that is too long or complex will be used poorly or not at all.

Third, the subject-matter focus of the evaluation must be considered. If a variety of subjects is to be covered, then a general form may be sufficient. If the focus is restricted, a general form may need to be modified or a special one created.

A fourth reason for modifying existing forms or creating new ones is that computer applications are appearing which can be neither used nor evaluated in traditional ways. Included in this group are generic applications programs such as word processing and database management software: these programs are used to conduct classroom activities that previously were not often undertaken because they were too tedious or difficult. Though they have no inherent instructional objective, these programs can be used to achieve a variety of learning goals. Some evaluation criteria from existing forms might be applied to such software, especially those criteria related to technical implementation, but others cannot.

A combined approach to evaluation.   The use of external and locally collected evaluation data can be combined to form a comprehensive evaluation process. The first step in this process is to search for existing evaluative data, which may be located through several sources. The RICE database includes the full text of MicroSIFT evaluations, as well as references to other sources. Printed MicroSIFT evaluation reports are available from over 250 state and local education agencies, ERIC centers, and the ERIC system. EPIE evaluations are available by subscription, which many state departments of education possess.

Another source of data, not available in every locale, is state-supported evaluation projects, conducted to evaluate courseware as a service to schools and to provide some measure of quality control over instructional materials. The results are not always available outside the state and, understandably, are designed to meet state needs. Two examples of this kind of resource exist under the auspices of the Texas Education Agency (TEA) and the North Carolina Department of Public Instruction. The TEA is funding a continuing effort, coordinated by the Region IV Service Center, to evaluate courseware in specific subjects with respect to objectives measured by the Texas Assessment of Basic Skills (TABS). These evaluation reports are available nationally in the TABS database and can be accessed through the BRS information utility. In North Carolina, the Media Section of the Department of Public Instruction conducts yearly software evaluation activities, reporting the results in a printed catalog distributed to all districts.

While the first evaluation stage involves gathering existing data, the second focuses upon generating local data. This second stage is necessary for several reasons. First, existing data may be sketchy because the package is new, has not been marketed effectively, or covers an area of limited interest. Also, the growing number of educational packages and the expense of evaluation make it impossible for national and state agencies to cover all available products. Second, local factors, such as those discussed above, and special considerations sometimes not included on existing forms need to be integrated with the evaluation process.

Special considerations for evaluating software.   Several special considerations in software evaluation are discussed in this section, and additional considerations can be identified by referring to the MicroSIFT evaluation form contained in the chapter appendix.

One evaluation consideration receiving increased attention is software licensing arrangements. These arrangements govern how particular software products can be used, and thus the match between these arrangements and district requirements should be carefully evaluated before the district makes a decision to purchase. Once it buys the software, the district will be legally and morally bound to adhere to these arrangements.

In making the selection, staff should determine what restrictions are placed on the use of the software and what provisions are made for the replacement of damaged copies. With respect to the former consideration, the license agreements controlling some products prohibit using the product on more than one machine at a time. Districts wishing to have several students working at different machines concurrently on the same drill-and-practice program will need to buy several copies of the program, even if the computer does not need the program once it is loaded into it. Recognizing that buying multiple copies can be costly, especially where classroom sets are concerned, some vendors offer "site licenses." For a fee that is more than that for a single package but less than the cost of a complete classroom set, the vendor agrees to permit the district to load the program into several machines concurrently. Other vendors sell at reduced price classroom packages that contain several copies of the master diskette but only one set of program documentation.

Districts must also determine if restrictions mesh with hardware requirements. For example, some districts arrange their hardware in a local area network in which the mass storage needs of several machines are served by one computer. Mass storage for the network is usually relegated to a hard disk. If the software license permits, a single copy of a program stored on the hard disk can be used by several students at the same time. Several vendors sell network versions of their packages for a price that is higher than that for a single copy.

Last, the manufacturer's provisions for replacing damaged software should be assessed. Copyright law protects most software products from being copied for other than archival (i.e., backup) purposes, and many vendors make their programs difficult to copy as an added preventative measure. Some vendors will provide a backup copy of the product, some will allow only a limited number of archival copies to be made, and some will place no limit on the production of backup disks. Other vendors will neither allow copies to be made nor provide any copies, but will furnish a replacement disk upon receipt of the damaged original and a nominal fee. Finally, some may make no replacement provisions.

A second special, and often overlooked, consideration in software selection is the teaching style and philosophy of those expected to use the software. If the software is primarily drill and practice, but drill is not a commonly used technique or is one in which teachers see little value, the use of that software likely will be resisted.

Third, cost should be considered, in terms of both the value and the affordability of the product. Cost-worthiness is a judgment that the apparent value of an item is worth the purchase price. This judgment depends greatly on the need perceived by the school. Because of differing need, the same drill-and-practice package may be worth $45 to one school but not to another. Affordability is a second local cost-related factor. A school may not be able to afford an item, regardless of the fact that it is judged to be well worth its cost.

Cost-effectiveness implies that one instructional method produces more learning for the same cost, or the same amount for less cost, than alternative methods. For most instructional software, practical problems have prevented the amount of learning produced from being measured and direct comparisons with alternative learning methods from being made. A somewhat more practical approach may be to view software in terms of the "value added" to traditional instruction. In this conceptualization, traditional methods are not replaced, but supplemented with computer-based techniques. No good tools are available to measure the value added, so it must be a judgment made within the context of local conditions.

Finally, an assessment of congruence should be included in software evaluation. That is, judgments should be made about the degree of overlap between the software and community values, local expectations for computer use, and other instructional materials used. Forms designed for general use typically do not provide for the evaluation of local contextual factors.

SUMMARY

Because selecting software is similar in many ways to selecting other supplementary instructional materials, the selection of software should be performed with the same care and systematicity as that of other instructional media.

The computer can be applied effectively to instruction in many ways. Knowledge of these applications is essential to making sensible software selection decisions. As objects of instruction, computer literacy, programming, vocational skills, and computer science can be taught. As a supplement to instruction, the computer can be used for drill, tutorial, simulation, problem solving, and generic applications purposes. Finally, the computer can be used in instructional management to help diagnose learning needs, set goals, and assess student progress and program performance.

The selection process begins with the identification of available software by subject and grade level. Software should next be matched with specific curricular objectives. For those programs that can be matched with curricular needs, a more thorough evaluation should be conducted.

Evaluation is the primary component of software selection, and it provides the information districts need in order to decide which software is most suitable for their needs. Evaluation may be conceived as a multi-level process involving screening, descriptive, review, and research levels. Most districts can implement the first three levels by either using existing evaluation information or gathering their own data through modified or newly created evaluation forms. A combined approach to evaluation is suggested, in which existing reviews are used as an initial screen and a more thorough evaluation then determines the appropriateness of software for local needs. This more thorough evaluation should consider such special factors as licensing arrangements, teaching style, cost, and congruence.

REFERENCES

Della-Piana, G., & Della-Piana, C. K. (1982). *Making courseware transparent: Beyond initial screening.* Portland, OR: Northwest Regional Educational Laboratory.

EPIE Institute. (1985). *TESS: The educational software selector.* New York: Teachers College Press.

Houston, J. E. (Ed). (1984). *Thesaurus of ERIC descriptors.* Phoenix, AZ: Oryx Press.

Jones, N. B. (Ed). (1983). *Evaluation of educational software: A guide to guides.* Austin, TX: Southwest Educational Development Laboratory.

Northwest Regional Educational Laboratory (NWREL). (1983). *Evaluator's guide for microcomputer-based instructional application.* Eugene, OR: International Council for Computers in Education (ICCE).

APPENDIX MicroSIFT courseware description and courseware evaluation forms

 micro SIFT **COURSEWARE EVALUATION**

 NORTHWEST REGIONAL EDUCATIONAL LABORATORY

Package title _____ Producer _____

Evaluator name _____ Organization _____

Date _____ ☐ Check this box if this evaluation is based partly on your observation of student use of this package

SA - Strongly Agree A - Agree D - Disagree SD - Strongly Disagree NA - Not applicable
Please include comments on individual items on the reverse page.

CONTENT CHARACTERISTICS

(1) SA A D SD | NA | The content is accurate.
(2) SA A D SD | NA | The content has educational value.
(3) SA A D SD | NA | The content is free of race, ethnic, sex and other stereotypes.

INSTRUCTIONAL CHARACTERISTICS

(4) SA A D SD | NA | The purpose of the package is well defined.
(5) SA A D SD | NA | The package achieves its defined purpose.
(6) SA A D SD | NA | Presentation of content is clear and logical.
(7) SA A D SD | NA | The level of difficulty is appropriate for the target audience.
(8) SA A D SD | NA | Graphics/color/sound are used for appropriate instructional reasons.
(9) SA A D SD | NA | Use of the package is motivational.
(10) SA A D SD | NA | The package effectively stimulates student creativity.
(11) SA A D SD | NA | Feedback on student responses is effectively employed.
(12) SA A D SD | NA | The learner controls the rate and sequence of presentation and review.
(13) SA A D SD | NA | Instruction is integrated with previous student experience.
(14) SA A D SD | NA | Learning can be generalized to an appropriate range of situations.

TECHNICAL CHARACTERISTICS

(15) SA A D SD | NA | The user support materials are comprehensive.
(16) SA A D SD | NA | The user support materials are effective.
(17) SA A D SD | NA | Information displays are effective.
(18) SA A D SD | NA | Intended users can easily and independently operate the program.
(19) SA A D SD | NA | Teachers can easily employ the package.
(20) SA A D SD | NA | The program appropriately uses relevant computer capabilities.
(21) SA A D SD | NA | The program is reliable in normal use.

QUALITY

Write a number from 1 (low) to 5 (high) which represents your judgement of the quality of the package in each division:

_____ Content
_____ Instructional Characteristics
_____ Technical Characteristics

RECOMMENDATIONS

☐ I highly recommend this package.

☐ I would use or recommend use of this package with little or no change. (Note suggestions for effective use below.)

☐ I would use or recommend use of this package only if certain changes were made. (Note changes under weaknesses or other comments.)

☐ I would not use or recommend this package. (Note reasons under weaknesses.)

Describe the potential use of the package in classroom settings

Estimate the amount of time a student would need to work with the package in order to achieve the objectives: (Can be total time, time per day, time range or other indicator.)

PLEASE SIGN THE FOLLOWING STATEMENT
The producers copyright was respected during this evaluation and I did not copy or attempt to copy any portion of this package.

Name: _____
Position: _____

micro SIFT COURSEWARE DESCRIPTION

NORTHWEST REGIONAL EDUCATIONAL LABORATORY

Title _____ Version Evaluated _____

Producer _____ Cost _____

Subject/Topics _____

Grade Level(s) (circle) pre-1 1 2 3 4 5 6 7 8 9 10 11 12 post-secondary

Required Hardware _____

Required Software _____

Software protected? ☐ yes ☐ no   Medium of Transfer: ☐ Tape Cassette ☐ ROM Cartridge ☐ 5" Flexible Disk ☐ 8" Flexible Disk

Back Up Policy _____

Producer's field test data is available ☐ on request ☐ with package ☐ not available

---

INSTRUCTIONAL PURPOSES & TECHNIQUES
please check all applicable

☐ Remediation   ☐ Tutorial
☐ Standard instruction   ☐ Information retrieval
☐ Enrichment   ☐ Game
☐ Assessment   ☐ Simulation
☐ Instructional   ☐ Problem Solving
   management   ☐ Other
☐ Authoring
☐ Drill and practice   _____

DOCUMENTATION AVAILABLE
circle P (program) S (supplementary material)

P S Suggested grade/ability level(s)   P S Teacher's information
P S Instructional objectives   P S Resource/reference information
P S Prerequisite skills or activities   P S Student's instructions
P S Sample program output   P S Student worksheets
P S Program operating instructions   P S Textbook correlation
P S Pre-test   P S Follow-up activities
P S Post-test   P S Other

                                                               _____

OBJECTIVES   ☐ Stated   ☐ Inferred

_____

PREREQUISITES   ☐ Stated   ☐ Inferred

_____

Describe package CONTENT AND STRUCTURE, including record keeping and reporting functions

_____

Strengths:

_____

Weaknesses:

_____

Other comments:

(Northwest Regional Educational Laboratory [NWREL]. [1983]. *Evaluator's guide for microcomputer-based instructional application.* Eugene, OR: International Council for Computers in Education [ICCE].) Reprinted by permission.

4
Choosing Hardware

Lud Braun
Stan Silverman

The first "affordable" personal computers came on the market in 1977, when Apple, Commodore, and Radio Shack released the Apple II, the PET, and the TRS-80. Since then, several things have happened (and continue to happen) to frustrate educators whose responsibility it is to choose a computer for their districts. On at least an annual basis, the costs of computers have dropped dramatically and their capabilities have increased just as dramatically. Educators are used to purchasing capital equipment and amortizing its cost over a decade. Many have said, year after year, "I'll wait till next year, when the prices are down and/or the performance has improved," but those who have opted for this philosophy still haven't bought their first computer!

To make matters worse, until about 1982, educators saw the computer as a drill-and-practice tool for weak students, or as a tool for very bright students to learn programming. The vast body of students was excluded from access to computers because of cost and lack of suitable materials. Since then, we have seen the development of word processing, spreadsheet programs, database programs, simulations, construction sets, and other exciting products which make computers attractive for creating learning environments for all students. Now, with the backing of research showing positive results for computers used in many ways by students with diverse characteristics (Education Turnkey Systems, undated; Kulik, Bangert, & Williams, 1983; Murphy & Appel, 1984; Ragosta, 1983), and with a spate of recent reports from national commissions recommending strongly that computers be integrated into all phases of school curricula (National Commission on

Excellence in Education, 1983; The National Science Board Commission on Precollege Education, 1983; Twentieth Century Fund Task Force, 1983), educators are looking seriously at the computer as a learning environment for all their students.

Unfortunately for educators, this increasing pressure (not always ameliorated by purchase funds) resolves only the question of whether or not to buy computers. It doesn't answer the question of which computer to buy. If educators want the cheapest computers (and they do), they probably would buy Commodore computers; if they want computers with the most available software (and they do), they would buy Apple computers; if they want to buy computers from the most stable company (and they do), they would buy IBM PCs; if they want the computers with the most exciting capabilities (and they do), they might buy Mindsets or Amigas.

But even choosing a company doesn't resolve the matter. Many companies have several models to further confuse the issue. As of this writing, Apple had the Apple IIe (in at least three slightly different versions), the Apple IIc, and the Macintosh; Commodore had the Amiga, the C-64, and the C-128; and IBM had the IBM PC, the PC XT, and the PC AT. Even within a company, the several models may or may not be mutually compatible (able to run the same software). New companies keep appearing, announcing computers that are more spectacular than anything on the market—and, then, many of them disappear. Established companies announce new computers, or "leak" information about forthcoming computers. Other companies appear with "clones," or act-alikes for some of the major computers. These clones sometimes are substantially cheaper than the machines they imitate, but the potential buyer must be wary when purchasing a clone. Manufacturers of clones say that their computer is compatible with computer XYZ, but is less expensive. If it is "95% compatible," that means that 95% of the programs written for XYZ will run on the clone, but if your program is in the other five percent, 95% compatibility is useless to you.

How is the computer-inexperienced educator to choose from this morass of possibilities? Even among experts with as much as two decades of experience in educational computing, one of the most hotly debated issues is that of the best computer to select for schools. There is no clear-cut answer, but there are approaches one may take which can help. That is what this chapter is about.

HOW CAN YOU USE THIS MACHINE?

Before deciding on the computer to buy for an educational application, the educator must be aware of the roles the computer can play in education. Some people propose that the educator decide on the software, find out what machines it runs on, and then choose the computer to run that software, but that seems to be a very narrow view. The quality of educational software has increased significantly since 1980, and, more importantly, the *kinds* of software available have also changed within the past few years. Because it is impossible to predict the ingenuity of the educational software developer, it is foolish to choose hardware based on today's software. Before 1982, for example, most people thought that word processing was something to be taught only to students in business courses in high school and college. Now, many teachers of writing see it as an excellent vehicle to teach writing to all students, starting in elementary school. Some developers have designed word processors specifically for young children, because those designed for professionals are too complex for young minds—their very power gets in the way of learning to write. Many other kinds of software have come into existence only recently, or have been modified only recently for young people. If we base our decisions on today's software, we may be precluding the possibility of using tomorrow's exciting new computer developments. The moral here: Buy the best, most up-to-date computers you can afford.

Many ways of using the computer have been put into practice since Patrick Suppes (1966, 1967) started his explorations; among them are drill and practice, teaching programming, computer literacy, vocational training, and intellect enhancement (simulations, construction sets, word processing, spreadsheets, databases, laboratory support, adventure games). Of the applications listed above, only vocational training requires special kinds of computers for proper learning experiences. The student in a business program needs access to computers which can run powerful word processors; students of auto mechanics need computer-based analyzers; and students of computer repair and maintenance need access to sophisticated computers and peripherals. For other students, all the computers mentioned above are useful; all have available software to cover the standard applications, so the kind of application is no longer a crucial factor in making the selection decision.

This leaves us right where we were—with no real basis for choosing. Fortunately, there are ways of making this decision. We will explore this question in the next section.

CHOOSING—PRELIMINARY CONSIDERATIONS

Before we look in detail at the question of making a choice among the available options, we must look at a few important questions. The first of these is that of configuration. We can buy stand-alone microcomputers, a local-area network of microcomputers, or a system using terminals or microcomputers "talking" to a minicomputer. Each of these has advantages and disadvantages. Each points the decision-making process in a particular direction.

Stand-Alone Microcomputers

A stand-alone microcomputer is a microcomputer which is connected only to the local AC power source. Such a computer is completely independent and can be set up anywhere the user wishes—even at the beach or on a mountain trail, if it is battery powered. The disadvantage, though, is that it has no access to other resources—although remote databases and information services such as the Source and CompuServe are becoming available through telephone linkages.

In educational situations, stand-alone computers can be moved anywhere in the building (or even district) depending upon the teachers' needs. Thus it is possible, over the summer, on weekends, or even overnight, to allow students, faculty, and community residents to borrow district computers.

An important advantage of such computers is that, since they currently are the most popular machines, most current software is being developed for them.

Perhaps the most important advantage of stand-alone computers is their inherent system reliability. In a school laboratory, where there may be twenty-five computers, each has its own disk drive and printer. If a printer or disk drive breaks down, that station is out of service, but the other twenty-four are still able to operate. In the operational modes described below, when a disk drive breaks down, the entire system is down and no one can use the computer.

Local-Area Networks

A local-area network (or LAN) is a collection of microcomputers that are connected together, usually in a single building, and that can communicate with each other. In some schools, local-area networks are set up in a room which is used as a computer laboratory.

A LAN has three major advantages: it permits sharing of peripherals (disk drives, printers, and other add-ons); it permits sharing of software; and it sometimes permits the teacher to view the activity of every student without leaving the central station. The first is an advantage which must be counted with care. Although it is true that peripherals may be shared, it also is true that, when they are shared, queues develop. If the printer, for example, is shared, it must be a faster printer than a printer used with a single computer—and faster means more expensive (although printer costs are going down, and large buffer memories are now available to store documents for later printing). A careful analysis must be made with LANs to choose peripherals which are fast enough to keep the queues short and inexpensive enough to effect a real savings.

The second advantage of LANs is the possibility of sharing software among all the computers in the network. If there are twenty stations in the LAN and all will use the same software, then it may not be necessary to buy twenty copies of the software. Theoretically, only one, loaded onto the LAN system disk, is needed. Everyone on the LAN may then access that package.

The third advantage, teacher access to any student terminal, is available in some LANs but not all. Where it is available, it is not clear whether this really is an advantage. One could argue that the teacher should not simply view the student's progress remotely: some people think that such remote access is Orwellian.

One major disadvantage of LANs is that the teacher loses flexibility. Because the computers share resources, they must remain where the peripherals are. It isn't possible to move them to where the students are, or to lend them out over a weekend. A related disadvantage is that typically there is only one disk drive and one printer, and when these break down, the entire system is out of commission. With stand-alone computers, only that machine whose drive breaks is out of action.

Another disadvantage of LANs is that many publishers of software do not permit use of their software on more than one computer at a time. It is necessary, therefore, to obtain a license from publishers before sharing software over a LAN.

Minicomputer/Terminal Systems

Systems consisting of a central minicomputer and terminals located remotely were very popular from 1970 until 1975 but have been overtaken by stand-alone microcomputers and LANs. Such systems have a place in education because they provide the user with access to a large main-frame memory (typically, over one million characters of information) and to as much as several hundred million characters or "bytes" of disk memory. With this much memory, large database systems and telecommunications systems can be maintained, as well as detailed records of educational progress for hundreds of students. These large systems also permit simultaneous use by students, teachers, and administrators (to keep academic and financial records, to schedule classes, bus routes, and so on).

Minicomputer systems have two major disadvantages: because they are not very widely used in education any longer, little software is being written for them; and they have little locational flexibility, although it is possible to communicate with them over the telephone by using a terminal and a modem (i.e., a device for converting computer symbols to sound and vice versa).

AN APPROACH TO DECISION MAKING

Educators, deciding which computers to buy for their classrooms, are faced with serious problems, some of which I have already identified. These educators are in a situation somewhat similar to those of us wishing to buy a car. We have an idea of our needs (four wheels, an engine, and a roof to keep out the rain are the basic ones) and of our budget limit, but we seldom have a firm grasp of either. Most of us go into the marketplace with prejudices. We all choose cars on the basis of a combination of objective and subjective criteria. Purchasers of computers do just the same. How are we to buy the "best" computer systems for our schools when we are faced with this dilemma, when no one seems to have the definitive answer?

Even though the computer-purchase decision cannot be made with total objectivity, it is possible to quantify the subjective and objective elements of the decision process and to arrive at a reasonable solution (Braun, 1979, 1981). Before we examine the specifics of this approach, four general guidelines should be considered.

1. Get the largest number of work stations that your budget permits. This is so obvious that it shouldn't need to be said; however, there are educators who buy very expensive systems when a simpler system will provide several times the number of work stations that the expensive system will. Educators are more and more concerned about equity in access to computers for females and for poor children. One essential element in addressing equity is to purchase less expensive systems, so that more children can get access to computers.

2. Do not choose a particular computer unless there is a body of users of that computer in your region. Because most educators don't have a great deal of expertise concerning computer hardware or software, there is great value in joining a community of users. Such communities frequently form clubs for exchanging experiences—good and bad. In a group, it is likely that you will find someone else who has had and solved a problem you may have. If you have the only XYZ computers in your area, you will be completely dependent on the manufacturer or the vendor for help, sources which have not always been reliable in the past.

3. Buy from a local dealer. In the computer magazines, ads from mail-order houses offer computers and peripherals at very attractive prices, prices that are frequently lower than those a local dealer can offer. Even so, it is usually wise to buy locally, because the dealer will frequently lend you a system while yours is out for repair, or will provide on-site training and advice. The turn-around time for repairs is much shorter with a local dealer than with a national mail-order house. Some local dealers offer seminars on computer use for teachers in their client districts which cannot be matched by mail-order houses.

The traditional requirement in schools for soliciting bids and choosing the lowest bidder may be cheapest in the short run, but you will have your computers for several years and must consider the long run as well.

4. Don't wait for breakthroughs in computer developments (lower prices or better machines) before buying. "Waiting till next year" may be a good policy in baseball, but not in education. Every year that goes by without access to an educational computer represents an irretrievable loss in the intellectual growth of a child (Braun, 1984).

COMPARING AND RATING COMPUTERS

The approach that I propose for comparing computers permits each educator to factor into the decision-making process the uniqueness of her or his environment and individual assessments of the extent to which each computer meets the educator's needs. The approach involves a three-step procedure:

1. Identify a set of capabilities of importance. Table 4–1 includes thirteen capabilities which I consider to be important in my environment. Some individuals may wish to add graphics animation to this table, or to eliminate memory expansion (the ability to increase internal storage). Any capabilities may be added to or subtracted from the table without invalidating the approach—indeed, it is this flexibility which makes the approach useful in a wide variety of situations. For illustrative purposes, the table presents information on each capability for seven microcomputers of interest at the time of this writing.

2. Assign a quality rating (Q) to each of the capabilities of Table 4–1 for each computer under consideration. Each quality rating is a number that expresses the machine's capability as compared with the other computers in Table 4–1. The ratings shown in Table 4–2 are computed as follows:

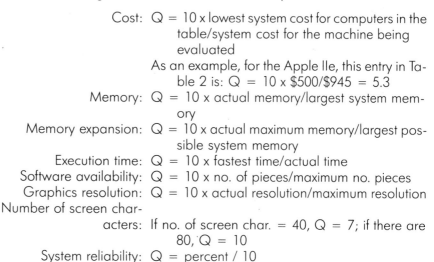

Cost: Q = 10 x lowest system cost for computers in the table/system cost for the machine being evaluated

As an example, for the Apple IIe, this entry in Table 2 is: Q = 10 x $500/$945 = 5.3

Memory: Q = 10 x actual memory/largest system memory

Memory expansion: Q = 10 x actual maximum memory/largest possible system memory

Execution time: Q = 10 x fastest time/actual time

Software availability: Q = 10 x no. of pieces/maximum no. pieces

Graphics resolution: Q = 10 x actual resolution/maximum resolution

Number of screen characters: If no. of screen char. = 40, Q = 7; if there are 80, Q = 10

System reliability: Q = percent / 10

$$\text{Music (voices): } Q = 10 \times \text{no. of voices/maximum no. of voices}$$
$$\text{Disk space available: } Q = 10 \times \text{disk space/maximum disk space}$$
$$\text{Colors available: } Q = 10 \times \text{colors available/maximum colors available}$$
$$\text{Disk access speed: } Q = 10 \times \text{access speed/maximum access speed}$$

Keyboard quality: The Q for keyboard quality is made up of two parts: number of keys and existence of a numeric keypad. Each factor was awarded a

TABLE 4–1   Capability information for several personal computers

Capability	Apple IIe	Apple IIe + 80-col card	Amiga	Commodore 64	Commodore 128	IBM PC	Macintosh
Cost[1]	$945	$1,100	$1,500	$500	$690	$1,900	$1,945
Memory	64K	128K	256K	64K	128K	256K	256K
Memory expansion	No	No	8M bytes	No	No	640K	512K
Execution time[2]	110 secs	110 secs	7.5 secs	121 secs	63/124 sec[3]	21.7 secs	19.5 secs
Software availability[4]	865	867[5]	0/365[6]	494	494[7]	405	46
Graphics resolution[8] (no. of pixels)	280x192 53,670	560x192 107,520	640x400 256,000	320x200 64,000	640x200 128,000	640x200 128,000	512x342 175,104
No. of screen characters	40[9]	80	80	40[9]	80	80	80
System reliability[10]	90%	90%	80%[11]	80%	80%[11]	99%	97%
Music (voices)	1	1	4	3	1	1	4
Disk space available	130K	130K	880K	170K	170K	360K	400K
Colors available[8,12]	6	16	4,096	16	16	16[13]	2
Disk access speed (bytes per sec)	1K/4.4K[14]	1K/4.4K[14]	8.6K	384K	500/1K/5K[15]	9K	8.6K
Keyboard quality							
No. of keys	63	63	89	66	92	82	58
Numeric pad	No	No	Yes	No	Yes	Yes	No

[1]These are the prices to educators in Fall, 1985. Since prices tend to decrease rapidly over time, current price information should be used in making comparisons.

[2]These timings were done using the Ahl Benchmark Program (*Creative Computing*, Sept. 1985, p. 6).

[3]These times represent times in the normal and fast modes.

[4]These are the number of pieces of software listed for each computer in the 1985 Soft-Kat Educational Software Catalog.

[5]Little educational software currently takes advantage of the features added by the 80-column card; however, virtually all Apple IIe software runs on this machine.

[6]Although there is little educational software currently available directly for the Amiga, it has an IBM emulator mode which appears to make most IBM educational software available for the Amiga. The second number assumes the typical 90% compatibility which exists in the industry.

[7]Little educational software currently takes advantage of the features of the C-128 which are not included in the C-64; however, all C-64 software runs on the C-128.

[8]Generally speaking, the number of colors available and the graphics resolution are inversely related (the higher the resolution, the fewer colors are available).

[9]Eighty-character displays are possible with added hardware or software.

[10]These numbers are based on a limited sampling of educational institutions, and will vary with the level of local maintenance.

[11]No data are available because these computers have been in the field only a limited time. Because of the apparent quality of these machines a reliability estimate of 80% seems reasonable.

[12]In general, only a limited subset of the available colors may be used at one time.

[13]Separate color card needed (cost, $180).

[14]The first speed is with Apple DOS 3.3 and the second is with ProDOS.

[15]The load speeds indicated are in normal, fast, and burst modes respectively.

maximum of 5 points, and the overall Q determined as the sum of the two parts. The Q for number of keys is 5 x no. keys/maximum number of keys. For the numeric keypad, Q = 10 if there is one, and Q = 0 if there is not.

3. Assign an importance weight to each of the capabilities included in Table 4–1. The importance of a specific capability may be chosen (arbitrarily) to range from 0 to 100, with 100 considered extremely important, and 0 considered to be of no importance. My assignments of importance are shown in Table 4–3 for two cases: Case 1 is a typical school system with a broad range of applications; while Case 2 is a school with a special interest in word processing and database systems for its students. These importance weights are assigned so that the total is 100, with individual assignments made to reflect the relative importance of each of the 13 capabilities. Software availability is much more important than color in both cases, while software availability is much more important in Case 1 than in Case 2.

TABLE 4–2   Quality ratings for computers listed in Table 4–1

Capability	Apple IIe	Apple IIe + 80-col card	Amiga	Commodore 64	Commodore 128	IBM PC	Macintosh
Cost	5.3	4.6	3.3	10	7.3	2.6	2.6
Memory	2.5	5	10	2.5	5	10	10
Memory expansion	0	0	10	0	0	0.1	0.1
Execution time	0.7	0.7	10	0.6	0.6/1.2[1]	3.5	3.9
Software availability	10	10	0/4.2	5.7	5.7	4.7	0.5
Graphics resolution	2.1	4.2	10	2.5	5	5	6.8
No. of screen characters	7	10	10	7	10	10	10
System reliability	9	9	8	8	8	9.9	9.7
Music (voices)	2.5	2.5	10	7.5	2.5	2.5	10
Disk space available	1.5	1.5	10	1.9	1.9	4.1	4.5
Colors available	0	0	10	0	0	0	0
Disk access speed	1.1/4.9	1.1/4.9	9.6	0.4	0.6/1.1/5.6	10	9.6
Keybd. Quality[2]							
No. of keys	3.4	3.4	4.8	3.6	5	3.2	3.2
Numeric pad	0	0	5	5	5	5	0
Keyboard total	3.4	3.4	9.8	8.6	10	8.2	3.2

[1]These numbers represent the normal and fast modes of the C-128.
[2]The number of keys and the numeric pad each have been assigned 5 points maximum, so that total keyboard quality is the sum of the two numbers.

TABLE 4–3 Importance weights for capabilities of Table 4–1

Capability	Case 1	Case 2
Cost	15	10
Memory	5	10
Memory expansion	0	5
Execution time	5	10
Software availability	30	10
Graphics resolution	5	10
No. of screen characters	5	10
System reliability	20	20
Music (voices)	5	0
Disk space available	0	5
Colors available	5	0
Disk access speed	5	5
Keyboard quality	0	5
	100	100

The relative worth of each computer in Table 4–1 is determined by combining the Quality ratings of Table 4–2 with the Importance weights of Table 4–3 and is shown in Table 4–4 for Cases 1 and 2. Mathematically, we may think of this process as multiplying for each computer each Quality rating by its associated Importance weight and summing the results. For example, the worth of the IBM for Case 1 is:

$$\text{Worth} = Q_{cost} \times I_{cost} + Q_{MEMORY} \times I_{memory} + Q_{memory\ expansion} \times I_{MEMORY\ expansion} + \ldots + Q_{keyboard\ quality} \times I_{keyboard\ quality}$$

or

$$\text{Worth (IBM)} = 2.6 \times 15 + 10 \times 5 + 0.1 \times 0 + \ldots + 8.2 \times 0$$

or

$$\text{Worth (IBM)} = 583$$

Table 4–4 has been generated by carrying out for each computer the calculations indicated above using the quality ratings of Table 4–2 and the Importance weights of Table 4–3. Clearly, in this case, the Apple IIe with 80-column card is superior to the others in Case 1, and the Amiga is superior to the others in Case 2. A word of caution is in order here, however: the assignments of Importance in Table 4–3 are totally subjective, and are specific to the proposed use of the computer. The assignments of Quality in Table 4–2 also are somewhat subjective. It is essential that the reader use her or his own criteria to set up Tables 4–2 and 4–3 to reflect the local situation. In this way, a set of values can be chosen from which an intelligent decision may be made.

TABLE 4-4 Worth of each computer in Table 4-1

Computer	Worth: Case 1	Worth: Case 2
Apple IIe	658	505
Apple IIe + 80 col. card	686	574
Amiga	679	827
Commodore 64	584	497
Commodore 128	588	589
IBM PC	583	668
Macintosh	499	619

To simplify the data presentation, the numbers in this table are the largest numbers of those generated from Tables 4-1, 4-2, and 4-3.

In Tables 4-5 and 4-6, the computers are rearranged in order of decreasing Worth for Cases 1 and 2 respectively. It is interesting to compare Cases 1 and 2 by studying Tables 4-5 and 4-6. In Case 1, system cost and software availability are much more important than in Case 2, and the Apple IIe with the 80-column display option leads, while the IBM PC is next to last. In Case 2, where these two characteristics are less important, the Amiga moves from second place to a commanding lead, while the IBM PC moves from sixth place to second.

To summarize the decision-making approach: A set of desirable capabilities is defined and information on these capabilities is gathered for several promising microcomputers. Next, each microcomputer is rated relative to the others on each capability, producing a Quality rating. Third, the capabilities are weighted in terms of their importance to the user. This results in an Importance weight. Finally, the worth of each machine is computed by multiplying the Quality rating for each capability by its associated Importance weight and summing the results.

An epilogue. Which machine in our example is best? The answer clearly depends on the characteristics important in your environment, and on the relative importance that you assign to each. No one can choose the best computer for your application for you. Only you know your environment well enough to set up Tables 4-1 through 4-4 for your case. The approach described here can help you to define your needs and to personalize your choice. Subjectivity is not eliminated in the characteristics to be included or in the Importance values assigned in Table 4-3, but the approach is consistent and orderly, and should be helpful in eliminating the influences of emotional attachment to particular machines or vendors and the sometimes misguided advice of "experts."

TABLE 4–5 Worths in descending order (Case 1)

Computer	Worth
Apple IIe +80 col. card	686
Amiga	679
Apple IIe	658
Commodore 128	588
Commodore 64	584
IBM PC	583
Macintosh	499

TABLE 4–6 Worths in descending order (Case 2)

Computer	Worth
Amiga	827
IBM PC	668
Macintosh	619
Commodore 128	589
Apple IIe +80 col. card	574
Apple IIe	505
Commodore 64	497

PERIPHERALS

A peripheral is a device which is connected to a computer to make it operable, to make it easier to operate, or to make it do things it could not do without the peripheral. We will look at some peripherals to identify them and to consider their value in learning environments.

Video Display Devices

Probably the most important, and most essential, peripheral is the video display device. It may take the form of a TV set or of a video monitor. Some microcomputers (e.g., the Apple II series and the Commodore 64) can be connected to a standard TV set. The advantage of this capability is that an existing video device can be used; when not connected to the computer, the device can be attached to an antenna to receive TV broadcasts. TV sets frequently are significantly less expensive than monitors because of the production volumes; however, the disadvantage of using a TV set is that images are not as sharp as they are with a monitor. Despite the added cost, most educators are equipping their computers with monitors to achieve the best image quality available. With some of the more powerful computers like the Apple Macintosh, the Commodore Amiga, and the IBM PC, TV sets are not even usable because the resolution capabilities of these machines are so high.

Having decided that a monitor is a better choice than a TV set, the educator must still choose between monochrome and color monitors. Many of the current packages use color (although not always for pedagogical reasons). The user with a monochrome monitor will not be able to take advantage of color. On the other hand, monochrome monitors develop crisper images than do color monitors. In applications where there will be a lot of reading of text (such as in word processing), monochrome monitors are preferable, and are cheaper, lighter, and easier to maintain.

Disk Drives

The disk drive is another essential peripheral. It is used to store programs and data until they are needed by the user. Most computer manufacturers also make disk drives which are compatible with their computers. Although it is possible to buy drives from other vendors for some computers, that seldom is a wise idea, even when the cost is lower. Such "foreign" devices usually are only "95% compatible" with the host computer, and are therefore not apt to work under all conditions.

The educator must also decide whether to use a single disk drive or two (or more) at each station. There are times when a dual drive is convenient but not a necessity; at other times a dual drive is required, as with some sophisticated word processing programs and some database systems. However, if dual drives are not required, it usually is better to use the extra money to buy more systems.

Printers

Printers are less essential than disk drives or monitors in some applications, but are just as important in others. In word-processing or programming applications, for example, they are a required part of the system.

Choosing a printer is almost as difficult as choosing a computer. Printer prices range from very affordable to quite expensive, although all printer prices have been dropping dramatically. The many kinds of printers include dot-matrix, color, near-letter-quality, letter-quality, ink-jet, and laser.

Dot-matrix printers print characters using sets of dots rather than a fully-formed character as does a typewriter. They are faster and less expensive than other kinds listed below, but do not have quite the print quality of the others. One of the more exciting dot-matrix printers on the market is the color printer, which has great promise especially for younger children working with graphics tools.

Near-letter-quality printers are able to produce copy which is nearly letter quality; that is, the print looks almost as good as that from a good typewriter. In some cases, they are distinguishable from type only with a magnifying glass. Near-letter-quality printers are dot-matrix printers which use a high density of dots to achieve good-quality characters. Usually, such printers have draft and near-letter-quality modes and print with lower dot density in the draft mode. Such printers usually are somewhat more expensive than dot-matrix printers and, in the near-letter-quality mode, are considerably slower than dot-matrix printers. (There is a trade-off between letter quality and printing speed.)

Letter-quality printers use fully-formed type like that of a typewriter. They produce high-quality output, but are substantially slower and more expensive than dot-matrix printers. In some installations, a dot-matrix printer is the workhorse at every station, and a small number of letter-quality printers are reserved for final drafts.

Ink-jet printers print by squirting a stream of ink through a template. They are very fast, but also quite expensive, and are seldom considered for educational settings.

Laser printers, which use laser beams to form their characters, are extremely fast and very flexible. They frequently can produce any of dozens of fonts in a range of sizes. Because of their high prices, they currently are out of the reach of educators.

Other Peripheral Devices

Many other devices may be used to enter information into a computer and have some educational value. Among these are joysticks, paddles, touch-sensitive tablets, light pens, and analog/digital interfaces.

Joysticks are similar in function to a pilot's control stick. These devices permit the student to move objects around the screen and provide tactile feedback, valuable in some educational circumstances.

Paddles are similar in purpose to the joystick, but have the advantage of a rotary motion which is preferable to joystick motion in some circumstances. Unfortunately, most commercially available paddles are of poor quality and are not popular with software developers.

Touch-sensitive tablets, such as the Koala Pad and the Power Pad, permit the user to indicate any point on the tablet and translate it to the screen. They are used widely as input devices for graphic art software packages.

Light pens are devices which point directly at the screen and tell the computer where the user is pointing. Although they are potentially among the most desirable input devices, the available ones typically are not of good quality.

Analog/digital interfaces permit the user to connect the computer to the real world to gather data and to manipulate those data (e.g., to do statistical analyses and to develop plots of the data). One of the better of these interfaces is the *Experiments in Human Physiology* by Human Relations Media.

MAKING THE PURCHASE

Selecting a Computer Vendor

Once the decision of which computer to buy has been made, it might seem that the work is done; but many schools have learned that the final stage, the selection of a computer vendor, can make or break a program.

In almost 100 percent of the cases, the local school does not deal with the computer manufacturer but, rather, must rely on a local computer dealer. The local dealer is responsible for the delivery, the warranty, and any post-warranty repair of equipment. In each case, this can lead to a successful program or one filled with pitfalls and hand wringing.

A dealer must first be able to obtain the appropriate hardware and software. While this seems trivial, given the glut of microcomputers on the market, in reality it is a major problem because of the traditional slow manner in which schools handle the payment of bills. This long procedure forces the local dealer to establish a credit line with the manufacturer. These credit lines range from zero to several million dollars, and a dealer may purchase equipment up to his credit limit. If a dealer suddenly receives $500,000 in purchase orders and has only a $300,000 credit limit, at least $200,000 worth of computers cannot be ordered immediately.

One should look for a dealer who has both a large credit line and sufficient leverage in the wholesale/retail market to obtain equipment. Schools which, in July, ordered equipment from dealers unable to stroke the supply lines have found their students still waiting to see a computer in May.

Once the computers are delivered, it is essential that the vendor be knowledgeable about the product. Make sure that the vendor knows both the hardware environment and how computers are used in schools.

No matter what anyone says, computers break down—and they break down when you can least afford to have it happen. A dealer must not only be able to fix the products, but also must be able to instruct you on how to maintain the computers. A few lessons in preventive maintenance will save thousands of dollars in repair bills.

When looking for a dealer one must look for one committed to the educational market. Our needs are unique and we need dealers who are willing to fill those needs.

Bid Preparation

Once the decisions to purchase a specific type of computer and peripherals have been made, it is imperative that the ordering process go smoothly. In most cases, this process involves bidding. Bidding has been adopted by most school systems to ensure that they pay the lowest price for materials purchased, but the school must make sure that the bid specifications ensure not only the lowest price, but also the best service, delivery date, and support. Sometimes, the "lowest price" turns out to be very expensive when one encounters months of delay, inoperative equipment and general confusion.

To avoid the pitfalls of the bidding process, one must clearly outline exactly what is required in terms of both materials and service. The first step in this process is to list all necessary equipment, making sure that all cables and peripherals are included. Many schools have received unpleasant surprises when ordering what they believed to be complete systems only to find that the bidder interpreted the specifications to mean just the main computer without disk drive, power supply, or electrical cords. When specifying equipment, make sure to include everything that you expect from the supplier.

Of critical importance is that you specify interfaces when ordering equipment. (An interface is the electronic logic needed to connect the computer to a printer or other peripheral.) It is insufficient simply to order a Commodore 64 and printer: there are many different printers, each requiring a different type of interface. The correct terminology is: "Commodore 64 with Epson FX 80 printer and Cardco +G interface." While it seems that this type of wording is required only when crossing brands, that is not always true and a little care at the outset will avert potential problems later.

Equally important to the bid specifications are the inclusion of the terms of delivery. How much time is the bidder allowed to have before delivery is expected? Is the equipment to be delivered inside the building or dropped on the front lawn? Who sets up the equipment, you or the vendor? Is there a penalty for late delivery? Each of these questions must be answered and each must be specified in the bid. Most dealers are reputable and will assume all the correct answers; however, some dealers who operate on very close margins will assume nothing, and you may in turn get nothing.

The last area of concern should be the post-delivery period. This includes service, technical information, and notice of updates and changes. Make sure you include the warranty period that you expect and the terms for carrying out the warranty service. It is wonderful for a company to say that they will repair anything for a period of one year; however, that promise becomes meaningless unless the repair is completed in a reasonable amount of time. Some districts have required 72-hour turn-around and/or loaner equipment; some insist upon on-site repair. Each is very valuable to the customer, but each is expensive to the bidder. You never get anything for nothing, so determine exactly what you want and then ask for it in your specifications. (See the chapter appendix for a sample bid.)

When the bids are answered you may be confronted with one of the most difficult parts of the bidding process—the substitution. In this case, the bidder has decided to substitute an item for one you had on your list. The problem is that although the substitute may be a duplicate, or for that matter a better product, many times it is inferior, or at least different enough to be unsuitable for your purposes. One way to avoid this is to specify "no substitutions"; however, this is illegal in many areas and may in fact prevent you from getting better equipment. The only way to ensure quality is to specify exactly what the item does and contains, and how it is expected to perform.

The bid process is long and can be a nightmare, but it will allow you to arrive at the best possible price for the materials that you need to run your program.

SUMMARY

In this chapter, we have identified one of the problems educators face when moving into the world of educational computing—the wealth of hardware options from which to choose, all choices being good, but some seeming better than others. Making this choice is very difficult, partly because of its subjectivity.

An approach is presented which is partly analytic and partly subjective, but which has the advantage that it can be customized to the particular situation faced by the educator. The approach depends upon choosing a set of hardware characteristics of value in the school setting, assessing the quality of each computer under consideration in terms of these characteristics, and assigning a relative importance to each characteristic. From these values, a relative worth for each machine can be computed and used as a guide to hardware selection.

The chapter concludes with an emphasis on the importance of choosing a vendor carefully, and with a set of guidelines to help in making that choice.

REFERENCES

Braun, L. (1979). How do I choose a personal computer? *AEDS Journal, 13,* 81–87.

Braun, L. (1981, November). Help!!! What computer should I buy??? *The Mathematics Teacher,* pp. 593–598.

Braun, L. (1984). I have a dream. *Proceedings of the Sixth National Conference on Communications Technology in Education and Training.* Washington, D.C.: Information Dynamics, Inc.

Education Turnkey Systems, Inc. (undated). *Computer-assisted instruction (CAI): The bottom line.* Fairfax, VA: The International Communications Industries Association.

Kulik, J. A., Bangert, R. L., & Williams, G. W. (1983). Effects of computer-based teaching on secondary school students. *Journal of Educational Psychology, 75,* 19–26.

Murphy, R. T., & Appel, L. R. (1984). *Evaluation of the Writing to Read instructional system.* Princeton, NJ: Educational Testing Service.

National Commission on Excellence in Education. (1983, April). *A nation at risk: The imperative for educational reform.* Washington, D.C.: U.S. Department of Education.

The National Science Board Commission on Precollege Education in Mathematics, Science, and Technology. (1983). *Educating Americans for the 21st century.* Washington, D.C.: National Science Board.

Ragosta, M. (1983). Computer assisted instruction and compensatory education: A longitudinal analysis. *Machine mediated learning, 1,* 97–126.

Suppes, P. (1966). The uses of computers in education. *Scientific American, 215,* 206–220.

Suppes, P. (1967, February). The teacher and computer-assisted instruction. *NEA Journal,* pp. 15–32.

Twentieth Century Fund Task Force on Federal Elementary and Secondary Education Policy. (1983). *Making the grade.* New York: Twentieth Century Fund.

APPENDIX   A sample bid

The Einstein Public School District is interested in obtaining bids for the following:

10 Microcomputers

Commodore 64 or equivalent—to include power supply, manuals, warranty cards, power cords, and TV connectors.

Microcomputer must support the following:

1   320 x 200 pixel resolution
2   16 colors
3   3-D sprites
4   3-voice, 9-octave sound
5   6510 software

10 Single Floppy-Disk Drives

Commodore 1541 or equivalent—to include serial connector, manuals, warranty cards, and power cords.

Disk drive specifications:

1   5.25-inch single-sided, single-density floppies
2   Storage 174,848 per disk
3   Sequential storage 168,656 bytes per disk
4   Relative 65,535 records per file
5   144 directory entries
6   Blocks 683
7   Drive must load all Commodore copy-protected software

10 Dot Matrix Printers

Epson RX 80 or equivalent—to include Centronics interface, manuals, warranty cards, and power cords.

Printer must support:

1   Roman and Italic print fonts
2   Six pitches
3   Two kinds of bold print
4   Superscripts and subscripts
5   Forms-handling capabilities
6   High resolution graphics
7   100 character-per-second print speed
8   Adjustable tractors
9   Disposable print heads
10 Cartridge ribbons

10 Printer Interfaces

Cardco + G or equivalent—to include manuals, warranty cards, and connectors.

Interface must support:

1   Commodore graphics
2   All Commodore special print codes
3   Bank Street Writer software

Vendor Support

1   Vendor must supply all equipment within thirty days of awarding the bid.
2   Vendor must replace, within 10 working days, any equipment found to be defective upon delivery.
3   Vendor must provide in-building delivery and set-up of all equipment.
4   Vendor must supply 90-day warranty work which must be completed within seven working days, or a loaner must be provided.

5

Planning a Computer Center

John F. DeGilio

Few instructional facilities are as complex as a school computer center. Not only does this space house delicate electronic equipment but it also must be integrated with a range of programs in the school. As an extension of the classroom, the computer center must accommodate different teaching and learning styles. Every detail of the center's design is important: the flexibility the facility will have is a direct result of the care taken in its planning.

This chapter focuses on how to plan a school computer center. Although such centers are most often found in secondary schools, those responsible for planning centers from elementary programs through college may also find the chapter content useful. The approach offered is intended to encourage thoughtful and systematic planning. Through such an approach, many pitfalls experienced by schools in establishing computer facilities can be avoided (Poirot, 1980).

BASIC CONSIDERATIONS IN ESTABLISHING A COMPUTER CENTER

For the purposes of this chapter, a computer center is any facility that contains between ten and 30 work stations. A facility with fewer than ten computers might best be considered an extension of the classroom, and one with more than 30 machines presents a different set of management problems, with vastly different implications for teaching and learning. As defined in this chapter a computer center serves a single class of about thirty students working singly or in pairs. Larger computer facilities are not conducive to the same type of teacher-student and peer interaction found in class-sized labs.

The tasks involved in establishing a computer center can be grouped into three major categories: establishing a planning team, planning for the management of human resources, and planning for the management of physical resources.

Establishing a Planning Team

When microcomputers first entered the schools, centers were created by removing machines from individual classrooms and assembling them in a single room called the computer center. Expensive modifications had to be made in these schools as the potential of the computer center became apparent to the instructional staff, and many schools still suffer because of their lack of insight as to what might be accomplished in the computer center. For example, many schools did not plan adequately for power needs, individual space adjacent to work stations, and storage for documentation and peripheral equipment. In the worst cases, some schools, in their zeal to launch themselves into the "brave new world," completely neglected systematic planning. Some formed their centers around a single local expert who promptly left the system for a higher paying job in industry. The result was a room full of expensive equipment that nobody knew how to use and that posed a security nightmare. Software disappeared, machines broke down, and the center limped along until the next teacher-hobbyist appeared to rescue it.

Computer centers must be carefully planned. To start planning a computer center, establish an ad hoc committee responsible for its overall development. This ad hoc effort might properly be directed by the assistant superintendent for instruction or by whatever administrator coordinates the efforts of all school departments. In the best of all possible worlds, a committee of administrators and teachers whose departments constitute the community of interest should be selected. Broad representation should be sought to ensure a sense of commitment to the success of the venture. It will be the committee's mission to make recommendations to school policy-makers regarding the goals and purposes the computer center should serve (see chapter 2 for more on establishing a purpose for computer education). These recommendations should clarify whether the center is intended to be a special-purpose one for learning such things as programming, CAI, or word processing, or a facility attempting to fulfill several purposes at once. In addition, this panel should set the size and composition of a standing committee to plan and to oversee the general operation of the center.

Forming the standing committee. Members of the standing committee should be selected to ensure balanced representation. It is important that each group of teachers expected to use the center be represented. Under some conditions, it may be advisable to involve interested third parties, such as a parents' organization that can provide a person with insight and contacts in the local computer community. In the early planning stages, the committee should organize itself into subcommittees to focus on two broadly different aspects of creating the computer center: the management of human resources and the management of physical resources.

Planning the Management of Human Resources

The tasks involved in planning the management of human resources can be grouped into several different categories: establishing staff responsibilities, defining the role of the classroom teacher, and integrating classroom and center activities.

Establishing staff responsibilities.   The subcommittee that focuses on the management of human resources needs to set up a personnel organization chart and generate a job description for each position required by the center. The chart should clearly indicate the "chain of command" responsible for making day-to-day management decisions. A question that should be answered early is how the staff of the computer center will fit into the existing school administrative structure. In many schools, the center is administratively located in an academic department, such as mathematics or business. In other cases, an entirely independent administrative structure is created. A case can be made for each approach, based on the size of the school, the available resources, the administrative model used by the school, and the role the computer will play in accomplishing the mission of the school.

Each model of center administration presents different problems. When organized under an existing academic department the computer center may become the territory of a single department: use by others is allowed on a limited basis, if at all. On the other hand, when the center is a separate administrative unit, it may become disconnected from the academic departments it serves. No matter which staffing model is used, many of the problems can be solved by carefully planning how the center will become integrated into the existing organization and making this plan clear to the school community (Calkins, 1982).

In addition to establishing explicitly the center's place in the school's administrative structure, the human resources committee must clearly outline the duties of each member of the computer center staff. Regardless of the size of the center, these duties will fall into four general categories: center coordination, software management, instructional support, and equipment repair and maintenance.

With respect to the first category, responsibility must be assigned for coordinating the activities of teachers from diverse departments and for ensuring that all departments have an opportunity for center use. This coordination may include producing regular bulletins to inform the entire school community about recent software and hardware acquisitions, user services, projected developments, housekeeping details, and other news that relates to the computer center's mission.

Second, the management of software and documentation used in the center will have to be assigned. Software is often costly and easily stolen or misplaced. Without careful management, the school's investment in this essential component of the computer center will quickly evaporate.

Third, someone will have to be responsible for supporting students and teachers in the center. This may involve training and supervising student aides, advising teachers, and helping to perform specialized computer center tasks. These tasks might include installing new software and hardware, maintaining computer communications networks, and performing a number of other computer-related activities.

Finally, responsibility must be assigned for preventive maintenance and equipment repair. There is no question that computers and printers will eventually break down. In addition, there is little doubt that enhancement boards and other add-on products will be purchased to extend the capabilities of the center's hardware. The repair of machines and installation of these enhancement products is, therefore, an important staff function.

It is vital that one or more persons be appointed to carry out these various tasks if the center is to operate effectively.

Defining the role of the classroom teacher.   Another aspect of the management of human resources is defining the role that the classroom teacher will play in operating the center. If, for instance, an English class is learning to use a word processor, what role will the English teacher play in teaching these students? Is the English teacher expected to teach students to use the word processing software or is that the duty of the center staff? If center staff are to take responsibility for word processing instruction, will the classroom teacher assist? Will the teacher's assignment be part of the regular duty schedule like other nonteaching duties, or is it to be an additional compensated duty?

Integrating classroom and center activities.   To integrate computers into the curriculum effectively, the activities of classroom and center staff must be carefully coordinated. For example, pre- and post-lab classroom activities should be developed to introduce and reinforce students' work in the computer center. If social studies students are to learn to use a spreadsheet program to analyze political opinion data, for example, a class lesson describing the purpose and basic characteristics of the spreadsheet program should be conducted before the students visit the lab. After students return to the class, a lesson focusing on the conclusions drawn from the data might be delivered. The articulation between what happens in the center and what happens in the classroom is critical. Without this linkage, the use of the computer in the center may become divorced from the discipline in which it is employed.

Planning the Management of Physical Resources

The major task in physical resource management is establishing the computer center itself. The ideal way to go about this task is to design the center and then locate the space within the school that can best accommodate the design. Where this ideal can be realized, it is all to the advantage of the computer-education program. Where it cannot—and this may be the more typical situation—the lab must be designed to fit whatever space is available. Under these conditions, the process of establishing a center entails locating the space, selecting a physical organization, designing workstations, providing for electrical and other wiring needs, controlling environmental conditions, establishing ancillary space requirements, taking security precautions, and developing scheduling priorities.

Locating the computer center.   While most schools will not have the luxury of building a computer center to the specifications dictated by an optimal design, they will be able to select a space for the center from among several possible sites. Before recommending a site, the physical resources subcommittee should meet to review the possible locations for the center. If the center is to be part of a newly constructed building, there may be a number of possible sites, since the selection is less likely to be constrained by space already allocated to other functions. If the center is to be located in an existing building, skillful negotiation may be required to get the most adequate space while still preserving the integrity of other programs within the building.

In selecting the site, the committee should consider space on an upper floor. The area should ideally have limited access from the outside of the building and should be in direct line-of-sight from the street. Such a location reduces security problems significantly. Since the computer center is the single largest concentration of capital equipment in the building, and computer equipment and software represent an easily disposable commodity, security considerations are crucial.

In addition to security considerations, the space chosen for the center should be large enough to accommodate the various functions that the center will perform. Obviously, the location must provide enough space for students to work comfortably at the computers. But in addition to this, space ideally should be available for undertaking small group work, presenting large group demonstrations, storing student belongings, housing software, repairing hardware, and performing administrative responsibilities.

Selecting a physical organization.   Once the space has been selected and approved, the next task the physical resources subcommittee should undertake is to make a scale outline of the entire space. This drawing should contain all pillars, load-bearing walls, windows, and any other structure that cannot be easily altered. Then, using paper cutouts, examine the possible placements that would optimize the available space. Locate the core student work area, software storage space, hardware maintenance area, office area, demonstration classroom, and any other special purpose sections that are consistent with the purposes of the center. Also locate the power lines, telecommunication lines and other electrical facilities.

Within the core student work area various work-station arrangements are possible. These arrangements are differentiated by the letters of the alphabet their formation suggests. Each arrangement has its own advantages and limitations.

One arrangement, the "I" (lying on its side), places work stations in rows as in the traditional classroom (see Figure 5–1). Under this arrangement, it is easier to manage classes working on the same task in unison. Students have a clear view of the instructor and easily can shift focus between the front of the room and the computer monitor. One drawback to this arrangement is in providing electrical power. If both ends of each row are left free for students to

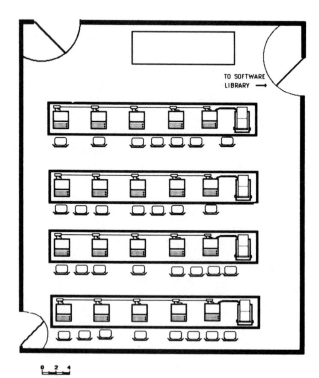

FIGURE 5–1   Work station arrangement "i"

walk around, the power must enter the middle of each row through the floor or from the ceiling, an arrangement requiring substantial remodeling work. A second limitation is that supervision of each student's work is more difficult since only one row at a time can be viewed and because the supervisor must stand at the rear of the room. Finally, communication between students is restricted to adjacent persons, thereby limiting opportunities for team projects.

A modification of this form is the letter "E," which for space reasons is presented in Figure 5–2 with two, instead of three, horizontal bars. Here the work stations are placed on the horizontal bars. The vertical bar (here a storage table) abuts a wall and makes the supply of electrical power to each peninsula easier. In some cases the peninsulas are double-width so computers can be located back to back (as in Figure 5–2). In this arrangement, the student can interact more easily with others. Supervision of students is also enhanced as an instructor standing between rows can monitor two rows of students at once. However, if machines are located back-to-back it will be difficult for students to work in unison since not all work stations will face the instructor.

A substantially different approach is to use the room periphery as the letter "O" or "U" (see Figure 5–3). In this case, the center of the room affords a

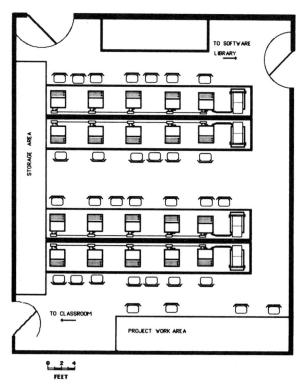

FIGURE 5–2 Work station arrangement "E"

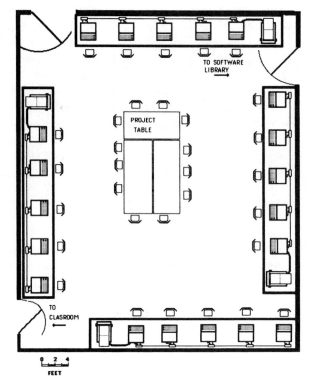

FIGURE 5–3   Work station arrangement "O" or "U"

clear view of all stations and a student in trouble can be identified easily. Once again the student is restricted to interacting with a neighbor on either side. All power cords and cables are located against the walls, out of the path of classroom travel. Work tables can be placed in the center of the room if space permits. Here students and aides can work on problems that do not require a work station.

A fourth model uses islands which, when paired, are shaped like the letter "H." These islands are strategically placed within the work area (as in Figure 5–4). This model affords some privacy as students cannot easily see one another's display screens. Social interaction may be facilitated, however, as each student can make eye contact with three others at the table. Disadvantages include the fact that at least half of the students will be out of the aide's view at any time, and that power must drop from the ceiling or come up through the floor. Finally, having all students perform a task at the same time is virtually impossible.

Designing work stations.   The number and arrangement of computers in the center is in part a function of the design and size of each work station. Because

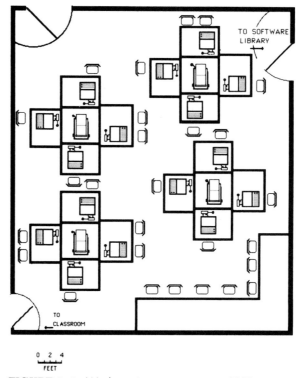

FIGURE 5-4 Work station arrangement "H"

of the wiring and stability requirements of computers, work stations should generally be designed around fixed, as opposed to movable, furniture. Whether the furniture is purchased or constructed in-house, it must be able to withstand the weight of computer equipment and heavy student use. Legs should be reinforced and work surfaces should be smooth and even. Finally, furniture with metal work surfaces should be avoided because of the potential shock hazard.

In terms of the unit space for each work station, one often-used rule-of-thumb is to allow a minimum of five linear-feet frontage for each computer and monitor. This provides adequate space for the machine and for a notebook or software manual. If, however, students will work in teams of two to accomplish assignments, up to six feet of frontage per work station may be necessary.

To accommodate most personal computers or terminals, a depth of two and a half feet is adequate. This depth allows access to the rear of the machine where cables and connectors are attached. If a security device is to be attached to each machine, access to lock and unlock the device also must be provided. Finally, when allocating space for machines, consider designing a few stations for left-handed students. For these students, leave work space adjacent to the machine on the left, rather than the right, side.

The optimum height for a computer work table for student users is about twenty-six inches above the floor. This height provides comfortable leg room with standard school furniture for most secondary-school students. For handicapped students, however, special design modifications may be needed. Space for wheelchairs and for such specialized data entry and output devices as expanded keyboards and large screen monitors may need to be provided.

Work-station design must consider the placement of the computer monitor. If the monitor is detached from the system unit and keyboard, it can be located on the system unit or placed on a shelf built into the work-station furniture. One important consideration in locating the monitor is the experience of the average user. Because beginners are constantly looking from keyboard to screen, they are often most comfortable with a distance of about two inches between the keyboard and the bottom of the screen. Experienced users may be more comfortable when this distance is about four inches. Because of the great variability in the heights of students, screen-tilting capability is a big advantage.

The inclusion of a printer will require added space for work-station design. An additional foot-and-a-half frontage should be included for these work stations. Be sure to provide easy access to the space behind the printer for storing paper and feeding it to the printer.

Except for continuous, heavy word processing applications, not all stations need to have a printer attached: a printer at every fourth or fifth station should meet most printing needs. When high-volume printing is required, the use of these stations can be controlled by cycling students to these machines during the work session. If more flexibility is desired, machines can be connected to a switch box that allows the output from a group of work stations to go, in turn, to a specific printer. This is a more expensive alternative because it requires specialized hardware and cables for connecting each machine to the switching mechanism.

Finally, consideration should be given to anticipated growth of the printing capabilities of the computer center. For example, if a plotter, extra-wide printer, or other specialized printing equipment is to be used at some future time, room should be reserved from the outset.

Providing for electrical and other wiring needs.   When arranging for electrical service to the computer center, plan to supply approximately 500 watts to each work station. Power can be supplied through a junction box of four grounded outlets at each station. One outlet can be used for a computer, one for the monitor (if it does not derive power from the computer), and one for a printer. The fourth outlet can be reserved for other peripheral equipment, a tape recorder, or other appliance. Whenever possible, outlets that serve machines should be at table height. This significantly improves safety and makes it easier for school maintenance staff to perform their cleaning tasks without interference from floor-level outlets and wires.

In some locations, the electrical service is not delivered in a smooth, steady supply or current. Often, other electrical equipment draws power from the same line affecting current throughout the building. Although most common appliances are unaffected by such momentary fluctuations in electrical power, the computer is not. Depending on the severity of the change in current, data can be lost or a microprocessor chip destroyed. If the building does not have protection from such power fluctuations, voltage regulators and surge protectors should be included in the center design. These devices are available from most electrical and computer supply houses.

Within the center, power should be delivered in three or four parallel branch circuits connected in series to a master switch. Having all circuits connected to a limited-access master switch will add to the safety and economy of the center. Shutting the switch off at the end of each day will ensure that all equipment is off even if someone forgets to turn off a particular unit, eliminating the danger of an off-hours fire caused by an overheated machine and the costs of unnecessary electrical consumption.

In addition to electrical power, wiring should be installed for at least one direct, outside telephone line. If not at the start, the center's computers will eventually need to communicate through a modem with computers outside the school. Installing the phone lines during the design stage is generally more convenient than having them put in after the center is completed.

A direct, outside line is needed for this purpose because lines routed through in-house phone systems typically cause data communication errors. The communications work station should generally be located on the periphery of the core work area so that it can be supervised more easily. The need for supervision comes partly as a result of the high cost of telecomputing. If the school has an account with an information utility like the Source or CompuServe, charges for use will include phone fees to get to the local utility node, as well as utility connect costs. Unless use is carefully regulated, the entire budget for computer communications could be spent in a very short time. Besides cost, security is also an important consideration. Many private databases are accessible by phone and it is the responsibility of the center to ensure that students do not abuse telecomputing privileges by breaking into these data banks. To limit access, the phone terminal block can be covered easily by a locked box.

Controlling environmental conditions.   Environmental conditions that need to be considered in center planning include lighting, noise, temperature, static electricity and dust (L'Hote, 1983). When considering the lighting requirements for a computer center, one major cause for concern is the glare created by natural lighting. Although natural light may be good for reading books, its reflection on monitor screens makes reading difficult. It is therefore sensible to locate machines so that sunlight will not shine on the screens. In addition, make sure that the center has an operating set of shades or blinds that can be adjusted as the direction and angle of sunlight changes.

A second environmental concern is noise. The major source of distracting noise in the computer center is the printer. To reduce the level of noise, position printers where possible in booths, best located away from the core work area. An inexpensive alternative to the printer booth is a lightweight wooden box with a plexiglass top and open back that covers the printer and printer stand. The inside of the box should contain sound-absorbing material. When the sound of a printer prevents students from concentrating, the printer cover can be put in place over the machine. Covers can be constructed in-house or purchased from computer supply houses. Finally, because a significant portion of printer noise comes from the transfer of sound to the printer stand, placing the printer on an inexpensive foam rubber pad can also reduce noise levels.

A third important environmental concern is temperature. Generally computers cannot withstand temperature extremes. It is therefore wise to consider the range of temperature conditions the center is likely to experience. The suggested range of temperatures for the proper operation of most microcomputers is from 55°F to 90°F. If room temperatures are frequently outside this range, air conditioning or special heating equipment may be necessary. Additional electrical service for this equipment should be installed while the room is being designed, rather than after the lines are in, walls are up, and computers are breaking down.

In relation to their bigger brothers, microcomputers suffer less from static problems, a fourth common environmental concern. Static charges can, however, cause microcomputer chip damage so some precautions against static buildup should be taken. The major source of static buildup is through contact with thick-pile nylon carpeting. If the computer center is carpeted, a relatively inexpensive spray can be obtained to reduce static. Under most conditions, spraying the carpet with a solution one-part water and three-parts fabric softener will prevent static problems. Low room humidity is also a source of static electricity. If the relative humidity is kept at 50 percent or above, this source of static will be eliminated too.

The final environmental condition to be discussed is dust. Most floppy disk drive failures can be attributed to contamination by dust particles. If the school building is known to contain a high concentration of dust, consider installing a filter on the air circulation system. In addition, a daily dusting of work surfaces and machines will prevent most problems with disk-drive mechanisms, disk read- and write-heads, and diskettes. A small hand-held vacuum cleaner might also be used in very active computer centers where printing is frequent. Finally, under no circumstances should a chalk board be installed in the center. Instead, install a liquid marker surface.

Establishing ancillary space requirements. Controlling environmental conditions in the center's core work area is critical to the center's efficient operation. Also fundamental is the availability of ancillary space. Ideally, the computer center should encompass a suite of rooms or a large work space capable of serving several concurrent functions aside from student computing. Among other things, such a center should contain space for students' belongings, for the storage of software, for hardware repair, for a demonstration classroom, for small group work, and for offices. Each of these areas need not be a separate room but could be delimited by partitions. Liberal use of glass in the partitions optimizes security and makes supervision easier.

Because few students come to the computer center empty-handed, space should be provided for purses, books, and other belongings. Either space near each work station, or a wall unit containing pigeonholes for the temporary storage of students' property, should be provided. Through the use of such pigeonholes the objects students bring into the core area can be controlled, thereby enhancing safety and security in the center.

A second problem that plagues most computer centers is the lack of hardware-related storage space. Space must be provided for equipment cartons, in the event that a unit is to be shipped to the manufacturer for service, as well as for spare parts, extra cables, and other items that may be used for special purposes. Most cartons and packing material can be stored offsite, but a few should be kept handy so that down machines can be quickly shipped for repair. Cables and other supplies can be kept in a small, well-secured closet located in the lab. The closet is best located near a work bench away from the core activity area.

In addition to space for personal effects and the storage of hardware-related materials, accommodation must be made for the storage of software. Software is constantly being removed and returned. When new software is delivered to the center, backup copies must be made (if the license permits), the originals must be filed, and the working copies inventoried and integrated with the rest of the collection. Some disks will need to be dispensed in class sets and others will be checked out one by one. Making sure that the software that leaves the library gets back at the end of the class session is a pressing concern. Without a librarian who can regularly attend to the cataloging and disbursement function, chaos results.

Ideally, an enclosed library should be established adjacent to the core work area. The library should be capable of being locked so that it need not be constantly staffed. Schemes to ensure that software does not get lost or stolen are as varied as the number of librarians. Most methods follow either the sign-out or collateral models. In the sign-out model, a signature is all that is required to take out software. In the collateral model, a school identification card, library card, or the like, is left with the librarian as collateral until the software is returned.

Although diskette sizes are standardized, few standards apply to the related documentation. Anticipating the shelving space needed for the library is, therefore, difficult. Using the IBM documentation as a standard is a somewhat risky but relatively conservative measure. Each of their diskettes comes with a loose-leaf type notebook about two inches wide. In an active school computer center it is not unreasonable that 100 to 500 pieces of software may be processed on a normal day. This may include some of the same diskettes used repeatedly by different students and different classes. Each time a package is used, some accounting should be done to ensure that the whereabouts of the center's property can be traced. Naturally, a microcomputer can be used for this type of accounting.

A fourth type of space important to computer center operations is an attached classroom. This space differs from the traditional classroom in that ideally it should contain a large-screen projection system—or one or more large-screen monitors mounted on rolling stands or fixed to the ceiling or walls—to permit easy viewing by an entire class. The teacher's desk should include a computer system similar to those in the core area. This facility is used principally for demonstrating software as part of pre-lab or post-lab activities. For example, if students are to learn to use graphing software, a demonstration of such software would be valuable before students try it in the lab.

A reasonable alternative to the computer classroom is a work station on a movable cart. This cart, along with a large screen monitor, can be transported to any classroom. The classroom teacher can then conduct the pre-lab or post-lab session in the regular class.

Finally, a portion of the center's space should be reserved for tables where students can work in small groups away from the work stations. Here, for instance, students can work on a mock-up of a newspaper, a poster, or other project without disturbing those at the computers.

Assuring center security.   The security of the computer center is in part determined by the general provisions taken to ensure security of the school building. There are, however, a few additional measures that every center can use to discourage vandalism and theft (Barbour, 1986). First, arrange entrances and exits so that students check in and out under the supervision of center staff. This stresses to students that center staff are concerned about protecting the school's investment and discourages petty theft. Second, fix entrance and exit doors with a double-lock system. At least one of the locks should be capable of being changed on short notice. A "key" list should be maintained in the main school administrative office and a policy for key authorization established. If funds are available and the situation warrants, an electronic combination lock and security system can be installed.

A variety of locking devices are also available to protect individual machines in the center. These devices range widely in price and sophistication. Unfortunately, once installed, these devices make it difficult to make minor adjustments in the placement of equipment. Before spending funds on such locking devices, some effort should be made to see if school carpentry staff can design a more economical and flexible locking system.

Developing scheduling priorities. The last aspect of physical resource management planning to be discussed relates to scheduling. As for all instructional facilities a schedule for lab use must be developed. In developing the schedule, the priorities assigned to different types of activities need to be established. What percent of the regular school day will be devoted to scheduled classes, student clubs, and free use by students? Will the center be open after school for clubs (e.g., school newspaper club, computer club), computer competitions, adult-education classes, or free-time use? In any event some tentative attempts at scheduling, modified as experience with the lab is gained, need to be made to ensure smooth operation.

SUMMARY

Creating a school computer center is a large and complex task (Cline, Bennett, Kershaw, Schneiderman, Stecher & Wilson, 1986). Unlike any other instructional space, the computer center must meet the needs of many departments and accommodate a wide range of teaching and learning styles. The major tasks involved in creating a computer center are establishing a planning team, planning the management of human resources, and planning the management of physical resources.

The planning team is responsible for making recommendations to school policy makers about the purposes of the center and for selecting a standing computer center committee. This committee is, in turn, charged with forming subcommittees to manage the two major aspects of center planning: planning the management of human resources and planning the management of computer resources.

Planning the management of human resources involves three tasks: establishing the responsibilities of center staff, defining the role of the classroom teacher, and integrating classroom and center activities. Establishing staff responsibilities requires locating the center in the school's administrative structure, and delineating and assigning responsibility for the recurring tasks that must be performed to operate the center effectively. Defining the role of the classroom teacher centers upon deciding whether the teacher will provide instruction to students in the center or whether this responsibility will be left to center staff. Last, integrating class and center activities involves making sure that some articulation between the class and center exists so that class activities can supplement those of the center, and vice versa.

Planning the management of physical resources entails locating the computer center, selecting a physical organization for work stations, designing work-station specifications, providing for electrical and other wiring requirements, controlling environmental conditions, establishing ancillary space requirements, taking security precautions, and developing scheduling priorities. These tasks are aimed at building the physical foundation for an effective computer facility.

The creation of a computer center requires careful planning. The information presented in this chapter should provide a useful beginning to this important planning process.

REFERENCES

Barbour, A. (1986). Protecting your micros. *Electronic Learning, 5*(7), 48–50.

Calkins, A. (1982). Sparring Over Computers, *Electronic Learning, 1*(4), 34–71.

Cline, H. F., Bennett, R. E., Kershaw, R. C., Schneiderman, M. B., Stecher, B. & Wilson, S. (1986). *The electronic schoolhouse.* Hillsdale, NJ: Lawrence Erlbaum Associates.

L'Hote, J. D. (1983). On Computers: Glitchproofing. *American School and University, 55*(10), 123–127.

Poirot, J. L. (1980). *Computers and Education.* Austin, TX: Sterling Swift.

6

Planning a Computer Education Curriculum

Gary G. Bitter

Computer education includes computer literacy, programming, computer science and, most of all, the infusion of the microcomputer as a tool in the curriculum. Infusion into the curriculum has always been a goal of microcomputer use. One of the first computer-literacy scope-and-sequence curricula for K-12 (Bitter, 1982a, 1982b, 1982c, 1983a, 1983b) includes many infusion ideas.

In the early 1980s, a few microcomputers were available in schools and their capabilities were largely limited to BASIC programming and drill and practice. These limitations understandably restricted the incorporation of the microcomputer in the curriculum. Since those early days, the microcomputer has gained significant new utility with the addition of application packages having database, spreadsheet, word processing, and graphic capabilities. Today's software offers drill and practice, simulation, remediation, testing, problem solving, instructional prescription, control of physical devices, and speech and sound capabilities, as well as improved user friendliness. Encyclopedias and dictionaries are also available. Finally, telecommunication is a new dimension still to be explored. As can be seen, significant changes since the early 1980s have made many of yesterday's microcomputer infusion ideas more feasible and desirable today.

The purpose of this chapter is to give educators guidance in developing school computer-education curricula and in integrating computers into existing curricula. The chapter accomplishes this purpose by outlining a set of steps for establishing a computer-infused curriculum and by providing detailed examples of infusion.

COMPUTER EDUCATION: A BRIEF OVERVIEW

Infusing the microcomputer into the curriculum reduces the need for computer-education courses. The topics included in most computer-literacy scope-and-sequence charts eventually will be infused into the subject matter of the K-12 curriculum (Bitter & Craighead, 1984, 1985). For the present, however, computer-education courses will be needed in grades 7–9 to meet the computer literacy requirements of students currently at the secondary level. A one-semester or one-year computer literacy course is utilized in several states (e.g., Texas, Tennessee, Utah) and many school districts for this purpose. The curriculum for this course usually includes the following topics: history, hardware, software, word processing, spreadsheets, databases, programming, societal implications, privacy, futures, ethics, and graphics. Several available commercial books satisfy this outline (e.g., Bitter, 1986).

High schools will continue to offer advanced courses in computing. Currently, several types of computer courses are provided, including computer literacy, business computing, computer mathematics, computer programming, and Advanced Placement Computer Science. General outlines for the three most common courses (computer mathematics, computer literacy, and computer programming) are presented in Table 6–1.

TABLE 6–1   General outlines for three common computer courses

Computer Literacy	Computer Programming (BASIC)	Computer Mathematics
History of computers	Constants/variables/ formulas	Elementary computer systems
Hardware	Naming variables	Applications
Software	Inputting information	Problem solving
Applications	Decision making	Structured programs
Word processing	Arrays	Programming
Spreadsheets	Graphics	Algorithms
Databases	Logical statements	Error analysis
Programming	String manipulation	Boolean algebra
Society	Applications	Mathematical applications:
Ethics	Structured programming	Algebra
Future		Geometry
Careers		Trigonometry
		Numeration
		Calculus

MICROCOMPUTER INFUSION

Many teachers are exploring the use of the microcomputer as a classroom tool in different subjects. The development of curriculum materials to assist this effort is essential. However, few established, well-researched materials exist.

The objective of infusion is to incorporate the microcomputer in the curriculum of an appropriate school subject. Included in this incorporation are courseware, the application of computer literacy concepts, and the use of applications packages and programming languages. The objective is to use the microcomputer to help achieve the goals of the school curriculum.

Curriculum Change

Many issues need to be addressed in the years ahead with respect to the curriculum changes implied by the availability of the microcomputer. Some of these issues are:

☐ The teaching of computation procedures beyond the basic facts and estimation should be reconsidered. Should we teach manual division of a 4-digit number by a 3-digit number when pocket calculators and computers can instantaneously perform this computation?

☐ The impact of word processing on writing and on the curriculum needs to be explored. What impact will the use of word processors have on writing skills? Will spelling checkers make unnecessary the inclusion of spelling lessons in the language arts curriculum?

☐ Algebra factorization can be done by some popular software packages. What is the impact on the teaching of algebra?

☐ Many science software packages provide laboratory simulations, as well as physical devices to carry out experiments. What potential do these packages have for the teaching of science and how effective are they?

☐ Graphics packages and the Logo programming language provide many opportunities for exploring geometric concepts. Should the geometry curriculum be altered to take advantage of these microcomputer capabilities?

☐ Databases will offer extensive information which can be immediately accessed. What does this imply for social studies and history curricula?

☐ Software packages are available to organize writing and research. Along with the use of databases, what will be the impact on the production of research reports in various subjects?

These are a few of the issues facing educators and curriculum developers. Will we make curriculum changes to meet the enormous capabilities that the microcomputer offers?

Curriculum Infusion

The microcomputer can be infused into the curriculum in many ways. For example, keyboarding skills can be taught as a precursor to computer writing or mathematics activities. Keyboarding is usually introduced by means of a district-wide plan. Some districts introduce this topic in the primary grades, while others delay formal instruction until the middle grades. Programming is another way in which computers can be infused. Logo is often used in elementary and middle school mathematics, and sometimes even up through grade 12. BASIC, the most popular programming language in the schools, is used throughout the grade range. Pascal, a popular language in colleges, is used in grades 11 and 12, usually for Advanced Placement Computer Science courses. Finally, infusion can be achieved by coordinating courseware with curriculum topics for tutorial instruction or drill and practice.

ESTABLISHING A COMPUTER-INFUSED CURRICULUM

To establish a computer-infused curriculum, a 12-step process is suggested:

1. Establish a planning committee.   The district should establish a committee to determine how best to utilize the available hardware. The committee should include citizens from the community as well as teachers and administrators. Including representatives of these various constituencies on the committee helps develop commitment to computer education among teachers, parents, and community members. The end result is usually broad support for computer education. (See Chapter 1 for more information on establishing a purpose for computer education.)

2. Develop a curricular plan.   The curricular plan should lay out in general terms the purpose, method, and expected results of the curriculum development effort. The plan should include a multi-year implementation schedule with specific objectives projected for each year. The objectives should focus on all subjects, and evaluation methods for each objective should be included (Chapter 10 provides more detail on the evaluation of computer-education efforts). Finally, issues such as finances, teacher training, and administrative responsibility should be addressed.

3. Identify goals for all subjects and levels.   Include teacher representatives from all subjects and grade levels in planning the curriculum. Work with this group to develop computer-related goals for each subject at each grade level; that is, goals that will encourage the development of computer competencies within the context of the subject-matter course. Second, identify subject-matter goals to which computers can be applied. Have administrators and parent representatives as well as school staff review these goals.

4. Develop microcomputer infusion ideas.   Specify exactly how the micro-computer will be utilized in each subject area. Keyboarding, programming, word processing, telecomputing, database management, graphics, and graphing are only a few ways in which computers can be used. For example, in high school mathematics, graphing programs can be used to help students develop an intuitive understanding of the meaning of various functions. Students can graph functions, change them, and immediately have the graphs redrawn to see how the shapes of various functions differ. Tie each suggested use to a particular computer competency or subject-matter goal.

5. Develop an integrated curricular scope-and-sequence guide and support materials.   Have subject matter experts work with computer educators to develop a microcomputer-infused scope-and-sequence guide for each subject-matter area. These individuals should organize themselves into sub-committees by subject area. Each subcommittee should develop sample lesson plans, data files, and student exercises to support ideas included in the curricular scope-and-sequence guide. Subcommittees should also recommend the purchase of appropriate software, print materials, films, video cassettes, and any other media that might be used to tie the computer meaningfully to particular curricular areas. Finally, each subcommittee should recommend when computers should be used in the laboratory instead of in the classroom.

6. Train teachers and administrators.   For infusion to be successful, the district will need to make a significant commitment to teacher training. Teachers must not only learn basic computer competencies, they must also be trained in using the computer to achieve specific subject-matter goals. Training should be provided over an extended time period to allow teachers to try computer activities in the classroom and return to discuss the results with trainers and with each other. (See Chapter 7 for a detailed treatment of the issues involved in planning a teacher in-service program.)

7. Implement the computer curriculum plan.   The plan to introduce computers into the curriculum should be implemented in small steps. Implementation in each subject-matter area should be guided by a computer infusion coordinator, who should take responsibility for helping teachers to incorporate the computer into subject-matter lessons. In addition to the support of the coordinator, the district must also provide basic hardware and software support: arrangements must be made for the maintenance and repair of hardware and for the cataloging and distribution of software and other instructional support materials.

8. Address equity issues.   Many computer-education programs underserve female, minority, and handicapped students. Through systematic planning, try to avoid perpetuating these inequities. For example, make sure that the use of computers is not limited to higher-level mathematics courses, which tend to be dominated by nonhandicapped, white, male students. Also, try to prevent after-school computer clubs from becoming male hang-outs. Limit the use of arcade-type, shoot-'em-up games, which appear to discourage female attendance, and, if necessary, establish clubs specifically for females.

9. Develop software ethics.   The district should promulgate a clear policy on when it is and is not permissible to copy software, and in this policy should clarify who has ownership of software developed by teachers for classroom use. This issue should be resolved to avoid conflicts over the right to market such software privately. Unless this issue is already dealt with in state law, district policy, or employment contracts, negotiation between school management and teaching staff may be required. Both copying and ownership issues should be formulated into a code of conduct for all school community members and explained clearly to staff in a seminar. Relevant portions of this code should be incorporated in the school conduct code and distributed to students. Such a code makes enforcement much more feasible.

10. Provide ongoing support to teachers.   The district should provide ongoing support for subject-matter teachers responsible for infusing the computer into their curricula. Such support would include release time for developing lesson plans and student exercises, meetings with computer resource teachers to discuss problems, and visits to other schools to observe computer-education activities. Books and software relevant to infusion in particular subject-matter areas should also be provided. Support for attending conferences focusing on subject-matter infusion might be helpful too. Finally, relevant infusion ideas should be continuously shared with teachers through in-service programs. (See Chapter 9 for more on facilitating the operation of computer-education programs.)

11. Evaluate progress.   The district should continuously monitor the progress of infusion activities. After computer activities have had a reasonable chance to become integrated into the routine of the curriculum, the district should evaluate the effects of that integration. This evaluation should be conducted with consultation from external evaluators. Among the effects that should be measured are academic success in particular curricular areas, attitude toward computers, and attitude toward subject-matter learning. Adjustments in the infusion program should be made on the basis of this research. (Chapter 10 provides a detailed discussion of the evaluation of computer-education efforts.)

12. Involve the school community.   The involvement of the community can be an asset to the school as well as to local businesses. The district should, therefore, make attempts to involve the community in computer education by providing information about and by promoting participation in school programs. Information on the progress of the infusion effort can be communicated through seminars for parents and through periodic research summaries. Training sessions for parents can also be offered to help them understand the computer's capabilities. Partnership arrangements with business and industry can be negotiated to obtain staff, faculty, and needed financial resources for school computer-education programs. Finally, parent/teacher groups can be asked to undertake activities (e.g., cake sales, flea markets, car washes) to help raise funds for software and other program purchases. In short, community support can help ensure the longterm success of a computer-infused curriculum effort.

MICROCOMPUTER INFUSION EXAMPLES

In this section, examples of the infusion of computers into curricular areas are provided for mathematics, English and language arts, social studies, science, and problem solving.

Mathematics

In a study conducted at the Arizona State University Microcomputer Research Clinic, currently available commercial courseware was assigned to the K-12 mathematics objectives used by one school district (Searcy, 1985). Examples from Grades 1 and 6 are presented in Tables 6–2 and 6–3 as an illustration of how available software can be integrated in the mathematics curriculum.

The matching of courseware to curricular objectives, as illustrated in Tables 6–2 and 6–3, can be done for most curricular areas. Of course, the courseware assigned must be appropriate in terms of content, level, and quality, and contrived uses of the computer must be avoided.

Aside from the use of instructional courseware, programming is another way in which the microcomputer can be applied to mathematics. For example, simple programs written in BASIC or Logo can be used to explore math concepts. At the fourth-grade level, the following BASIC program might be used:

```
10 PRINT ''Exploring Area''
20 INPUT ''Radius = ''; Radius
30 PRINT ''Area = ''; 3.14 * Radius ^ 2
40 END
```

This program can be used to explore both the formula for the area of a circle and the concept of how changes in radius affect area; the program il-

TABLE 6–2   Microcomputer infusion for mathematics, grade 1

NUMERATION

Objective: Given a model for the numerals 0–9, the learner will form each numeral correctly.
Koala Pad Touch Tablet (Koala Technologies Corporation)
Counting Skills: Number Recognition 5–10 (Aquarius Publishers, Inc.)

WHOLE NUMBERS

Addition

Objective: Given an addition fact in horizontal or vertical format, sums through 12, the learner will identify the sum.
Elementary Volume 7: Getting Ready to Read and Add Spaceship (Minnesota Educational Computing Consortium)
Alien Addition (Developmental Learning Materials, 1982)

Subtraction

Objective: Given a subtraction fact in horizontal or vertical format, minuends through 12, the learner will identify the difference.
Minus Mission (Developmental Learning Materials, 1982)
Alligator Mix (Developmental Learning Materials, 1982)
Edupak: Frenzy (Milliken Publishing Company)

FRACTIONS

Objective: Given regions divided into equal parts, the learner will color one-half, one-fourth, or one-third, or identify those regions already shaded.
Koala Pad Touch Tablet (Koala Technologies Corporation)

GEOMETRY

Objective: Given examples of a square, triangle, rectangle, and circle, the learner will identify the correct figure.
Gertrude's Puzzles (The Learning Company, 1982)
Logo, any version
Gertrude's Secrets (The Learning Company)

TABLE 6–2 Continued

MEASUREMENT

Time

Objective: Given pictures of clock faces, the learner will identify the time to the hour.
Clock (Hartley Courseware, Inc.)
A Tick Tock Tale (Hickory Stick, Inc.)
Time Master (Micro Power & Light Co., 1982)

Linear

Objective: Given three objects, the learner will identify the longest, shortest, or tallest.
No software located

Area

Objective: Given three regions, the learner will identify the one which is the largest or smallest.
Koala Pad Touch Tablet (Koala Technologies Corporation)
Comparison Kitchen: Which is Less (Developmental Learning Materials)

Volume

Objective: Given two or more containers, the learner will identify the ones which hold the most or the least.
No software located

Weight

Objective: Given a set of objects and a balance, the learner will identify the lightest or heaviest.
No software located

APPLICATIONS

Objective: Given an incomplete pattern sequence, the learner will complete the sequence.
Gertrude's Secrets (The Learning Company)
The Game Show (teacher-modifiable) (Advanced Ideas, Inc.)
Create-Lessons (teacher-modifiable) (Hartley Coursework, Inc., 1983)

TABLE 6–3   Microcomputer infusion for mathematics, grade 6

NUMERATION

Objective: Given a numeral through billions, the learner will identify the numeral in a given place.
The Game Show (teacher-modifiable) (Advanced Ideas, Inc.)
Create-Lessons (teacher-modifiable) (Hartley Courseware, Inc., 1983)

WHOLE NUMBERS

Addition

Objective: Given an addition fact in horizontal or vertical format, sums through 18, the learner will identify the sum.
Alien Addition (Developmental Learning Materials, 1982)
Alligator Mix (Developmental Learning Materials, 1982)
Mathsheet (teacher tool) (Houghton-Mifflin)

Subtraction

Objective: Given a subtraction fact in horizontal or vertical format, minuends through 18, the learner will identify the difference.
Minus Mission (Developmental Learning Materials, 1982)
Mathsheet (teacher tool) (Houghton-Mifflin)
Math Blaster (Davidson and Associates, 1983)

Multiplication

Objective: Given a multiplication fact in horizontal or vertical format, products through 81, the learner will identify the answer.
Dragon Mix (Developmental Learning Materials, 1982)
Meteor Multiplication (Developmental Learning Materials, 1982)
Mathsheet (teacher tool) (Houghton-Mifflin)

Division

Objective: Given a division fact, dividends through 81, the learner will identify the quotient.
Demolition Division (Developmental Learning Materials, 1982)
Dragon Mix (Developmental Learning Materials, 1982)
Mathsheet (teacher tool) (Houghton-Mifflin)

TABLE 6–3 Continued

FRACTIONS

Meaning

Objective: Given a proper fraction, the learner will identify an equivalent fraction.
Mathematics Activities Courseware 5: Fraction Maze (Houghton-Mifflin)
Early Games: Fraction Factory: Equivalent Fractions (Springboard)
Math Blaster (Davidson and Associates, 1983)

Addition

Objective: Given two proper fractions with unlike denominators, the learner will identify the sum.
Early Games: Fraction Factory: Adding Fractions (Springboard)
Adding Fractions (Microcomputer Workshops)
The Game Show (teacher-modifiable) (Advanced Ideas, Inc.)

Subtraction

Objective: Given two proper fractions with unlike denominators, the learner will identify the difference.
Early Games: Fraction Factory: Subtracting Fractions (Springboard)
The Game Show (teacher-modifiable) (Advanced Ideas, Inc.)
Create-Lessons (teacher-modifiable) (Hartley Courseware, Inc., 1983)

Multiplication

Objective: Given two proper fractions, the learner will identify the product.
Success With Math Fractions: Multiplication and Division (CBS Software)
The Game Show (teacher-modifiable) (Advanced Ideas, Inc.)
Create-Lessons (teacher-modifiable) (Hartley Courseware, Inc., 1983)
Multiplying Fractions (Microcomputer Workshops)

Division

Objective: Given a whole number and a proper fraction, the learner will identify the quotient.
The Game Show (teacher-modifiable) (Advanced Ideas, Inc.)
Create-Lessons (teacher-modifiable) (Hartley Courseware, Inc., 1983)

lustrates the fact that four simple lines of code can be used to explore relatively complex math concepts.

BASIC and/or Pascal programs also can be used to explore concepts in algebra. For instance, the programs and output presented in Figures 6–1 and 6–2 illustrate the linear function $f(x) = 2x - 1$ (Bitter, 1983c).

```
BASIC Version                           Pascal Version

5  Input X                              Var
10 If X = 99 then 30                       X,FX:INTEGER;
15 LET F = 2 * X − 1                     BEGIN
20 PRINT "X=";X,"F(X)=";F                   WHILE X < > 99 DO
25 GOTO 5                                      BEGIN
35 END                                            WRITELN('?');
                                                  READLN(X);
                                                  FX: = 2*X − 1;
                                                  WRITELN('F(X) = ':25,FX);
                                               END
                                        END
```

FIGURE 6–1   Programs for exploring the concept of a function

```
BASIC Version                           Pascal Version

?-5                                     ?-5             F(X)=-11
X=-5          F(X)=-11                   ?-2             F(X)=-5
?-2                                      ?-1             F(X)=-3
X=-2          F(X)=-5                    ? 0             F(X)=-1
?-1                                      ? 1             F(X)=1
X=-1          F(X)=-3                    ? 2             F(X)=3
?0                                       ? 5             F(X)=9
X=0           F(X)=-1                    ?99             F(X)=197
?1
X=1           F(X)=1
?2
X=2           F(X)=3
?5
X=5           F(X)=9
?99
```

FIGURE 6–2   Sample output from programs for exploring functions

Again, different numbers can be entered to explore the nature of the function.

English and Language Arts

In English and language arts, word processing programs of various types can be used for a variety of purposes. At the lower grade levels, story-writing programs are available that combine graphics capabilities and text editing. These programs allow young children to compose and illustrate their own stories, thereby developing creative writing and artistic skills. More advanced word processing and print utilities are being used by older students to create classroom and school newspapers and school yearbooks. Word processors also are being used widely to write compositions, research reports, and creative pieces.

The following exercise exemplifies the type of assignment that might give the middle school student the opportunity to develop both writing and word processing skills:

> Using a word processor, write a three-paragraph story about some person or event in your life. Some possible topics:
> A. My best friend's overnight visit
> B. My family's summer trip
> C. Learning to ride my bike (or other skill)
> D. My older brother or sister
> E. My favorite pet
> After your story is completed, print it out and make a backup copy of your file. Then, use your word processor's block-move facility to rearrange the order of the paragraphs in your story. When you are done, give a copy of the file and the printed copy of your story to your neighbor. Ask him or her to use the word processor to put your story back in the proper order.

Social Studies

Databases that incorporate facts drawn from a variety of areas are now available to help students learn research skills and explore concepts and relationships in social studies. For example, election results and voting patterns, the history of inventions, and the backgrounds of the framers of the constitution are all available in databases. Using a database management program, students can get answers to such questions as how campaign spending relates to election results and how different regions of the country have voted historically. Perhaps more importantly, students can learn to formulate and answer their own questions. As the value of such databases is recognized, additional disk-based fact files undoubtedly will be created for use with the social studies curriculum.

Science

In science, software for simulating laboratory experiments and for collecting real-time data is becoming quite common. Laboratory simulation software allows students to perform experiments that would normally be too costly, dangerous, or otherwise impractical to implement. Software for collecting real-time data works in conjunction with such physical devices as a thermometer linked to a microcomputer. The data collected can be analyzed immediately and illustrated graphically to allow better understanding of science concepts. Other physical devices (e.g., sound and motion probes) can also be connected to the microcomputer to allow many different types of actual data collection experiences.

Problem Solving

Problem solving is being emphasized in many different ways across curriculum areas. The microcomputer provides a powerful tool for supplementing these problem-solving activities. For example, database activities can teach students questioning, searching, and analytical skills. Assignments can present problem-solving experiences similar to those faced in real-life situations. Students can use databases in such diverse subjects as law, medicine, and government in learning to attack real-world problems.

These are only a few examples of how the microcomputer can be infused in the curriculum. Commercial materials are rapidly being developed for using the microcomputer in all grades and all curriculum areas. Until these materials are made available, educators will need to experiment with the microcomputer, trying different activities to determine those that work best in given curricular areas (Ford, 1984).

SUMMARY

This chapter has provided guidance in incorporating the microcomputer in the existing curriculum. A 12-step process for developing a microcomputer-infused curriculum was outlined and examples were provided to illustrate infusion into several subject areas. Microcomputer infusion will be the goal of education in the 1980s and '90s. Educators must develop thoughtful, long-term plans if this infusion process is to be successful. The microcomputer's potential as teaching tool is only limited by our imagination.

REFERENCES

Bitter, G. G. (1982a, September). The road to computer literacy: A scope and sequence model. *Electronic Learning, 2*(1), 60–63.

Bitter, G. G. (1982b, October). The road to computer literacy: A scope and sequence model. *Electronic Learning, 2*(2), 34–37, 85–86.

Bitter, G. G. (1982c, November/December). The road to computer literacy: A scope and sequence model. *Electronic Learning, 2*(3), 44–48, 90–91.

Bitter, G. G. (1983a, January). The road to computer literacy: A scope and sequence model. *Electronic Learning, 2*(4), 40–42, 46–48.

Bitter, G. G. (1983b, February). The road to computer literacy: A scope and sequence model. *Electronic Learning, 2*(5), 54–60.

Bitter, G. G. (1983c). *Microcomputer applications for calculus.* Boston, MA: Prindle, Weber, and Schmidt.

Bitter, G. G. (1986). *Computer literacy: Awareness, applications, and programming.* Menlo Park, CA: Addison-Wesley.

Bitter, G. G., & Craighead, D. (1984). *Teaching computer literacy—Lesson plans and activities for your classroom (K-4).* Austin, TX: Sterling Swift Publishing Company.

Bitter, G. G., & Craighead, D. (1985). *Teaching computer literacy—Lesson plans and activities for your classroom (5–8).* Austin, TX: Sterling Swift Publishing Company.

Ford, M. S. (1984). *The effects of computer programming on the problem solving abilities of sixth grade students.* (Ph.D. Dissertation). Tempe, AZ: Arizona State University.

Searcy, J. (1985, July/August). Integrating software into a math curriculum (K–8). *AEDS Monitor, 24*(1 & 2), 17–20.

APPENDIXES MATERIALS FOR PLANNING A COMPUTER-EDUCATION CURRICULUM

The resources that follow are books and general references that can be used to plan a computer-education curriculum. New resources are continually available, so be sure to check with commercial publishers, related journals, magazines, and computer conferences at which the most recent microcomputer applications are reported.

Appendix A Computer Books for Teachers

Programming

Turtle Geometry: The Computer as a Medium for Exploring Mathematics
Hal Abelson & Andrew DiSessa
M.I.T. Press, 1981

Primarily Logo
Donna Bearden
Reston, 1984

The Turtle's Sourcebook
Donna Bearden
Young People's Logo Association, 1982

Apple Logo Primer
Gary G. Bitter & Nancy R. Watson
Reston, 1983

Commodore 64 Logo Primer
Gary G. Bitter & Nancy R. Watson
Reston, 1984

CyberLogo Primer
Gary G. Bitter & Nancy R. Watson
Reston, 1984

IBM Logo Primer
Gary G. Bitter & Nancy R. Watson
Reston, 1985

Introduction to Computers and BASIC Programming
Kathleen M. Brenan
West, 1984

Logo: An Introduction
Dale J. Burnett
Creative Computing, 1983

Exploring Apple BASIC: A Problem-Solving Approach
Ronald L. Culbertson
Hayden, 1984

Instructional Computing Fundamentals for IBM Microcomputers
George Culp
Brooks/Cole, 1985

An Apple for the Teacher: Fundamentals of Instructional Computing
George Culp
Brooks/Cole, 1983

Programming in BASIC
Jeffrey Frates
Prentice-Hall, 1985

Creating Adventure Games on Your Computer
Tim Hartnell
Ballantine, 1984

How to Program Your Apple IIe
Tim Hartnell
Ballantine, 1984

How to Program Your Commodore 64
Tim Hartnell
Ballantine, 1984

Microcomputer Graphics for the IBM PC
Roy E. Myers
Addison-Wesley, 1984

Using Microcomputers: An Apple Lab Manual
Keiko M. Pitter
Mitchell, 1984

Using Microcomputers: An IBM PC Lab Manual
Keiko M. Pitter & Richard L. Pitter
Mitchell, 1984

40 Easy Steps to Programming in Logo and BASIC
James L. Poirot & Clark R. Adams
Sterling Swift, 1983

Astounding Games for Your Apple Computer
Hal Renko
Addison-Wesley, 1984

Introduction to TRS–80 BASIC
Robert T. Specht
Houghton Mifflin, 1985

Nudges: IBM Logo Projects
Steven Tipps
College, 1984

Practical BASIC for Teachers
Jim Thompson
Merrill, 1985

Discovering Apple Logo: An Introduction to the Art and Pattern of Nature
David Thornburg
Addison-Wesley, 1983

Picture This: PILOT Turtle Geometry
David Thornburg
Addison-Wesley, 1982

Learning With Logo
Dan Watt
McGraw-Hill, 1983

Apple IIe User's Handbook
Weber Systems, Inc.
Ballantine, 1983

Computer Literacy

Computers in Today's World
Gary G. Bitter
John Wiley & Sons, 1984

Teaching Computer Literacy: Lesson Plans and Activities for Your Classroom (K–4)
Gary G. Bitter & Donna Craighead
Sterling Swift, 1984

Teaching Computer Literacy: Lesson Plans and Activities for Your Classroom (5–8)
Gary G. Bitter & Donna Craighead
Sterling Swift, 1984

Using a Microcomputer in the Classroom
Gary G. Bitter & Ruth A. Camuse
Prentice-Hall, 1984

Best of Educational Software for the Apple II
Gary G. Bitter & Kay Gore
Sybex, 1984

Microcomputer Applications for Calculus
Gary G. Bitter
Prindle, Weber, and Schmidt, 1983

Bank Street's Family Computer Book
Barbara Brenner
Ballantine, 1984

Sources and Development of Mathematical Software
Wayne R. Cowell (ed.)
Prentice-Hall, 1984

Database for the IBM PC
Sandra L. Emerson
Addison-Wesley, 1984

Bits and Codes
Marjorie A. Fitting
Midwest Publications, 1983

Bytes and Memory Computation
Marjorie A. Fitting
Midwest Publications, 1983

Bases and Computation
Marjorie A. Fitting
Midwest Publications, 1983

Run: Computers in Education
Dennis O. Harper & James H. Stewart
Wadsworth, 1983

Bits 'n' Bytes Gazette
Rachelle Heller & Dianne Martin
Computer Science Press, 1983

Microcomputer Applications in the Classroom
Alan Hofmeister
Holt, Rinehart and Winston, 1984

My Students Use Computers: Learning Activities for Computer Literacy
Beverly Hunter
Reston, 1983

Computer Strategies for Education
Kinzer, Sherwood, & Bransford
Merrill, 1986

Microcomputer Courseware for the Classroom: Selecting, Organizing, and Using Instructional Software
Ann Lathrop & Bobby Goodson
Addison-Wesley, 1982

Mathematics and Logo
Kathleen Martin
Reston, 1985

Microcomputers in Education: Conference Proceedings
Microcomputer Research Clinic, Arizona State University, 1982, 1983

Microcomputers in Education Conference: Tomorrow's Technology
Donna Craighead (ed.)
Computer Science Press, 1985

Microcomputers in Education Conference: Literacy Plus +
Donna Craighead (ed.)
Computer Science Press, 1984

About the Best of the Proceedings: 1982–1984 Microcomputers in Education Conference
Donna Craighead (ed.)
Computer Science Press, 1985

Mindstorms: Computers, Children, and Powerful Ideas
Seymour Papert
Basic Books, 1980

Computers and Mathematics
James Poirot & David Groves
Sterling Swift, 1979

Computer Number Systems & Arithmetic
Norman R. Scott
Prentice-Hall, 1985

The Computer in the School: Tutor, Tool, Tutee
Robert P. Taylor (ed.)
Columbia University, Teachers College Press, 1981

Appendix B   Computer Magazines and Newsletters

General

Compute
The Journal for Progressive Computing, Circulation Dept.
515 Abbott Dr.
Broomall, PA 19008

Creative Computing
P.O. Box 789 M
Morristown, NJ 07960

Education Practice and Research

AEDS Journal and AEDS Monitor
Association for Educational Data Systems
1201 Sixteenth St. NW
Washington, DC 20036

Apple for the Teacher
5848 Riddio St.
Citrus Heights, CA 95610

Classroom Computer Learning
19 Davis Dr.
Belmont, CA 94002

Computers in the School
The Haworth Press
28 East 22 St.
New York, NY 10010

The Computing Teacher
Dept. of Computer and Information Science
University of Oregon
Eugene, OR 97850

Educational Technology
140 Sylvan Avenue
Englewood Cliffs, NJ 07632

Electronic Education
Electronic Communications, Inc., Suite 220
1311 Executive Center Dr.
Tallahassee, FL 32301

Electronic Learning
Scholastic, Inc.
902 Sylvan Avenue
Englewood Cliffs, NJ 07632

Family Computing
P.O. Box 2512
Boulder, CO 80321

The Logo and Educational Computing Journal
1320 Stony Brook Road, Suite 219
Stony Brook, NY 11790

Microzine (a magazine on a floppy disk for students)
Scholastic, Inc.
730 Broadway
New York, NY 10003

Teaching and Computers
Scholastic, Inc.
902 Sylvan Ave., Box 2001
Englewood Cliffs, NJ 07632

Curriculum Specialization

The Journal of Computers in Mathematics and Science Teaching
P.O. Box 4455
Austin, TX 78765

The Journal of Computers, Reading, and Language Arts
NAVA
3150 Spring St.
Fairfax, VA 22031

School Science and Mathematics
School Science and Mathematics Association, Inc.
Bowling Green University
126 Life Science Bldg.
Bowling Green, OH 43403

Newsletters

Computer-Using Educators Newsletter
Computer-Using Educators
Independence High School
1776 Education Park Dr.
San Jose, CA 95133

Logophile
College of Education
MacArthur Hall
Queen's University
Kingston, Ontario K71 3N6

National Logo Exchange
Posy Publications
P.O. Box 5342
Charlottesville, VA 22905

Turtle News
Young People's Logo Assn.
1209 Hillsdale Dr.
Richardson, TX 75081

Appendix C   Books for Students

Computer Literacy

Computer Literacy: Awareness, Applications, and Programming
Gary G. Bitter
Addison-Wesley, 1986

Chip Mitchell: The Case of the Stolen Computer Brains
Fred D'Ignazio
Dutton, 1983

Computer
Ian Graham
Watts, 1983

Computer Craziness
Paul Somerson
Scholastic, 1984

A Computer Dictionary for Kids and Other Beginners
David Fay Smith
Ballantine Books, 1984

Computer Awareness Books—A Series
Watts, 1983
  Careers in the Computer Industry   Laura Green
  Computers in Our World   Sandy and Martin Hintz
  Data Processing   Melvin Berger
  Invent Your Own Computer Games   Fred D'Ignazio
  Programming in BASIC   Christopher Lampton

Katie and the Computer
Fred D'Ignazio & Stan Gillian
Creative Computing, 1979

One Computer 30 Kids
Kay Richardson
Meka, 1980

The Computer That Said, "Steal Me"
Elizabeth Levy
Four Winds, 1983

The Wish Card Ran Out!
James Stevenson
Greenwillow, 1981

What Can She Be? A Computer Scientist
Esther and Gloria Goldreich
Lothrop, Lee, & Shepard, 1979

Computers
Neil Ardley
Watts, 1983

Computers for Kids
Sally Greenwood Larson
Creative Computing, 1981

Computers: How They Work
Nigel Hawkes
Watts, 1983

Computer Monsters
Paul Somerson
Scholastic, Inc., 1984

Computer Space Adventures
Paul Somerson
Scholastic, Inc., 1984

Creative Kids Guide to Home Computers
Fred D'Ignazio
Doubleday, 1978

Exploring With Computers
Gary G. Bitter
Julian Messner, 1983

Every Kid's First Book of Robots and Computers
David Thornburg
Computer Books, 1982

*Picture This Too: An Introduction to Computer
  Graphics for Kids of All Ages*
David Thornburg
Addison-Wesley Publishing, 1982

Drawing and Painting With the Computer
Dan Bolognese & Robert Thornton
Watts, 1983

Invent Your Own Computer Games
Fred D'Ignazio
Watts, 1983

Programming

Introduction to Programming in BASIC (Apple
  Version)
Gary G. Bitter
Random House, 1985

BASIC Beginnings
Susan Drake Lipscomb and Margaret Ann
  Zuanich
Avon, 1983

*BASIC Fun: Computer Games, Puzzles, and
  Problems Children Can Write*
Susan Drake Lipscomb & Margaret Ann
  Zuanich
Avon, 1982

BASIC Programming for Kids
Rosalie Sain
Houghton Mifflin, 1983

Programming in BASIC
Christopher Lampton
Watts, 1983

Programming in BASIC for the IBM PC
Gary G. Bitter & Salvatore Severe
Addison-Wesley, 1986

Programming in BASIC for the TRS–80
Gary Bitter & Salvatore Severe
Addison-Wesley, 1986

Programming in BASIC for the Apple II Series
Gary Bitter & Salvatore Severe
Addison-Wesley, 1986

Programming in BASIC for the Commodore 64
Gary Bitter & Salvatore Severe
Addison-Wesley, 1986

TRS–80 For Kids from 8 to 80
Michael P. Zabinski
Howard W. Sams & Co., 1983

Drawing and Painting With the Computer
Dan Bolognese & Robert Thornton
Watts, 1983

Computer Basic
Hall Hellman
Prentice-Hall, 1983

Introduction to Computer Programming
Brian R. Smith
Osborne

*It's BASIC: The ABC's of Computer Program-
  ming*
Sheley Lipson
Holt, Rinehart & Winston, 1982

I Speak BASIC
Aubrey B. Jones, Jr.
Hayden

Appendix D   Logo Software

Atari Logo
Atari Computer Corp.
1312 Crossman Dr.
Sunnyvale, CA 94086

Atari Pilot Educator Pak
Atari, Inc.
1265 Borregas Ave.
Sunnyvale, CA 94086

Atari Pilot Student Pak
Atari, Inc.
1265 Borregas Ave.
Sunnyvale, CA 94086

Commodore 64 Logo
Commodore Business Machines, Inc.
1200 Wilson Dr.
West Chester, PA 19380

CyberLogo
Cybertronics
One Lincoln Plaza
New York, NY 10023

Delta Drawing
Spinnaker Software Corp.
215 First St.
Cambridge, MA 02142

Kidstuff
Thomas R. Smith
P.O. Box 345
Dedham, MA 02026

LCSI's Apple Logo
Logo Computer Systems, Inc. (LCSI)
Apple Computer, Inc.
20525 Mariani Ave.
Cupertino, CA 95014

M.I.T. Logo
Commodore Computer
487 Devon Park Dr.
Wayne, PA 19087

M.I.T. Logo
Krell Software Corp.
1320 Stony Brook Rd.
Stony Brook, NY 11790

M.I.T. Logo
Terrapin, Inc.
380 Green St.
Cambridge, MA 02139

PC-Logo
Harvard Associates, Inc.
260 Beacon St.
Somerville, MA 02143

TI Logo 11
Texas Instruments
P.O. Box 53
Lubbock, TX 79408

Toddler's Turtle
Young People's Logo Assn.
P.O. Box 855067
Richardson, TX 75085

TRS–80 Disk Color LOGO
Radio Shack Education Division
1400 One Tandy Center
Fort Worth, TX 76012

TRS–80 Program Pak
Color LOGO
Radio Shack
Education Division
1400 One Tandy Center
Fort Worth, TX 76102

Vanilla Pilot
Computer Marketing Service
300 W. Marlton Pike
Cherry Hill, NY 08002

Appendix E   Logo Newsletters

Logophile
College of Education
MacArthur Hall
Queen's University
Kingston, Ontario K71 3N6

National Logo Exchange
Posy Publications
P.O. Box 5342
Charlottesville, VA 22905

Polyspiral
Boston Computer Society
Three Center Plaza
Boston, MA 02108

The Logo and Educational Computing Journal
Interactive Education Foundation
1320 Stony Brook Road
Stony Brook, NY 11790

TI Source and Logo News
Microcomputer Corporation
34 Maple Avenue
Armonk, NY 10504

Turtle News
Young People's Logo Association
1209 Hillsdale Drive
Richardson, TX 75081

Appendix F   Audiovisual Materials

Addison-Wesley
General Books Division
Reading, MA 01867
  Computer Graphics Calendar (visual display)

Alameda County Superintendent of Schools
Learning Resource Services
Public Sales
685 A St.
Hayward, CA 94541
  Classroom Applications of Microcomputers
    (video)
  Using a Computer in the Elementary School
    (video)
  Education Software (video)
  Teaching Computer Literacy and Program-
    ming (video)

Audio Visual Center
Indiana University
Bloomington, IN 47405
  The Personal Touch (film)
  Hardware and Software (film)
  Speaking and Language (film)
  Data Processing, Control, Design (film)
  For Better or Worse (film)
  Extending Your Reach (film)

Bell Laboratories
Film & Tape Library
150 J. F. Kennedy Parkway
Short Hills, NJ 07076
  Microworld (film)
  Incredible Machine (film)
  The Thinking???Machines (film)
  Communications Milestone: Invention of the
    Electrical Digital Computer (film or
    videotape)
  The Quiet Revolution (videotape)
  (all loaned free)

Charles Clark Co., Inc.
168 Express Dr. S.
Brentwood, NY 11717
  All About Computers (filmstrips)
  Computer Literacy Series (filmstrips)
  Computer Concepts (filmstrips)

Churchill Films
662 N. Robertson Blvd.
Los Angeles, CA 90069
  Computers: The Inside Story (film)
  Computers: Tools for People (film)

Educational Activities
P.O. Box 392
Freeport, NY 11520
  Advanced BASIC Techniques (filmstrips)
  BASIC for Elementary Grades (filmstrips)
  BASIC for Microcomputers (filmstrips)
  Careers in Computers (filmstrips)
  Computer Literacy and Understanding
    (filmstrips)
  Discover Logo (filmstrip)
  Know Your Computer (cassette/worksheet)
  Operating the Microcomputer (video)

Encyclopedia Britannica Educational Corp.
425 North Michigan Ave.
Chicago, IL 60611
  Computers in Our Society (filmstrips)
  Understanding Computers (filmstrips)

EPCOT Educational Media
  Skills for the New Technology: What a Kid
    Needs to Know (film)
  Futurework (film)

Films Incorporated
733 Green Bay Rd.
Wilmette, IL 60091
  The Computer Programmer (video)

FlipTrack Learning Systems
Box 711
526 N. Main St.
Glen Ellyn, IL 60137
  FlipTrack Training Course for PC (cassettes)

Follett Library Book Co.
4506 Northwest Highway
Crystal Lake, IL 60014
  Computer Basics (filmstrips)
  Computers: From Pebble to Programs
    (filmstrips)
  Computer Hardware: What It Is and How It
    Works (filmstrips)
  At Home with Computers: What It Can Do
    for You (filmstrips)

The Computers (filmstrip)
Understanding Computers (filmstrips)
Microcomputers (filmstrip)

January Productions
124 Rea Ave.
Hawthorne, NJ 07506
Computers: What They're All About (filmstrip)

Marshfilm
P.O. Box 8082
Shawnee Mission, KS 66208
Computer Literacy Series (filmstrip)

Modern Talking Picture Service
5000 Park St. N.
St. Petersburg, FL 33709
About Computers (film)
Computers in Your Life (film)
The Information Machine (film)
(all loaned free)

Prentice-Hall Media
150 White Plains Rd.
Tarrytown, NY 10591
An Introduction to Computers and Data Processing (filmstrip)
Apple Computer Basic (filmstrip)
TRS-80 BASIC (filmstrip)
Introduction to Microcomputers (filmstrip)
Getting to Know the Micros (filmstrip)
Computer Components (filmstrip)
The Computer Glossary (filmstrip)
Terminology for Computer Literacy (filmstrip)
Programming Basic (filmstrip)
Robotics (filmstrip)
Our Computer Society (filmstrip)

Sunburst Communications
39 Washington Avenue
Pleasantville, NY 10570
Careers with Computers: Jobs for Today (filmstrip)
How a Computer Works (filmstrip)
Understanding the Computer (filmstrip)

Time-Life Video
Distribution Center
100 Eisenhower Dr.
P.O. Box 644
Paramus, NJ 07652
Computers and the Future (film)
Computers, Spies, and Private Lives (film)

Walt Disney Educational Media Co.
500 South Buena Vista St.
Burbank, CA 91521
A Hard Day's Hardware (filmstrip)
Computers: The Truth of the Matter (film)
Computers: The Friendly Invasion (film)
Software to the Rescue (filmstrip)
The Computer: A Proper Introduction (filmstrip)
The Computer Kid (filmstrip)
Tron (film)

7

Training Teachers to Incorporate Computers into the School Curriculum

Howard Kimmel

The proliferation of microcomputers in schools has far outpaced the ability of colleges, state departments, and school districts to train teachers to use the machines effectively and to teach about them. In too many instances, school districts have purchased computers without developing a plan for adequately training teachers to integrate them into the curriculum. The result often has been to find the computers sitting in a corner or storage closet collecting dust.

In many cases, the training of teachers in computer education has been modelled after earlier National Science Foundation (NSF) projects, with postsecondary institutions offering courses and/or workshops for school staff. For several reasons, this model has not been applicable to computer education.

First, the NSF model generally focused on a specific subject area for teachers already certified and teaching in that or a related discipline. In most states, however, certification criteria for computer education are still under development. In addition, teachers work within a wide range of disciplines; many will not necessarily teach about computers or programming, but will want to use the capabilities of the computer to augment their classroom instruction. Thus, a large number of subjects may need to be covered in training a diverse group of teachers.

Second, teacher training in computing must be specific to the available hardware as well as to the particular needs of the teacher and the school district. These limitations were not usually placed on NSF projects, which provided a fixed training program at all locations.

In short, teacher training should be an integral part of a custom-built district plan for implementing computer education. This chapter will discuss the various issues related to teacher training and the approaches necessary for developing computer competency in teachers. The presentation is meant to provide the school or district computer administrator with basic guidance in the construction of an in-service program.

THE "COMPUTER-LITERATE" TEACHER

Although there seems to be little difficulty in defining "scientific literacy" or "reading literacy," there is no clear, conventional definition of "computer literacy," if such a condition can be considered to exist. Microcomputers are being rapidly incorporated in elementary and secondary schools, and in-service programs for teachers are continually being developed to make them "computer literate," or more appropriately, competent in the use of microcomputers.

In-service training is being provided in spite of a lack of agreement on what these competencies should be. One school of thought advocates that teachers should be able to program proficiently in a computer language or two. Others argue that programming is not essential to computer literacy.

The intent here is not to get involved in a debate over the meaning of computer literacy. Rather, it is to arrive at a graduated set of microcomputer competencies that can form the basis for in-service education. Such competencies can vary according to the needs and disciplines of teachers, as well as the curricula and grade levels they teach. For example, Moore (1984), in a comprehensive study involving specialists from elementary, secondary, administrative, and college/university levels, developed competency guidelines for preparing teachers to teach about computing; these guidelines were developed for teachers of all subject areas, as well as for teachers of computing at the elementary and secondary levels. (The guidelines for teachers in various subject areas did not include programming as a competency.) Other major efforts to provide similar competency guidelines include work by Zalewski (1982) for the School Science and Mathematics Association, work by Baird (1984) that utilizes seven categories of end uses for computers in education, and recommendations of the National Council of Teachers of Mathematics (1984).

One means of bridging the gap among various competing definitions of computer competency is to pose a simple but flexible definition: Competency is the set of specific skills needed by teachers to fulfill their functions in the classroom. If the competency is in reference to computing, then teachers should have the necessary skills to use microcomputers effectively in the classroom. Teacher training provides the means to develop these skills and acquire competency.

Ideally, teacher training in computing should be more than a process that has a beginning and an end, and that communicates a finite amount of information. In-service training in computer education should include, in addition to the core workshop or seminar experience, on-going consultation, opportunity for in-depth study, and the collection of pertinent references and resource materials; that is, the long-term support needed to integrate the computer into a teacher's own curriculum and style of teaching. Without such long-term support, it is highly unlikely that teachers will feel comfortable or competent enough to incorporate computers into the classroom routine. (See Chapter 9 for more details about providing long-term support.)

In order to define the most appropriate and effective in-service program, planners must identify clearly the needs and concerns of their teachers. Gressard and Loyd (1985) confirmed that teachers' attitudes toward computers and computerized instruction are a key factor in the successful implementation of training programs. Further support for this view is offered by Killian (1984), who studied factors associated with the professional growth of teachers in attaining computer competency. Killian used survey data to compare "average" teachers with computer literacy "seekers" in terms of computer knowledge and skills, interests, attitudes, and sources of encouragement. Those who attained a higher level of professional growth in computing, the "seekers," were very positive in their perception of computers' influence on schools and teaching, as well as on their own teaching careers. On the other hand, those who attained less growth (the "average" teachers), showed a fear of computers and of the possibility that the machines would replace teachers in the classroom.

It is clear that in-service programs must respond to the specific affective needs of those taught; such needs are as important as basic computer competency—learning about the equipment, discovering how it works, and becoming informed about its potential and its limitations. In this respect, the typical approach of delivering a single, brief in-service program to a large heterogeneous group of teachers can do more harm to developing computer competency than no training at all (Baird, 1984) because such a program cannot possibly respond to the affective needs of so diverse a group. Rather, teacher training programs should be designed for homogeneous groups based on expressed needs and skills. The following discussion will offer basic guidance in the development of these programs.

THE IN-SERVICE TRAINING OF TEACHERS

The complexity of needs and issues that must be addressed in planning and operating in-service programs in computer education makes it difficult to develop good programs. One reasonable approach to this problem is to develop a minimum list of knowledge and skills that should be possessed by a "computer-competent" teacher. A synthesis of the competency lists developed by Baird (1984), Zalewski (1982), and Moore (1984), produces the following levels of skill:

1 knowledge of the importance of the computer in business, education, and society;
2 ability to understand and use microcomputer hardware and software terminology;
3 knowledge of the basic operation of a microcomputer;
4 knowledge of the uses and limitations of microcomputers in the classroom (including software copyright issues);
5 ability to operate a microcomputer in order to run prepared programs;
6 ability to find, select, and use microcomputer software;
7 ability to make informed choices about a microcomputer system's hardware;
8 ability to read and write simple programs;
9 ability to write large programs in a high-level language using a procedural approach;
10 ability to apply principles of computer science to the selection of appropriate data structures and algorithms, and to conduct a College Board Advanced Placement Course in computer science.

Most would agree that all teachers, regardless of subject area, should develop skill levels 1–6. However, in designing a program to develop these competencies, each competency must be defined in terms of the teacher's specific responsibilities for using computers. For example, the training program should include only that terminology (skill level 2) necessary for the teacher to understand and use the computer effectively in the classroom. Overuse of computer "jargon" can turn teachers away from the computer (Fincher, 1984).

If the school district is providing training for selected teachers prior to purchasing microcomputers (for instance, to those who will coordinate the computer-education program), skill level 7 may be critical, as teachers should be involved in the hardware purchase process. Even though most districts first purchase the equipment and then train teachers, instruction in making hardware decisions still may be helpful because peripheral equipment and more computers eventually will be purchased.

Skill levels 9 and 10 are most appropriate for teachers of computing, with level 9 necessary for most computing teachers and 10 only for those high-school instructors teaching computer-science courses. This demarcation of competencies appropriate for the specialist (teachers of computing) from those of the non-specialist (teachers who use the computer in subject-matter areas) is expanded upon in the following sections.

The Specialist

For the purposes of this chapter, the concept of a computing "specialist" includes a range of responsibility. Near one end of this range is the middle-school instructor, responsible for teaching such fundamentals as computer history, operations, basic applications, and introductory programming. At the other end is the high-school teacher, who provides instruction in computer science—the study of algorithms and advanced programming, among other topics. Although this range of responsibility implies a fairly broad range of competency, the depth and breadth of knowledge required is generally substantially greater than that of the non-specialist. Hence, the specialist position is treated here as a group of positions sharing a set of core competencies.

Training for teachers of computing is conceptually similar to training for teachers in other disciplines. To teach this subject, prospective specialists would have to take the coursework necessary to develop competencies 1–10, and to meet any certification requirements promulgated by the state education agency. (An example of the development of a university-based program that would meet certification requirements is provided by Sherwood, Connor, and Goldberg, 1981; an extensive study of preparation issues is reported by Moore, 1984.)

The breadth and depth of competency required to be a computing specialist suggests that teachers can best be trained through a long-term, state-certified course of study, usually provided by a college or university. The shortage of computing specialists, however, has forced some of the larger districts to establish their own in-service computing-specialist programs. Table 7–1 presents a sample curriculum for training those teaching about the more fundamental aspects of computing. The curriculum was developed by the Houston Independent School District (HISD) (Sclafani, Smith, & Arch, 1984) and requires 296 hours of instruction. (Readers interested in developing their own in-service curricula should recognize that this or any other curriculum should not be used unless it can be adapted to local needs and constraints.)

As noted, most school districts will not have the faculty, equipment, or financial resources to mount as comprehensive an in-service effort as Table 7–1 proposes. Too, the programs they are able to offer usually will not be able to meet the certification criteria increasingly required by state education departments. Therefore, most districts will have to turn to colleges and universities to fulfill their training needs for computing specialists.

The Non-Specialist

The non-specialist, who may or may not be interested in many of the topics under the umbrella of computer studies, wants to know how the machine

TABLE 7–1   A sample in-service training curriculum for specialists

---

☐ **Instructional applications (68 hours)**

    Hands-on training
    Computer as tool, tutor, and tutee
    Math applications
    Reading applications
    MECC software

☐ **Computer literacy (32 hours)**

    History and social impact
    Information resources
    HISD Computer Literacy Curriculum K–12

☐ **Computer as a tool (52 hours)**

    Database management
    Electronic spreadsheet
    Word processing
    Authoring languages
    Printer functions

☐ **Computer languages (80 hours split between two languages)**

    Logo
    BASIC
    Pascal

☐ **Planning and implementation (64 hours)**

    Planning and decision making
    Classroom organization
    Hardware troubleshooting
    Software evaluation
    Emerging technologies
    Future trends
    Building in-service training

Sclafani, S., Smith, R. A., & Arch., J., 1984. A model for a computer literacy project. *The Computing Teacher,* 12(3), 39–41. Used by permission.

can be used to help students achieve subject-matter goals. Or, as one teacher said, "If it meets the learning needs of my students in my classroom, I welcome it. If it doesn't meet those needs, I don't want it" (Fincher, 1984).

Unlike specialists, non-specialists can be created through a level of in-service education within the resources of many, if not most, school districts. Even so, in-service programs designed to create non-specialists must be substantial undertakings, carefully planned and carried out. Developing computer competency takes time and effort, and ongoing support services must be provided, both during the in-service process and after formal training is concluded, to ensure that competencies are developed and consolidated.

Four questions can be used to guide the planning of an in-service program: planners must resolve how the program will be conducted, what it will provide, who will provide the program, and where and when the program will be delivered.

How will the program be conducted?   The characteristics of effective adult education present a useful foundation on which to design the in-service program. Building these characteristics into computer education in-service programs should result in smoother, more effective training experiences. These characteristics, summarized by Bennett (1984), include the following:

- ☐ Staff development activities should be part of an overall organizational plan.
- ☐ Staff development efforts should be based on an assessment of learner needs.
- ☐ Explicit goals for staff development should be established based on the results of needs assessment.
- ☐ Staff development activities should actively engage the learner.
- ☐ Staff development programs should be continuous.
- ☐ Staff development programs should be evaluated.

Each in-service session should have simple, direct goals. In addition, each session should emphasize hands–on experiences, with a minimum amount of lecture for the introduction of concepts and applications. Novices tend to overload very quickly when working with a computer. Therefore, ample time must be provided to practice skills, to assimilate concepts, and to develop strategies for integrating computers into the learning process. Finally, the sessions should focus on activities teachers can use in their classrooms.

The presentation of instruction by a human instructor has been the standard mode of in-service delivery for many years. However, other delivery modes are available to supplement, and in some cases, replace this method (see chapter appendixes). Videocassette tapes are available for teaching the history of computing and hardware concepts. Software tutorials exist for training novices in the use of computers, in basic computer literacy, and in specific applications (for instance, word processing, spreadsheets). In addition, some software packages come with audiotape training materials, and comprehensive packages for training teachers in computer education also exist. These in-service resources might best be used to supplement instructor demonstrations and supervised practice. For example, a session on basic computer concepts might be introduced by a video tape, followed by an interactive operating-system tutorial, and concluded with supervised hands–on practice in carrying out operating system commands.

In some situations, such as in highly rural locations where competent in-service faculty are not available, alternative methods may be needed to deliver the program. For example, audiovisual conferencing can be used to bring a single trainer simultaneously to several remote sites. Such conferencing would use television or, if TV is not available, the telephone for delivery of audio and slides (provided in advance) for the visual presentation. Once trainees have learned the computing basics, telecomputing can be used for follow–up dialogue between the instructor(s) and the trainees, as well as for directly teaching computer competencies. Indeed, telecomputing has been used to teach courses in programming, computers and society, and other related areas. The fact that participants can communicate through electronic mailboxes at any time and from any location means that teaching and learning can occur at the participants' convenience. A continuous support mechanism for teachers can also be made available efficiently through this medium.

What will be provided?   The definition of competency—the set of specific skills needed by teachers to effectively use microcomputers in their classrooms—and the list of minimum knowledge and skill levels needed by teachers, provide a good starting point for setting objectives for in-service programs. Objectives for in-service training in computer education can be organized into three areas: objectives for all teachers regardless of subject taught; objectives relevant to a specific subject area or group of subject areas; and objectives relevant to a set of grade levels (e.g., elementary or secondary).

For teachers of all disciplines, the following objectives are suggested:

☐ *Learn to operate a computer and run computer programs.* Teachers should learn how to operate the brand of computer that they will be using in their classrooms. Such instruction should include the different components of the computer, related terminology, and the different types of input and output devices, among other things. Teachers should know how to turn the computer on and off, how to load programs and data, and how to output the information to disk, tape, or to a printer. In addition, they should know how to use the system disk and its various utility programs to copy or move files, format disks, check available disk space, and check the catalog or directory.

☐ *Develop appropriate strategies for using the computer in the classroom.* The integration of the microcomputer in the curriculum offers enormous potential for enhancing the educational process. Two aspects of integration involve the different uses of the computer in instruction and the management of computers in the classroom.

Teachers should be familiar with the major instructional uses of the computer and their advantages and limitations. The types of software that facilitate these uses include computer-assisted instruction (CAI) (both drill-and-practice and tutorial), educational games, simulations, and utilities and applications.

Classroom management techniques will depend on whether computers are located in the classroom or in a separate computer laboratory. Advantages and disadvantages of a computer lab have been summarized by Bitter (1985). The teaching of skills such as word processing, spreadsheets, or programming, for example, are often best accommodated by a computer lab. But putting computers in the classroom should be the more effective way to ensure that teachers fully integrate computers in their instructional routines.

☐ *Learn how to evaluate computer software.* The classroom teacher is in the best position to judge which materials or equipment should be used to augment classroom instruction. Guidelines for evaluating print materials have focused on such concerns as the scope and sequence of topics, instructional approaches, type of student activities involved, readability, societal issues (e.g., equity), durability, cost, and ease of use by both teacher and student. The need to evaluate computer software may be greater than that of print materials because software is often used independently of teacher control and because its unit cost is higher.

Thus, teachers must know the difference between good and poor software. Software evaluation forms and guides are readily available from professional organizations such as the International Council for Computers in Education (ICCE) (1982). Among other things, training in software evaluation should treat educational content, quality of presentation, level of student interaction with the computer, and teacher usability (availability of record keeping, modifiability of program content, etc.). Also important is documentation and the availability and quality of supplementary materials for students. Differences in evaluation concerns according to the type of software (e.g., tutorial vs. simulation), and how the software will be used (with a single student or group, or as a demonstration to the entire class) should be emphasized. Sample software should be provided to demonstrate desirable and undesirable characteristics, and evaluation forms made available for hands-on practice. (See Chapter 3 for information on software evaluation.)

☐ *Learn the minimal amount about programming to be able to do program editing and to write simple programs.* Though a basic level of programming skill is not absolutely necessary, many teachers will find it useful. Even quality programs cannot be "all things to all people." Teachers with some programming capability often will be able to edit programs; that is, they occasionally will be able to make modifications in programs to better meet the needs of their students, thus allowing the software to be used more effectively.

☐ *Learn to use application packages and teacher utilities.* Application packages such as word processors, spreadsheets, and database managers were once of very limited interest. For example, several years ago, word processing software was of interest only to those teaching secretarial studies. Now application packages are used across a variety of disciplines and grade levels. Database systems are being employed for classification and for storage and retrieval of information in science, English, and social studies. Spreadsheets are being used in science classes to analyze experimental data and in math classes to perform complex computations. Word processors are used in many disciplines for completing research papers and other writing assignments.

Aside from application programs, teachers may find simple utilities very useful. Utilities can make tests and keep grades and records, among other things. Authoring languages (e.g., Pilot) and software for creating custom learning exercises are becoming easier to use and more powerful. Teachers should be aware of the availability of these utilities and how they can be employed.

In-service training should address the availability, purpose, use, and limitations of application packages and utilities. Sessions should allow for demonstrations and extensive hands–on experience with these packages. Sample data files built around the appropriate disciplines and the grade levels of teachers should be provided for training. Teaching strategies, lesson plans, data files, and student exercises tailored to particular subject areas should also be developed so teachers can readily integrate applications programs in their instructional areas.

A sample outline for training in the use of application software is shown in Table 7–2. The outline is sufficiently general for use in any subject area in which the software is applicable and specific examples and exercises are available.

In summary, the major objectives suggested for all teachers include learning to operate a computer and run computer programs, developing appropriate strategies for using the computer in the classroom, learning

TABLE 7–2 Sample outline for educational utility programs and applications

☐ **Introduction to the computer and related terminology**

☐ **Introduction to utility programs and application packages**

What is meant by "utility program" and "applications package"
Simple utility routines and applications packages; advantages and disadvantages of each type
General considerations for using utility programs

☐ **Simple utility routines**

Materials generator
Specific database managers: inventory, student records, etc.
Gradebooks
Others

☐ **Applications packages**

Word processing
1. Introduction, description, and terminology
2. Teacher use
3. Integration into existing curricula
4. Examples and exercises

Electronic Spreadsheets

Databases

Others

☐ **Sources of public domain and commercial utilities and applications packages**

how to evaluate computer software, learning rudimentary programming skills, and learning to use applications programs and teacher utilities. A sample training program that covers most of these objectives is outlined in Table 7–3. The outline can be adapted to the needs of teachers of any subject or grade level, and can be the starting point for a more comprehensive program built around local requirements.

In addition to objectives for all teachers regardless of their subject areas, some training for teachers in specific disciplines should be offered. At the very least, teachers in a given subject area should be helped in examining

TABLE 7–3 Sample outline for a training program for the non-specialist

---

☐ **General concepts involved in computing**

Historical perspective
Introduction to vocabulary
Operating a computer, including hardware and software components, input and output of information, and using the system disk

☐ **Computers in the classroom**

Introduction to types of programs: CAI (drill and practice, tutorial), games and simulations, teacher utilities, and application packages
Integration of computer materials into existing curricula

☐ **Computer operations**

Running commercial computer programs; hands-on experience with computer activities and materials available for classroom use
Using teacher utilities

☐ **Software evaluation**

☐ **Ethics/legality of copying software**

☐ **Rudimentary computer programming**

---

software related to their discipline and in developing strategies for integrating that software into the curriculum. In addition, topics of special interest for certain subjects should be provided; for example, a session on linking the computer to laboratory equipment likely would be of interest to science teachers. Examples for other disciplines are available (for instance, see Roth and Tesolowski, 1984, for additional competencies needed by vocational teachers). Needs assessment will suggest additional objectives for teachers of specific subject areas.

Obviously, elementary- and secondary-school teachers need somewhat different training. One clear difference is the use of Logo, a simple but very capable language commonly used in the elementary grades. A 1985 survey by the New Jersey Department of Education (Braun, 1985) found that teachers most frequently cited instruction on how to teach children Logo as their greatest need. Readers interested in teacher training in Logo and its implementation in the classroom should consult Martin and Heller (1984), Heller and Martin (1985) and Schulman and Hrelja (1984). The Heller and Martin (1985) syllabus for a training course, "Introduction to Logo for Educators," is shown in Table 7–4. Though it is not widely used in secondary schools, Logo can be applied in secondary mathematics and science.

Who will provide the program? In-service training can be provided by equipment vendors, universities or colleges, professional societies, educational agencies, or the local school district. It is critical that the trainers, regardless of affiliation, have experience in training teachers, in using microcomputers, and in working with school curricula. The trainers must be sensitive to the fears novices have about computers, must have the ability to communicate in simple terms, and must understand the classroom teacher's work situation and needs.

Training programs delivered by vendors can vary widely. One unusual training program delivered by a vendor had all the ingredients necessary for success (Cline & Anderson, 1984; Cline, Bennett, Kershaw, Schneiderman, Stecher, & Wilson, 1986). In this program, IBM established twelve teacher-training institutes (TTI) at colleges, universities, and other educational organizations located near major IBM installations. First, a cadre of 24 teacher trainers from the twelve TTIs underwent two weeks of intensive training in the educational use of computers. Subsequently, these teacher trainers instructed teachers and administrators from 89 secondary schools that had received hardware and software donations from IBM. In turn, these teachers and administrators conveyed what they had learned to colleagues at their respective schools. During the course of the school year, local TTIs provided educational and technical support for school staff. The net effect of this vendor-sponsored program was to create a large number of non-specialist teachers in a relatively brief period of time.

In-service training by colleges and universities is usually delivered through regularly scheduled courses. The quality of such courses will vary, but most will not provide the follow-up support teachers need in order to implement the technology in the classroom, nor will the content of the courses necessarily respond to the particular needs of the participants. One approach to the latter problem is offered by Friske (1984): a series of eight-hour workshops offered on consecutive Saturdays during the school year, with teachers able to choose the sessions most suited to their needs.

University training models that include follow-up support have been reported by DeVault and Harvey (1985) at the University of Wisconsin, and Masat (1984) at Glassboro State College in New Jersey. The University of Wisconsin model includes hands-on experience, experience in teaching children, discussion among professionals, extensive examination of software, and curriculum development. Although the primary activities were undertaken during the summer, the teacher–training aspects continued year-round. The pro-

TABLE 7–4 Syllabus: Introduction to Logo for Educators

Week	Topic
1	Using a Computer to Solve Problems
2	How Computers Are Used in Education
3	Logo as a Procedural Language
4	Logo Graphics
5	Use of Variables in Logo
6	String Manipulation Capabilities in Logo
7	Random Selection and Recursion in Logo
8	Logo Geometry
9	Logo Language Exam
10	Looking at Logo Resources
11	Project Development Lab
12	Project Development Lab
13	Social Impact Lecture; Presentation of Projects
14	Round Table Discussion: Logo Implementation

Heller, R. S., & Martin, C. D., 1985. Analyzing teacher training in Logo using a stages-of-concern taxonomy. *LOGO/85 Conference,* pp. 1–5. Used by permission.

gram at Glassboro begins with a summer session that focuses on teaching and subject-related problems in classroom and microcomputer laboratory situations and provides extensive hands-on experience. The participants receive further training at the college during the school year, and the Glassboro staff visit the schools as needed.

Among the professional organizations that have offered training programs is the American Chemical Society (ACS). Through its Division of Chemical Education's Project Seraphim, the ACS evaluated and disseminated software; coordinated workshops given by local educators; and offered one-day workshops on classroom strategies and software evaluation, on the use of utilities and application packages for the chemistry curriculum, and on linking computers to laboratory components.

The best-known educational agency offering teacher training is the Minnesota Educational Computing Consortium (MECC), now the Minnesota Educational Computing Corporation. Although its initial efforts were with Minnesota schools, it now delivers services across the country and overseas. Though it began largely as a developer and distributor of educational software, MECC now provides a wide variety of teacher-training services.

A cooperative effort between a university and a state education agency was generated by the University of Texas under contract from the Texas Educational Computing Cooperative (Baird & McClanahan, 1985). A two-day training module was made available through the twenty Texas Educational Service Centers. The sessions provided demonstration, discussion and active participant involvement in the use of microcomputers in science laboratories and classrooms, and the instructors encouraged teacher–teacher interaction in order to promote the development and sharing of effective teaching strategies.

Each of these programs was effective for a particular group: planners must realize that the most suitable way to meet both the specific needs of teachers and those of their school district is through in-service training developed and operated by the school or district. Such programs assume that the local staff has attained the high levels of competency needed to train teachers and to provide the follow-up support teachers need to use the technology effectively in the classroom. (See Chapter 13 for a description of an extraordinary program of this type.)

Where and when will the programs be delivered? The success of in-service training should not be jeopardized because of poor location and timing of the program. Schedules and facilities, as far as possible, should be selected to facilitate the success of the in-service effort. The site chosen should have at the very least adequate hardware and software for the purpose of the training. If the training sessions are held away from the school, the site should have the same hardware and software that teachers will be using in their classrooms.

A major issue in the timing of in-service sessions is whether to hold summer or school-year programs. Programs presented during the school year allow teachers to try ideas out immediately. On the other hand, an intensive, full-time program, not generally possible during the year, can be offered during the summer. Whether programs are offered during the summer or during the school year, hardware must be conveniently available between sessions so that teachers can practice what they learn. In the course of the school year, computer time must be reserved for teachers. During the summer, teachers should be able to borrow equipment so that they may learn at their convenience in their homes.

Developing an in-service program is not a simple task, but it will be made easier and the program more effective if it is based on a plan consistent with the needs of teachers and the school district. This chapter has addressed the major considerations for those developing such a plan. Planners should start by contacting the state education agency, as most agencies offer technical assistance, and many can offer the outline of a plan that can be adapted to the needs of the district or sample plans from comparable districts in the state. A sample plan developed by the Wisconsin Department of Public Instruction (Anderson, 1985) is shown in Table 7–5.

SUMMARY

A computer-competent teacher is one who has the skills necessary to use microcomputers effectively in the classroom. Teachers can be motivated to learn to use computers by being shown that the computer is both easy to use and an aid to effective teaching. Even though all educators do not have to master programming to teach with computers, all must be trained in the basic competencies they need to use the computer effectively in the classroom.

Teacher-training programs should be built around several basic considerations: the content of the sessions; how the programs should be conducted; who should develop and present the training; and where and when sessions should be held. The ideal teacher-training program should consist of instruction offered over a significant period of time. The opportunity for substantial hands-on experience with the microcomputer should be provided during and between sessions. Follow-up, continuous support, and appropriate resources should be available to help teachers integrate the computer into the classroom.

A minimum list of competencies was suggested as a guide for developing teacher training programs. Different sets of competencies were specified for the specialist (someone who teaches computing), and the non-specialist (someone who feels comfortable enough to use the microcomputer in the classroom to enhance the learning experiences of students). The non-

TABLE 7–5 Sample in-service training plan

☐ **Introductory Concepts**

General understanding of social and economic effects of computers and how technology is influencing the changes occurring in society today.

Basic knowledge of how computers work, common computer terminology, and various applications of computers, including how computers are used in everyday living, transportation, communication, merchandising, banking, business, and manufacturing.

Understanding the computer as a tool in computer–aided learning, including evaluation of software and classroom implementation strategies.

Exposure to a programming language, including the writing of simple programs in Logo or BASIC.

☐ **General Applications**

Ability to use applications software such as word processing programs, databases, and spreadsheets.

General understanding of computer applications in various occupations related to content areas.

☐ **Specific Content–Area Applications**

Understanding of computer applications in occupations related to the specific content area.

Working knowledge of computer applications which may be used in instruction for a specific content area.

Experience using the computer in all aspects of computer–aided learning.

Ability to plan, implement, and evaluate activities which integrate the computer into classroom instruction.

Anderson, M. E. (Ed.), 1985. *Wisconsin guidelines for instructional computer use in education K–12.* Madison, Wisconsin: State of Wisconsin Department of Public Instruction.

specialist should be able to operate a computer and run computer programs, to integrate the computer in the classroom, evaluate educational software, and to use application packages and simple utilities; he or she should also have some simple programming knowledge for program editing.

REFERENCES

Anderson, M. E. (Ed.). (1985). *Wisconsin guidelines for instructional computer use in education K–12.* Madison, Wisconsin: State of Wisconsin Department of Public Instruction.

Baird, W. E. (1984). Road atlas for computer literacy and teacher training. *The Computing Teacher,* 12(3), 11–16.

Baird, W. E., & McClanahan, G. (1985). Microcomputers in secondary science instruction—A training module. *The Computing Teacher,* 12(9), 51–52.

Bennett, R. E. (1984). Personnel development. In J. E. Ysseldyke (Ed.), *School psychology: The state of the art.* Minneapolis, MN: National School Psychology Inservice Training Network.

Bitter, G. (1985). Computer labs—Fads? *Electronic Education,* 4(7), 17.

Braun, R. J. (1985, July 22). Computer questioned as teaching panacea. *The Newark Star-Ledger,* p. 1.

Cline, H. F., & Anderson, J. A. (1984). A program for teaching the teachers. *Perspectives in Computing,* 4(2/3), 39–46.

Cline, H. F., Bennett, R. E., Kershaw, R. C., Schneiderman, M. B., Stecher, B., & Wilson, S. (1986). *The electronic schoolhouse.* Hillsdale, N.J.: Lawrence Erlbaum Associates.

DeVault, M. V., & Harvey, J. G. (1985). Teacher education and curriculum development in computer education. *THE Journal,* 83–86.

Fincher, J. (1984). Jousting with jargon. *The Computing Teacher,* 12(3), 18–21.

Friske, J. C. (1984). Microcomputer Saturdays for educators. *Proceedings NECC '84, 6,* 323.

Gressard, C., & Loyd, B. H. (1985). Age and staff development experience with computers as factors affecting teacher attitudes toward computers. *School Science & Mathematics,* 85(3), 203–209.

Heller, R. S., & Martin, C. D. (1985). Analyzing teacher training in Logo using a stages–of–concern taxonomy. *LOGO/85 Conference,* 1–5.

International Council for Computers in Education (ICCE). (1982). *Evaluator's guide for microcomputer–based instructional packages.* Eugene, Oregon: Author.

Killian, J. E. (1984). Computer literacy among teachers: Factors associated with professional growth. *Proceedings NECC '84, 6,* 249–253.

Martin, C. D., & Heller, R. S. (1984). Teaching Logo to teachers: A look at the issues. *Proceedings NECC '84, 6,* 39.

Masat, F. E. (1984). Computer education for teachers: A regional approach. *Proceedings NECC '84, 6,* 291–294.

Moore, M. L. (1984). Preparing computer–using educators. *The Computing Teacher,* 12(2), 48–52.

National Council of Teachers of Mathematics (1984). *The Impact of computing technology on school mathematics—Report of an NCTM conference.* Reston, VA: Author.

Roth, G. L., & Tesolowski, D. G. (1984). Microcomputer competencies for vocational teachers. *The Computing Teacher,* 12(3), 64–66.

Schulman, E., & Hrelja, V. (1984). The development of a successful LOGO program. *Proceedings 1984 AEDS Convention,* pp. 74–79.

Sclafani, S., Smith, R. A., & Arch, J. (1984). A model for a computer literacy project. *The Computing Teacher,* 12(3), 39–41.

Sherwood, R. D., Connor, J. V., & Goldberg, K. P. (1981). Developing computer literacy and competency for preservice and inservice teachers. *Journal of Computers in Mathematics and Science Teaching,* 1(2), 23–24.

Zalewski, D. L. (Ed.). (1982). *Microcomputers for teachers—with application to mathematics and science.* Bowling Green, Ohio: School Science and Mathematics Association.

APPENDIXES*

These resources comprise a brief list of materials for training teachers how to use and integrate computers into the curriculum. Because new resources are constantly becoming available, check publishers' catalogs, educational computing journals, and conferences for more recent releases.

APPENDIX A Comprehensive teacher-training packages

Computers in the Mathematics Curriculum
MECC
3490 Lexington Ave. N.
St. Paul, MN 55126 (1984)

Computer Literacy: Instructional Interactive Videodisc Series
Tescor, Inc.
461 Carlisle Drive
Herndon, VA 22070

Integrating Computing into the Curriculum
MECC
3490 Lexington Ave. N.
St. Paul, MN 55126 (1985)

Microcomputers in Education: A Scholastic In–Service Training Program
James L. Poirot and Karen Billings
Scholastic Book Services
730 Broadway
New York, NY 10003

New Horizons: The Educator's Computer Literacy Series
South-Western Publishing Company
Consumer/Professional Products Department
5101 Madison Road
Cincinnati, OH 45227

Teaching Writing with a Word Processor
MECC
3490 Lexington Ave. N.
St. Paul, MN 551236 (1985)

Using the Computer in the Classroom
MECC
3490 Lexington Ave. N.
St. Paul, MN 55126 (1983)

APPENDIX B Audiovisual materials

A Statewide Educational Computing Network: The Minnesota Educational Computing Consortium (MECC) (video recording)
Washington, DC: The Center, 1983.

An Introduction to Computer Literacy (video recording)
Miami, FL: Big Orange Video Library, 1983.

Apple Computer BASIC (filmstrip)
Tarrytown, NY: Prentice-Hall Media.

Classroom Applications of Microcomputers (video recording)
Haywood, CA: Learning Resource Services.

Computer Applications: Education (motion picture and video recording)
Chicago, IL: Encyclopedia Britannica, 1982.

Computer Literacy: A New Subject in the Curriculum (video recording)
Washington, DC: The Center, 1983.

Computer Literacy Series (filmstrip)
Shawnee Mission, KS: Marshfilm Enterprises, 1983.

The Computerized Classroom (filmstrip)
Stamford, CT: The Group, 1983.

Don't Bother Me, I'm Learning (motion picture and video recording)
Del Mar, CA: McGraw-Hill Films, 1981.

Educational Software (video recording)
Haywood, CA: Learning Resource Services.

The Microcomputer as a Teaching Tool (filmstrip)
Chicago, IL: The Society, 1984.

School District Experiences in Implementing Technology (video recording)
Washington, DC: The Center, 1983.

---

*Compiled by Susan Wilson

Talking Turtle (motion picture and video recording)
New York, NY: Time-Life Video, 1984.

Teacher Training Experiences and Issues (video recording)
Washington, DC: The Center, 1983.

Teaching Computer Literacy and Programming (video recording)
Haywood, CA: Learning Resource Services.

Terminology for Computer Literacy (filmstrip)
Tarrytown, NY: Prentice-Hall Media, 1984.

TRS–80 BASIC (filmstrip)
Tarrytown, NY: Prentice-Hall Media.

Using a Computer in the Elementary School (video recording)
Haywood, CA: Learning Resource Services.

The VideoSoft Instructional Programming Series (video recordings)
Little Rock, AR: VideoSoft, Inc., 1985.

APPENDIX C   Books

A Beginner's Guide to the Apple
B. Presley and T. Deckel
Albany, NY: Delmar, 1985

A Beginner's Guide to the Commodore 64
B. Presley and T. Deckel
Albany, NY: Delmar, 1985

Computers, Education, and Special Needs
E. Paul Goldenberg, Susan Jo Russell, Cynthia J. Carter, et al.
Reading, MA: Addison-Wesley, 1984

Computers and Teacher Training
Dennis M. Adams
New York, NY: Haworth Press, 1985

Computers in Curriculum and Instruction
M. Tim Grady and Jane D. Gawronski (Eds.)
Alexandria, VA: Association for Supervision and Curriculum Development, 1983

Computers in the Classroom
Stephen Radin
Chicago: Science Research Associates, 1984

Computer Programming for the Compleat Idiot
Donald H. McCunn
San Francisco: Design Enterprises, 1985

The Electronic Schoolhouse
H. Cline, R. Bennett, R. Kershaw, M. Schneiderman, B. Stecher, & S. Wilson
Hillsdale, NJ: Lawrence Erlbaum Associates, 1986

Instructional Computing
J. Richard Dennis
Glenview, IL: Scott, Foresman, 1984

Instructional Computing for Today's Teachers
Edward Vockell
New York, NY: Macmillan Press, 1984

Kids, Teachers, and Computers
Mindy Pantiel
Tarrytown, NY: Prentice-Hall, 1984

Microcomputers and Exceptional Children
Randy Elliot Bennett and Charles A. Maher
New York, NY: Haworth Press, 1984

Microcomputers and Teachers
Ruth Hoffman
Denver, CO: Love Publishing, 1983

Microcomputer Applications in the Classroom
Alan Hofmeister
New York, NY: Holt, Rinehart, Winston, 1984

Mindstorms: Children, Computers, and Powerful Ideas
Seymour Papert
New York, NY: Basic Books, 1980

Run: Computer Education
Dennis Harper and James Stewart
Monterey, CA: Brooks/Cole, 1983

A Teacher's Companion to Microcomputers
John A. Niman
Lexington, MA: Lexington Books, 1985

Teaching Computer Literacy
Gary Bitter and Donna Craighead
Austin, TX: Sterling Swift, 1985

The Computer in the School: Tutor, Tool, Tutee
Robert Taylor
New York, NY: Teachers College Press, 1980

APPENDIX D   Magazines and journals

A+
Ziff-Davis Publishing
One Park Ave.
New York, NY 10016

AEDS Journal and AEDS Monitor
Association for Educational Data Systems
1201 Sixteenth Street NW
Washington, DC 20036

Classroom Computer Learning
Peter Li, Inc.
2451 E. River Rd.
Dayton, OH 45439

Compute
The Journal for Progressive Computing, Circulation Department
515 Abbott Dr.
Broomall, PA 19008

Computers in the Schools
The Haworth Press
28 E. 22nd St.
New York, NY 10010

Computers, Reading and Language Arts
Modern Learning Publishers
1308 E. 28th St.
Oakland, CA 94602

Commodore Magazine
Computer Systems Division, Commodore Business Machines
681 Moore Rd.
King of Prussia, PA 19406

Commodore Microcomputers
Commodore Publishers
1200 Wilson Dr.
Westchester, PA 19380

Computers and Education
Pergamon Press
Maxwell House, Fairview Park
Elmsford, NY 10523

Computronics Monthly Magazine for TRS-80 Owners
H & E Computronics, Inc.
5020 North Pascack Rd.
Spring Valley, NY 10977

The Computing Teacher
Department of Computer and Information Science
University of Oregon
1787 Agate St.
Eugene, OR 97403

Creative Computing
Creative Computing
P.O. Box 789 M
Morristown, NJ 07960

Educational Computer Magazine
EdComp
10439 N. Sterling Rd.
Cupertino, CA 95015

Educational Technology
Educational Technology Publications
720 Palisade Ave.
Englewood Cliffs, NJ 07632

80 Microcomputing—the Magazine for TRS-80 Users
Academic Computing Center
3737 Brooklyn Ave. NE
Seattle, WA 98105

Electronic Education
Electronic Communications, Inc. Suite 220
1311 Executive Center Dr.
Tallahassee, FL 32301

Electronic Learning
Scholastic, Inc.
730 Broadway
New York, NY 10003

Family Computing
Family Computing
P.O. Box 2512
Boulder, CO 80321

inCider
CW Communications/Peterborough
80 Pine St.
Peterborough, NH 03458

Instructional Innovator
AECT
1126 Sixteenth St. NW
Washington, DC 20036

Journal of Computers in Mathematics and Science Teaching
Association for Computers in Mathematics and Science Teaching
P.O. Box 4455
Austin, TX 78765

Journal of Special Education Technology
Council for Exceptional Children
1920 Association Dr.
Reston, VA 22091

Nibble: The Reference for Apple Computing
MicroSparc, Inc.
45 Winthrop St.
Concord, MA 01742

PC: The Independent Guide to IBM Personal Computers
Ziff-Davis Publishing
One Park Ave.
New York, NY 10016

School Microcomputing Bulletin
Learning Publications
3030 South Ninth St.
Kalamazoo, MI 49009

Teaching and Computers
Scholastic, Inc.
730 Broadway
New York, NY 10003

THE Journal
Information Synergy, Inc.
2922 South Daimler St.
Santa Ana, CA 92705

APPENDIX E College and university graduate programs*

Alaska
University of Alaska, Juneau

California
San Diego State University, San Diego
San Francisco State University, San Francisco
United States International University, San Diego

Adapted from Ekhaml, Leticia. (1985, October). A study of universities offering graduate degree programs in computers in education. *THE Journal,* vol. 13, 98–102. Used by permission.

University of California, Santa Barbara
University of La Verne, La Verne

Colorado
University of Colorado, Colorado Springs
University of Denver, Denver

Delaware
University of Delaware, Newark

Florida
Barry University, Miami Shores
Jacksonville University, Jacksonville
University of Miami, Coral Gables

Georgia
Georgia State University, Atlanta

Illinois
National College of Education, Evanston
Southern Illinois University, Carbondale
University of Illinois, Champaign

Indiana
Purdue University, West Lafayette
University of Evansville, Evansville

Iowa
Clarke College, Dubuque

Maryland
Johns Hopkins University, Baltimore

Massachusetts
Boston College, Chestnut Hill
Harvard University, Cambridge
University of Massachusetts, Amherst

Michigan
Eastern Michigan University, Ypsilanti
University of Michigan, Ann Arbor

Missouri
Webster University, St. Louis

New Jersey
Seton Hall University, South Orange

New Mexico
University of New Mexico, Albuquerque

New York
Bank Street College, New York City
Long Island University, Greenvale
State University College of Arts and Sciences, Potsdam
State University of New York at Oswego
State University of New York at Stony Brook
Teachers College, New York City

Ohio
John Carroll University, Cleveland
Ohio State University, Columbus
Xavier University, Cincinnati

Oklahoma
University of Oklahoma, Norman

Oregon
University of Oregon, Eugene

Pennsylvania
Lehigh University, Bethlehem
Pennsylvania State University, University Park
University of Pennsylvania, Philadelphia

Texas
Texas Tech University, Lubbock
University of Houston—University Park, Houston

Utah
University of Utah, Salt Lake City

Washington
Eastern Washington University, Cheyney
St. Martin's College, Lacey
University of Washington, Seattle
Western Washington University, Bellingham

APPENDIX F   Software

Beginning Applesoft BASIC and *Advanced Applesoft BASIC* (Apple II series)
MECC
3490 Lexington Ave N.
St. Paul, MN 55126

Computer Discovery: A Computer Literacy Program (Apple II series, IBM PC)
Science Research Associates, Inc.
155 North Wacker Drive
Chicago, IL 60606

Computers in Teaching (Apple II series)
MECC
3490 Lexington Ave N.
St. Paul, MN 55126

Discovering BASIC: An Introduction to BASIC Programming (Apple II series, IBM PC)
Science Research Associates, Inc.
155 North Wacker Drive
Chicago, IL 60606

Introduction to Logo for Teachers (Apple II series)
MECC
3490 Lexington Ave N.
St. Paul, MN 55126

The Instructor (IBM PC)
Individual Software Inc.
24 Spinnaker Place
Redwood City, CA 94065

Logo, Words, and Ideas (Apple II series)
MECC
3490 Lexington Ave N.
St. Paul, MN 55126

Micros Made Easy: An Introduction to Microcomputers for the Absolute Beginner (Apple II series, IBM PC)
Science Research Associates, Inc.
155 North Wacker Drive
Chicago, IL 60606

PC Tutor (IBM PC)
Comprehensive Software
P.O. Box 90833
Los Angeles, CA 90009

Professor DOS (IBM PC)
Individual Software, Inc.
24 Spinnaker Place
Redwood City, CA 94065

Programming Presentations (Apple II series)
MECC
3490 Lexington Ave N.
St. Paul, MN 55126

Structured Design and Programming (Apple II series)
MECC
3490 Lexington Ave N.
St. Paul, MN 55126

8

Estimating the Cost of Computer Education

Brian Stecher

Neither superintendents nor principals can have all the staff and supplies they would like. Instead, as experienced school administrators, they try to combine teachers, aides, textbooks, materials, facilities, and support staff in ways that will produce the best educational results within a given budget. Their overall task is to decide how to use limited resources in the most effective manner.

For computer educators, cost considerations are particularly important. Most computer–education programs require the purchase of new equipment, and funding for capital expenditures is limited. Moreover, the equipment itself is expensive. In addition, most educational applications of computers require that only one or two students at a time work with a computer. A program's success depends on the availability of a large number of computers. Thus, a computer laboratory that could be used by a full class of students, even two to a machine, would cost many thousands of dollars. Furthermore, additional costs beyond the computer hardware include peripheral devices, software, supplies, repairs, and teacher training. Many of these are recurring costs, and resources must be found to support these costs year after year. For all these reasons, computer educators should be concerned about cost considerations.

One tool for calculating program demands is cost analysis, a technique for summarizing the value of all of the components of a project or activity. A thorough cost analysis can increase understanding of the nature of a program and the manner in which it functions, and it can provide crucial information for making better educational decisions.

Cost analysis can be useful in at least two ways, by providing information for planning and implementing new programs and for improving existing projects. For example, consider a situation in which a school principal must decide between two different approaches to teaching writing. The first method is computer based and relies upon word processors and structured lessons. The second approach requires new textbooks that emphasize personal expression. Assume that the cost for the former approach is $12,500 over five years, while the latter costs only $8,700 for the same period. If there is reason to believe that the programs yield comparable benefits, then the text-based approach is clearly the better use of funds. If, on the other hand, evaluation shows that the gains from the computer-based method are twice as great as the second, then this project will provide more growth for each dollar spent. In either event, the principal cannot make a good choice without assessing the costs involved.

Of course, in real life decisions are likely to be far more complex than this example. Certain resources may be easily obtainable, others not. Staff may support one program over another. The fact that initial costs are higher for computer programs may cause a problem. But administrators cannot make informed choices without good information about the costs of the alternatives.

This chapter explains, to computer educators unfamiliar with the process of evaluating costs, how cost-analysis procedures can be used to generate useful information for program planning and decision making. The meaning of the term *cost*; the scope of cost analysis; procedures for cost analysis; a cost worksheet and two complete examples of computer-education cost analyses; the use of cost information in decision making; and information on methods that educators have used to meet the costs of·computer education will all be discussed.

INTRODUCTION TO COSTS

When educators talk about the cost of computer education, they generally limit their attention to the purchase price of computer hardware and software. Thus, for example, they might describe a computer project involving fifteen microcomputers, word processing software for each machine, and three printers as costing $18,000 ($900 each for the computers, $100 each for the software, and $1,000 each for the printers). In this case the word *cost* is used synonymously with *expenditure*.

However, this notion of costs is quite narrow, as it ignores many other necessary project components—such things as classroom space, security, electricity, and staff training. Equipment expenditures are only one element in a complex collection of effort, activities, and materials that must be combined to produce a functioning computer project. Administrators need a broader notion of costs, one that acknowledges the value of all program components, for effective decision making and program improvement.

For this reason the cost of an activity is defined as the total value of all of the ingredients used to make the activity happen: the money that is spent on materials and supplies as well as the value of all of the other resources that go into the project—planning time, facilities, training, maintenance, furniture, and so on. These values are then expressed in dollar terms.

An economist would give a technical definition of cost in terms of "opportunities foregone:" that is, the value that resources used for this purpose would have in any alternative use. This formulation stresses the fact that the value of a thing is derived from its scarcity and the alternative ways in which it might be used. Dollars are a convenient meter for expressing and comparing these values, and the marketplace is an efficient way of establishing in dollar terms exchange rates for most commodities.

The working models of cost analysis presented here cannot answer all questions in all situations. In an actual cost analysis two general types of problems may arise. The first type of problem is conceptual: for example, what is the best way to determine the cost of a resource for which no market exists, such as the space in a school building? The second type is mechanical: what is the best way to determine the average teacher's salary, so that an accurate estimate of staff costs can be made? General cost analysis procedures can be made clear, but certain complex conceptual issues are beyond the scope of this discussion. Similarly, most of the difficult mechanical problems will be left for other sources. By reading this chapter and reviewing the examples provided, computer educators will be able to begin to use cost analysis to illuminate program issues; those who wish to attempt a comprehensive cost analysis that will be the basis for major decisions should seek expert assistance.

COST ANALYSIS PROCEDURES

The Ingredients Approach

The procedure described here is called the "ingredients" approach or the "resource" approach to cost estimation. The first step in the process is to list all of the components (ingredients) that comprise the activity. The second step is to determine the value, in dollars, of each ingredient and assign these costs to the different agencies that will bear them.

For example, Apple Computer donated one microcomputer to each school in California under a program called "Kids Can't Wait," and many schools built computer-education programs around their computers. A cost analysis can be conducted to find out the actual cost of such a program.

The first step in the cost analysis is to list all program ingredients. Consider a typical school, Tyson Elementary. Although their microcomputer was free, their program had additional components. A review of the school's budget shows that $225 was spent for additional software—a word processor and some arithmetic drill-and-practice programs—and $150 was spent for a locking device to secure the computer. In addition, other elements of the project did not show up as items on the school's budget: teacher time, volunteer time, space in school buildings, consultation with the district computer-resource teacher, maintenance, and other costs. The program at Tyson involved more ingredients than might first be imagined.

In general, the elements in a computer-education program can be grouped into a few major categories: equipment and materials (hardware, software, text and other print materials, supplies, etc.), facilities (classroom space, furniture, etc.) personnel (teachers, staff training, consultants, etc.) and other miscellaneous elements (security, insurance, travel, etc.). All of the ingredients that are needed for the project to function should be listed, and only then should administrators proceed to the second step—assigning values to the ingredients.

Valuing Resources

How are dollar values assigned to the ingredients once the list is completed? In some cases this is quite simple. If a commodity is commonly bought and sold, then the marketplace price is a meaningful measure of value. In the "Kids Can't Wait" example, the purchase price of the software ($225) is a fair measure of its value. Similarly, the purchase price is the best measure of the value of such things as the paper, printer ribbons, and other supplies. The value of most goods and services that are bought and sold on the open market is their market price.

Similarly, staff costs are relatively easy to estimate, since salaries are market-based prices for the time of professionals and support staff. Of course, one must estimate the proportion of time devoted to the program compared to the total amount of time devoted to school duties. For example, if a teacher is responsible for coordinating a computer laboratory and spends approximately ten percent of his or her time on this task, then ten percent of the salary is a fair measure of the cost of this ingredient. In the same way, the cost estimate may include a portion of administrative time and support-staff time. Generally, average salaries, not the salaries of specific individuals, should be used, because the average is the best estimate of what will occur under typical circumstances.

Do ingredients that are not purchased, such as school buildings or parents' time volunteered have a cost? Yes, they do, and that cost must be included in the cost analysis because the program could not have functioned as it did without these components. However, other procedures must be used to estimate their value.

One method for determining the value of an ingredient with no market or with constraints in the market is to use shadow prices, estimates of fair market prices based upon similar situations. For example, the shadow price for volunteer staff is equal to the amount that would have to be paid to hire classroom aides or teacher assistants to fill these positions. This hourly rate can be used as a measure of the cost of the volunteers. In the same way, the cost of classroom space is roughly equal to the rental rate of similar facilities.

Another, broader way to determine a resource's value is to calculate its opportunity cost: the value of the opportunities that are foregone by using the resources for one purpose instead of any other. A computer-education program claims resources that others might use. Lacking any market price, these resources can be assigned a dollar value equal to the amount they would be worth in their most productive alternative use.

Normally program planners will not have to worry about opportunity costs, but when a program involves a large capital expenditure or when neither direct nor shadow markets exist for estimating the cost of an ingredient, opportunity costs may be relevant. For example, if a school purchases a portable classroom for $20,000 to serve as a computer laboratory, the true cost of this choice is actually more than $20,000: the $20,000 would be worth more in another use. Left in the bank, it would earn interest and increase in value over time. The cost of the building, then, is $20,000 *plus* the earning potential lost by using these resources for a building—altogether, say, $22,000 for the first year of the structure's useful life. This value will differ according to the current interest rate.

Finally, planners must be concerned about establishing the value of an asset that is acquired in one year but lasts for many years. In the "Kids Can't Wait" example, the software that cost $225 probably would be used for four or five years. Should the software cost be averaged out over its useful life or viewed as a lump sum?

Which cost a planning committee uses—full purchase price or yearly average—depends upon the question they are trying to answer. For example, if they want to make comparative judgments of operating cost, then they need to calculate average annual costs. In general, the best long-term measure of program resource demands is the average annual cost.

To calculate annual cost, the purchase price and the length of time the asset will last, or its useful life, must be known. It is relatively easy to determine the former figure, but not so easy to know the latter. Nevertheless, planners must use the best available data to estimate the useful life of an asset and then divide the price by the useful life to determine annual cost. For example, the annual cost of the software described above would be only $45 ($225/5 years = $45).

This procedure will provide a rough estimate of annual cost. However, it ignores the fact that capital resources have alternative uses, and this omission can be a problem: the opportunity cost of a capital resource may be greater than its purchase price. For example, the real value of the portable classroom computer laboratory mentioned above was greater than its initial cost. Annualization tables that provide simple multiplier factors allow easy calculation of annual costs for capital resources, based upon their useful life and the prevailing interest rate.

Initial Cost vs. Continuing Cost

In computer education, one must consider initial and continuing costs. The average annual cost of a project and its actual cost in any one specific year frequently differ. Many programs involve large capital expenditures for computers, so schools must pay during one year for equipment that will be used for many years to come. For example, the initial cost for computer hardware might be $50,000. This hardware might be expected to last at least five years. Thus, the annual cost of this same hardware is roughly $10,000. How should administrators treat these differences in continuing and initial costs?

Initial costs cannot be forced to equal annual costs; instead, planners must decide whether to use an initial-cost analysis or a continuing-cost analysis. On the one hand, annualized costs are more appropriate measures for making comparative and cost-benefit judgments: the average cost per year over the projected life of the program more accurately reflects what facilities and equipment are needed to operate the program on a sustained basis and is also the best way to make program–by–program comparisons.

On the other hand, because capital expenditures usually have to be paid for in a single year, even though they may be used for many years, it is also important to know what the initial cost of a project is likely to be. A district might be able to afford the average annual cost of a computer project, but might not have enough available funds to purchase the hardware during the first year. Since school financing is provided on a year–to–year basis, the initial costs of a project are an important concern.

Planners interested in assessing both initial and continuing costs will need to conduct two cost analyses, one describing initial or "start-up" costs that would be incurred in the first year of operation of the new project and the other calculating the average annual cost of operating the program. Because administrators are subject to both absolute and relative constraints, they need both types of information. Annual costs are useful for long-range evaluation and start-up costs are critical in developing new programs.

Who Bears the Cost?

A final consideration in any cost analysis is the assignment of costs to different groups. Many of the costs identified by the ingredients approach are not borne by the school itself. For example, classroom space is a necessary ingredient in any computer-education program, so it should be included in the analysis, but it is usually not a cost that must be paid for by the individual school. In most cases the school district is responsible for these facilities. Is it fair to include an estimate of the cost of classroom space in an analysis of the cost of the program? Yes, it is. In fact, its omission would yield a misleading result. On the other hand, aggregating into a single sum costs that actually are paid by different groups would also be misleading.

The best way to account for costs is to differentiate between the three or four major cost "centers" and calculate subtotals for each relevant entity. Normally costs are apportioned among key groups such as the sponsoring agency, governmental bodies, private contributors, and so on. Meaningful categories are chosen according to the particular situation under investigation. For a public-school computer-education program the natural breakdown would be: school costs, district costs, government agency costs, private donations, and student/family costs. Obviously, categories that provide no support can be eliminated.

COST ANALYSIS EXAMPLES

Cost Analysis Worksheet

Information from a cost analysis can be summarized on a simple cost analysis worksheet (see Figure 8–1). The worksheet itself is a two-dimensional matrix with categories of ingredients on one side and organizational units on the other. Most general models of cost analysis use four major categories of resources; additional subcategories, the types of ingredients common to computer-education programs, have been added to this computer-education worksheet. On the worksheet, ingredients are linked to the source which supplies them and the cost of each ingredient is indicated in the appropriate column. The total cost is simply the sum of the individual agency subtotals.

Completing the worksheet aids in structuring the cost-analysis process and in displaying the results. It prompts the user to specify ingredients carefully and attribute them to their proper sources, and it summarizes the results of the analysis and allows comparisons between alternatives.

Two examples will be provided to illustrate how the process is carried out. The first is an analysis of the start-up costs of a new computer literacy program; the second, a review of the annual costs of a computer-assisted instruction project.

Start-up Costs: An Example

This example is adapted from a project that was initiated in 1983–84 in a California elementary school: the program focused on computer literacy for

FIGURE 8–1 Cost analysis worksheet

Category	School Cost	District Cost	Gov't Agency Cost	Private Donated Cost	Total Cost
Personnel					
Instruction and Support					
Training					
Facilities					
Equipment and Supplies					
Hardware					
Software					
Security					
Miscellaneous Repairs Blank Disks					
Other					
Insurance Electricity					
Totals					

students, staff, and parents, using the curriculum model proposed by Bitter and Camuse (1984) and stressing computer awareness, BASIC programming, and the use of word processing software to enhance written communication skills. Most of the costs were paid out of a special government grant, though other sources were used to meet some expenditures.

The cost analysis presented might be used in summarizing the project at the end of its first year, when the staff would be concerned about initial costs for the first year rather than annual costs. Figure 8–2 summarizes the start-up costs of this project.

Personnel. Special project funds were used to pay most personnel costs, including salary differentials so that two teachers with previous computer experience could serve as computer coordinators. The two put in extra hours each week to supervise the running of the project. The project also hired a teacher's assistant for three hours each day to provide support for the computer-education activities. Substitute teachers were employed to release all twenty elementary-school teachers to attend two days of intensive in-service training at the beginning of the year. An outside consultant was retained to conduct the staff development sessions. The district covered the cost of its computer resource specialist, who visited the school on four occasions to conduct training sessions for classroom aides (during their regular working hours) and for parent groups after school. Volunteers donated their time.

Facilities. Since the computers were being placed in existing classrooms no additional space was needed. Available furniture was used to set up small computer centers in each classroom, and the overall resource impact was negligible. In addition, a book storage room, fitted with new locks, was converted into a secure facility for computer and software storage.

Equipment and supplies. Twenty microcomputers and five dot–matrix printers were purchased with project funds. In addition, word-processing software was purchased for each computer. As a security precaution, locking devices were installed to fasten each computer to its table. During the year the school purchased a daisy-wheel printer and printing supplies, including paper, ribbons, and additional daisy wheels. A computer-literacy workbook for each student and an instructor's guide for each teacher were provided out of project funds. Miscellaneous computer-education books and a subscription to a computer magazine were donated by the principal and various teachers from their own funds. Blank disks, some purchased by the school, others by the parent support group, were provided for student work. Finally, the school had to pay for repairing two disk drives which broke after their warranties expired.

FIGURE 8–2 Start-up costs for a computer literacy project

Category	School Cost	District Cost	Gov't Agency Cost	Private Donated Cost	Total Cost
Personnel					
Computer coordinators (2)			$ 2,500		$2,500
Teaching assistants (½ time)			3,000		3,000
Volunteer class aides (200 hours)				$1,600	1,600
Training					
Consultant (3 days)			600		600
Substitutes (20 @ $70/day)			1,400		1,400
Resource specialist (2 days)		$ 500			500
Facilities					
Storage room (400 sq. ft.)		500			500
Equipment & Supplies					
Hardware					
Microcomputers (20)			18,000		18,000
Dot-matrix printers (5)			2,500		2,500
Daisy-wheel printer (1)	$ 750				750
Printer supplies, cables, etc.	100				100
Software					
Word processing software (20)			1,000		1,000
Security					
Locking devices (20)			1,600		1,600
Miscellaneous					
Magazines & books				50	50
Repairs (2 disk drives)	100				100
Blank disks	300			300	600
Teacher's guides (20)			300		300
Student workbooks (600)			4,200		4,200
Other					
Insurance		100			100
Electricity		50			50
Consultant travel			450		450
Totals	$1,250	$1,150	$35,550	$1,950	$39,900

Other. The consultant's travel costs were paid out of project funds. In addition, electricity use and the district's insurance rate both increased slightly as more and more microcomputers were acquired.

Summary. From the subtotals on the cost-summary sheet it can be seen that the special grant covered $35,550. The school's own budget covered $1,250 and the district provided resources that were valued at $1,150. Private support worth $1,950 was contributed. In combination, these four sources financed the first year of this project.

Annual Costs: An Example

This analysis examines the annual costs of a project designed to deliver computer-assisted instruction (CAI). A pilot project was undertaken by a large urban school district, and the analysis reported here is adapted from the evaluation of the project commissioned by the National Institute of Education (Levin & Woo, 1982).

In this project a minicomputer with 32 terminals delivered drill-and-practice instruction in mathematics, reading, and language arts for students in grades 1–6. Instruction was delivered in ten-minute segments, and students received at least one segment each day. The computer center was staffed by a full-time coordinator who was responsible for operating the system, scheduling students, and reporting to teachers. In addition to the coordinator, a full-time teaching assistant monitored students and answered questions.

As this was an experimental program to examine the efficacy of CAI as an instructional medium, all direct expenditures were paid by a government agency. The developers were interested in making comparisons between this approach and other instructional models, so they needed an estimate of the annual costs of minicomputer-based CAI. Figure 8–3 presents the results of the analysis.

Personnel. A specially trained teacher served as the full-time coordinator for the CAI center. Two part-time teaching assistants were hired on an hourly basis as helpers. These personnel requirements did not change from year to year, so the teacher's salary and the assistants' wages are annual costs. In addition, general administrative responsibilities had to be performed each year for the program to succeed: among these were negotiating contracts, managing fiscal matters, and providing general supervision. A small portion of the school administrator's time must, therefore, be included as an annual cost to the project.

Because training needs vary from year to year, the annual staff development costs are difficult to estimate. During the first year all thirty teachers had to be trained for a half day each. Substitutes were hired for the half day for $35 each. However, in subsequent years, only new teachers needed to be trained.

FIGURE 8–3 Annual costs for a CAI project

Category	School Cost	District Cost	Gov't Agency Cost	Private Donated Cost	Total Cost
Personnel					
Computer coordinator			$27,000		$27,000
Teaching assistants (2 @ ¼ time)			5,000		5,000
Principal (1/20th time)			2,000		2,000
Training					
Teacher training (annualized over 5 years)			450		450
Training consultant (1 day/year)			150		150
Facilities					
Classroom (annualized over 25 years)	$5,500				5,500
Remodeling (annualized over 15 years)			2,450		2,450
Equipment & Supplies					
Hardware					
Computer (annualized over 6 years)			27,550		27,550
Software					
Curriculum rental			6,500		6,500
Security (included in remodeling)					
Miscellaneous					
Repairs (maintenance contract)			12,000		12,000
Supplies			500		500
Other					
Insurance			3,000		3,000
Electricity			1,500		1,500
Totals	$5,500		$88,100		$93,600

On the average, teachers in this district remain at a school for five years. Thus, the initial training costs can be thought of as an investment with a five–year life, and the annualized rate can be estimated. (All calculations are based on an interest rate of ten percent.) Since the value of this ingredient is small compared to the overall value of the project, minor errors of estimation in this resource are not a worry. Last, a consultant was hired for one day each year to conduct the teacher-training sessions for new teachers.

Facilities.   The district provided a large classroom to serve as the CAI center. (When the project began, the district estimated that it would cost $50,000 to replace this classroom: such a replacement would have a useful life of 25 years.) The room was modified to accommodate the computer system at a cost of $15,000 of project funds; the modifications would be useful for ten years. The annual cost is computed from a table of annualization factors, using these numbers and the same estimated prevailing interest rate, ten percent.

Equipment and supplies.   The computer system, with 32 terminals, high-speed printer, and delivery and installation, cost $120,000. The useful life of the system is only six years. The drill-and-practice software was not purchased outright, but was rented on an annual basis. Similarly, a maintenance contract was signed annually; in general, yearly computer maintenance contracts vary in price from seven to fifteen percent of the total purchase price of the system, and in this case, maintenance costs were $12,000 per year. Finally, the cost of paper, ribbons, and other supplies, fairly constant from year to year, was estimated to be $500.

Other.   A number of other resources were needed for the program. The largest of these were insurance and electricity. The school's insurance costs increased as a result of the computer system, and this increase was estimated to be $3,000 per year. Energy costs for operating the equipment, and providing light, heat, and air conditioning for the classroom were estimated to be $1,500 per year.

Summary.   The total annual cost of the CAI pilot project was $93,600. The district absorbed the $5,500 cost of the classroom, but all other costs were borne by the sponsoring agency. This $93,600 figure can be used for estimating the cost per pupil of the instructional innovation. Furthermore, combined with information about average growth in performance, this figure could be used to estimate the cost per unit of achievement.

Some Final Notes on Cost-Analysis Procedures

Cost analysis can be a useful tool for program planning and decision making: just compiling the list of ingredients is often very revealing, and it certainly encourages more accurate and careful program planning. Completing the cost analysis by assigning dollar values to ingredients yields further valuable information.

The cost–analysis process may seem complex, but it need not be overwhelming. Errors of estimation will occur in every cost analysis, for it is not possible to determine the "true" cost of every component. The techniques should be adapted to fit the needs of each particular situation. For example, administrators need not worry about complex adjustments in the value of capital investments over time when preparing a small proposal for a local foundation. Similarly, small improvements in the accuracy of the estimation of minor components are not worth large amounts of effort: do not spend forty percent of available time trying to estimate an item that represents only ten percent of the total cost.

Readers interested in learning more about the procedures of cost analysis should consult a fine introductory book on the subject by Henry Levin (1983).

USING COST INFORMATION

Cost information and analysis can be used very effectively in planning, evaluating and improving computer-education programs.

The most obvious use of these estimating procedures is in planning for new computer-education projects. Because the initial costs of computer education are higher than those of other educational innovations, fiscal planning is crucial. Accurate estimates of start-up costs will ensure that necessary resources are provided and new computer-education projects have better chances of success.

Much can be learned in this regard from the experience of others. Generally, in the past, educators focused on the cost of computer hardware and underestimated the cost of essential support services. Research suggests that the start-up costs for hardware are not, however, the most significant element in the long-term cost of computer education: support costs have proven to be quite high. In a minicomputer-based CAI project, Levin (1985) found that the cost of computer hardware was a mere one–ninth of the cost of providing CAI services on a yearly basis. Similarly, analyzing a microcomputer project that focused on the use of the computer as a general purpose tool, Stecher (1986) reported that the non-hardware expenditures were a substantial proportion of overall expenditures, and that contributed teacher time was the largest component of all: teachers spent hundreds of hours learning to use the computers. The conclusions of Levin (1985), regardless of the computer application, are worth remembering:

> The purchase of a microcomputer configuration is a necessary condition—but not a sufficient one—for providing ... services. For every dollar spent on such hardware, some four or more dollars of other resources will be needed [sic] such as supporting software maintenance, personnel, and special facilities. (p. 35)

One lesson that program planners should draw from these cost analyses is that non-hardware needs of the project—and their costs—need to be carefully examined. The first step in the cost analysis—compiling a thorough list of ingredients—should help in identifying these needs.

Along with analyzing start-up costs, planners would be wise to carry out a multi-year analysis, projecting program growth and costs over a three- or four-year period. Fisher (1983) described a model for gradual computer–program implementation in which the acquisition of hardware and software was staggered over three or four years. Considering the need for staff training and other support services, this staggering is educationally sound; moreover, this approach is often the only fiscally reasonable one in many districts. A careful multi-year cost projection based on this approach will allow for more precise estimates of the actual yearly costs and, as a result, will allow the program to be implemented more smoothly.

Cost analysis can also be a valuable evaluation tool, particularly as part of a summative evaluation. Comparing a program's benefits with its costs provides a useful measure of the worth of the activity. For example, consider a computer-based language arts program which produced greater gains in achievement than an alternative non-computer program. Adding cost information to this comparison would indicate the relative cost of the achievement gains obtained by each group. For example, each month of growth may have cost $150 per student in the computer–based program, compared to $50 in the non-computer program. This disparity in the cost of achievement might make a significant difference in decisions about the two programs.

Levin (1985) gives an actual example of using computer-education costs in evaluation. Comparing CAI with three other special projects for improving achievement in reading and mathematics, Levin used the number of months of improvement in achievement for each $100 of project costs as a measure of cost effectiveness. CAI produced more achievement per $100 than either adult tutoring or increased regular instructional time, but less achievement growth per $100 than peer tutoring. Reducing class size was more cost-effective than CAI in mathematics but less cost-effective in reading.

Of course, such data must be interpreted carefully: for instance, doubling the exposure to one alternative may not automatically double the growth achieved. Moreover, other important project outcomes may not be incorporated in the analysis, such as attitudes and personal interactions. But even with these limitations, cost-based comparisons can be quite useful in helping educators decide which activities to provide. After all, schools operate on limited budgets. It makes sense to try to achieve maximum impact with available resources.

The process of combining cost information with outcome data—cost-effectiveness analysis—is a powerful analytic technique that can be used in situations where outcomes (effectiveness) can be measured reliably and quantitatively. The cost–analysis component of cost–effectiveness analysis is identical to the procedure outlined in this chapter.

MEETING THE COSTS OF COMPUTER EDUCATION

People who are interested in determining the costs of computer education are also likely to be interested in the problem of obtaining funds to defray them. A number of institutions are willing to contribute funds to establish and expand computer-education programs, but, unfortunately, few sources will cover the substantial ongoing costs of operating a computer program. This problem will certainly attract greater attention in the future. Some of the methods that are commonly used to finance computer education are outlined in this section.

Both public and private sources have been used to support computer education. Many state education departments earmark funds for such programs, sometimes linking funds to specific mandates for computer training, sometimes awarding money on a competitive basis for new pilot projects. In addition, other state grant programs are used sometimes to support computer education. The best example of this is staff development: state programs earmarked for in-service training often can be used to train teachers to operate computers or to familiarize them with computer activities being offered at their schools.

This example illustrates an important point: funding a computer-education program may involve layering contributions, donations and/or grants from different sources. Although obtaining layers of funding may involve more work in the initial stages, in the long run it is likely to be a more effective approach for obtaining funds. Because certain functions are more attractive to different funding agencies, targeting parts of one's appeal will increase the likelihood of a favorable response. Moreover, many funding agencies like to be involved in collaborative efforts and respond well to projects that can demonstrate support from other quarters.

State funds are not the only public resources that can be used to support computer education; individual school districts are already supporting many computer-education activities. For example, districts participating in the IBM Secondary School Computer Education Program agreed to provide substantial resources as a condition of receiving a donation of hardware, software, in-service training, and support (Cline, Bennett, Kershaw, Schneiderman, Stecher, & Wilson, 1986). District resources may well support computer education, especially when that support is linked to a donation from another source.

Public grants are only gotten by hard work. Because of the growing competition for available funds, large grants do not usually fall into the laps of worthy school administrators without some effort. The process of obtaining grants involves more than just writing proposals: it begins with awareness. Effective fund raisers need to keep abreast of any developments in the state legislature and the state department of education that may relate to computer education. This awareness can be accomplished through personal contacts, but it is more easily gained through organizations of computer-using educators and through computer magazines and journals. The International Council for Computers in Education (ICCE) has affiliated organizations in most parts of the country, and many computer educators are members.

In addition to courting public funds, educators can also obtain private support for computer education from foundations, corporations, and individual donors. Cash grants are most likely to be obtained from foundations, equipment from local corporations, and services from individuals with ties to the school or the community. Of course, these lines are often crossed. For example, private schools have long relied upon the local community to provide equipment and services as well as cash contributions.

The process of obtaining grants from foundations is very similar to the process of obtaining competitive state funds. The foundation usually requires a proposal, which sets out the program goals and objectives, the activities that will be undertaken to achieve these goals, the budget that will be required, and the means that will be used to judge the success of the project. Because most foundations have very specific charters limiting their support to projects of a certain type or subject, planners will need to conduct research to identify foundations that are likely to support computer education.

It is difficult to specify guidelines for raising funds through other private sources. There are probably as many creative approaches as there are computer educators. Three activities described by Stecher (1986) deserve special mention because they might become continuing sources of funds, not just one-time grants. First, in many jurisdictions, schools can offer classes on a fee basis for community members interested in learning about computers, and the profits from these classes can be used to support school activities. For example, a software fund could be maintained with the fees paid by adults for computer literacy classes. Second, by purchasing in quantity, a school can buy blank disks at wholesale prices and resell them at normal prices in the student store. Finally, student fund-raising drives—from car washes to cake sales—can be used to raise money to improve the computer-education program.

These are some of the methods that can be used to meet the costs of computer education. However, no educator can develop a sensible plan for meeting these costs without first carefully analyzing what the costs of computer education are likely to be. Such an analysis is usually an important part of any grant application because it suggests that the applicants have carefully planned the structure of the program and determined what they need to carry it out.

SUMMARY

Cost analysis is a beneficial tool for computer educators, as it can help in both program planning and evaluation. The basic techniques of cost analysis are not complicated. First, all the ingredients of the program are specified—from hardware and software to facilities and indirect support. These resources are then categorized according to the organization or agency that will provide them—the school, the district, an outside governmental agency, or a private donor. Next, dollar values are assigned to each resource, according to its market price, the market price of similar commodities, or the value of the resource in alternative uses. Finally, total costs for each agency and for the overall project are calculated. Different, but complementary analyses examine start-up costs and continuing annual costs.

The results of a cost analysis, shown program planners, administrators, or funding agencies, will help them make better decisions about the project. These cost data can be part of the planning process for a new or continuing project, part of an application for funding, or part of an evaluation of an existing computer-education program.

REFERENCES

Bitter, G., & Camuse, R. A. (1984). *Using a microcomputer in the classroom.* Reston, VA: Reston Publishing.

Cline, H. F., Bennett, R. E., Kershaw, R. C., Schneiderman, M. B., Stecher, B., & Wilson, S. (1986). *The electronic schoolhouse.* Hillsdale, N.J.: Lawrence Erlbaum Associates.

Fisher, G. (1983, January). Developing a district-wide computer-use plan. *The Computing Teacher, 13*(9), 52–57.

Levin, H. M. (1983). *Cost-effectiveness: A primer.* Beverly Hills: Sage.

Levin, H. M. (1985, Spring). Cost and cost-effectiveness of computer-assisted instruction. *Public Budgeting & Finance, 5*(1), 52–57.

Levin, H. M., & Woo, L. (1982, April). An evaluation of the costs of computer-assisted instruction. In M. Ragosta, P. W. Holland, & D. T. Jamison, *Computer-assisted instruction and compensatory education: The ETS/LAUSD study. The final report.* Princeton, N.J.: Educational Testing Service.

Stecher, B. (1986). Costs of computer-based education. In H. F. Cline, R. E. Bennett, R. C. Kershaw, M. B. Schneiderman, B. Stecher, & S. Wilson, *The electronic schoolhouse.* Hillsdale, N.J.: Lawrence Erlbaum Associates.

9

Facilitating and Monitoring a Computer Education Program

Terence R. Cannings
John F. McManus

The successful implementation of any computer-education program depends on effective facilitating and monitoring: these activities will provide the basic support teachers need to use computers in their classes and will let program administrators know the extent to which more or different supports are needed.

The process of facilitating and monitoring a computer-education program involves six major activities: promoting a building-site concept of implementation, involving appropriate individuals in the implementation process, defining the role of the principal, defining the roles of the school-site and district-level coordinators, facilitating equal access, and monitoring program implementation. Attempts to implement a new computer-education program are, in essence, a study of the impact of change. Therefore, this six-step approach recognizes the influence of the school's culture in determining the course of program implementation and its eventual incorporation in the school curriculum.

PROMOTING A BUILDING-SITE CONCEPT OF IMPLEMENTATION

Our observations, supported by research findings, suggest that the school site should be the primary focus of facilitating and monitoring efforts. Because teachers, parents, administrators and students create their own culture at each school, it is extremely important to involve all of these groups in implementation planning and decision making.

In *The Culture of the School and the Problem of Change,* Sarason (1982) maintains that each school has its own particular culture, with its own unique organizational arrangements, patterns of behavior, and assumptions. In order to facilitate an effective computer-education program, planners must first understand the behavioral and programmatic regularities of the school and recognize the importance of the principal's role. Heckman, Oakes, and Sirotnik (1983) echo this view:

> The local school is where social, political, and historical forces are translated into practice, and at each school that is likely to happen in different ways. Change efforts based only on an understanding of a general school culture, and not on its particular form at the local school, will ignore what is most critical, the particular structures, behaviors, meanings, and belief systems that have evolved in that school.
>
> (p. 27)

Thus, if the computer-education program is to have more than a trivial impact on the school, the particular culture must be understood and its behavioral and programmatic regularities recognized. Most schools' regularities involve number of subject areas offered, number of periods per day, number of minutes spent on each subject, classroom rules (e.g., students raising hands to answer teacher's questions), and classroom organization (e.g., children sitting at desks facing the teacher). An understanding of these regularities at each site and how the computer-education program meshes or conflicts with them will help facilitate the implementation of the new program.

In many cases, some of the regularities that compose the culture of the school will need to be changed for the program to succeed. Terence Deal (1982), in *Corporate Cultures,* says that "culture is the barrier to change . . . the stronger the culture, the harder it is to change" (p. 118).

How can cultural regularities be changed? Applying to education the eight attributes of excellence set forth in the book, *In Search of Excellence* (Peters and Waterman, 1982), *Businessweek* ("Corporate Cultures," 1984) recommends that the superintendent and school board "encourage local principals and other staff to develop and carry out building level plans"; that the school principal "give autonomy to teachers to carry out their jobs consistent with school priorities"; and that the classroom teacher "encourage students to show initiative in planning and carrying out learning and leadership activities." In other words, projects that depend upon large-scale, district-wide, top-down strategies—that is, those that ignore the needs and the culture of individual schools—are not likely to succeed.

INVOLVING APPROPRIATE INDIVIDUALS IN THE IMPLEMENTATION PROCESS

Initiating, facilitating, and implementing any new program, including a computer-education program, is a continuing process that requires substantial cooperation among professionals. Administrators and teachers cannot carry out the various elements of the program—staff development, curriculum integration, evaluation—individually. Rather, teachers and administrators must work together to implement a new computer program effectively.

In attempting to involve teachers in implementation, school-site facilitators must recognize that teachers adapt to new programs gradually and that they differ in their ability and willingness to adapt to change. At first, not all teachers may agree that educational computing is needed, and a few may be reluctant to participate in implementation plans. Technology is threatening to some teachers; the principal must recognize this anxiety and be patient. As Hall and Loucks (1978) put it: "Change takes time and is achieved in small steps" (p. 37).

This developmental adaptation to change is summarized in a Concerns-Based Adoption Model (CBAM) proposed by Loucks and Hall (1979). CBAM can serve as a guide in supporting teachers and planning further implementation activities. This research-based, conceptual model defines seven Stages of Concern (SoC) that teachers and administrators go through as they implement a new program (see Figure 9–1). When the program is first introduced, self-concerns predominate (How will this affect me?). Once they begin to use computers, teachers become concerned with management issues (Will I ever get organized?). Only when these issues are resolved do concerns about the impact of the program emerge (Are my students learning what they need to know?). Thus, teachers move from a focus on self to one on task, and finally to a concern with impact.

A "planned-change" approach to facilitating this developmental process combines cooperative decision making with continuing staff development and support. Cooperative decision making refers to the need to involve teachers in program implementation decisions that will affect them, directly or indirectly; it brings faculty members together and promotes a sense of ownership of and commitment to the program. The faculty's ownership and commitment are necessary if the program is to become fully integrated in the school routine and culture.

With respect to staff development, Berman and McLaughlin (1977) suggest that training activities for computer-education programs should:

☐ be concrete and aimed at specific skills;
☐ emphasize demonstrations and opportunities for staff to practice the new skills and to receive feedback;

☐ be individualized to address the requirements of each participant and to relate to on-the-job needs;

☐ be ongoing, stretching throughout the school year;

☐ include opportunities to observe other teachers who have mastered the skills being taught;

☐ involve teachers in choosing program content and in acting as helpers and planners;

☐ include principals as participants as well as trainers and supporters; and

☐ make use of local resource personnel as trainers rather than external consultants.

FIGURE 9–1 Stages of Concern: Typical expressions of concern about the innovation

Stages of Concern	Expressions of Concern
0 Awareness	I am not concerned about it (the innovation).
1 Informational	I would like to know more about it.
2 Personal	How will using it affect me?
3 Management	I seem to be spending all of my time in getting material ready.
4 Consequence	How is my use affecting kids?
5 Collaboration	I am concerned about relating what I am doing with what other instructors are doing.
6 Refocusing	I have some ideas about something that would work even better.

Hall, G. E., & Loucks, S. F., 1978. Teacher concerns as a basis for facilitating staff development. In A. Lieberman and L. Miller (Eds.), *Staff development: New demands, new realities, new perspectives*. New York: Teachers College Press. Reprinted by permission of the publisher. © 1978 by Teachers College, Columbia University. All rights reserved.

Berman and McLaughlin's suggestion that staff development continue throughout the implementation process is worth emphasizing. Teachers will need training from the time the program begins until it finally becomes incorporated in the school's curriculum and culture. This is because staff development and program implementation are inextricably intertwined: teachers will learn as a result of implementing the program and will need help in learning as they implement the program. They will constantly encounter new issues and problems that will need to be addressed. Divorcing staff development from implementation, by first training teachers and then asking them to implement the program, ignores this critical interrelationship.

Staff development should be planned and conducted by the same people who are involved with developing curriculum goals and content, purchasing the necessary hardware and software, and setting up computer classes and centers; that is, by those who are most intimately involved in the computer-education program. As Berman and McLaughlin suggest, teachers should play a significant part in this process, as they should throughout the implementation effort. Teachers can be used as local resource personnel and can participate in cooperative decision making with respect to in-service education planning. (See Chapter 7 for more information on staff development.)

Finally, facilitating the involvement of teachers means providing them with continuing administrative and educational support. Such support is necessary because computing represents a new set of skills for many teachers. Even with ongoing staff development, these skills will take time to learn, and the learning process will not always be easy. Furthermore, teachers will have additional responsibilities: they will need to develop new lessons and student exercises, they will need to preview and learn new software, and they will need to consult new informational sources in order to keep up with computer-education developments. The key to such support is the school principal.

DEFINING THE ROLE OF THE PRINCIPAL

Most authorities agree that the principal sets the tone of the entire school. The principal determines what is permitted to happen and what behavior is rewarded. He or she plays an especially crucial role in the elementary school, where the chain of command is short and the principal's actions are felt directly. In the secondary school, a larger staff and student body require that department chairs and assistant principals share the leadership role, and so these individuals will have an important influence on the program's implementation.

As the central figure in the school, the principal can facilitate implementation of the computer-education program by communicating to the faculty that the program is important, by attending workshops to demonstrate commitment, and by becoming involved directly in planning and implementation. Principals should bear in mind the points suggested by Lieberman and Miller (1984):

☐ Effective program implementation requires attention to all relevant aspects of school life: norms, the reward system, structural arrangements, and human and material resources.

☐ The change process comprises three stages: initiation (i.e., engagement, awareness), implementation (i.e., managing or changing), and incorporation (i.e., institutionalization). Movement from one stage to another is not automatic. Motivation, needs, conflicts, and rewards change over time and will affect this movement.

☐ Although there is some disagreement over the role teachers should play in program implementation (e.g., as initiators vs. primary decision-makers vs. collaborators), their continuous participation is essential to school improvement.

☐ School leaders must be sensitive to the needs and concerns of individual teachers, must be aware of the conditions under which teachers work, and must give teachers the support they need to enhance their skill repertoires and to integrate their training into practice.

☐ Implementation is the critical stage for teachers (as opposed to the first stage of initiation and the final stage of incorporation), because they must actually do something different in the classroom and find it more effective than past practices.

An administrator may not find it easy to internalize and apply these concepts, but they are essential to the success of any new computer-education program. The principal's attitude toward the program is the most critical element: he or she must convey to school staff a sense of the program's importance.

Key administrators can facilitate program implementation in some practical ways. With respect to training, they can schedule in-service education for the week prior to the students' arrival for the new school year; offer workshops for teachers on student-free days during the year; make machines available for teachers during lunch hours, free periods, and after school; and allow faculty to take computers home over weekends and on holidays. By way of support, administrators can give teachers incentives to integrate computers in their classroom activities (e.g., rewards and public praise); provide funds for their staff to attend local conferences; appoint a person to help carry out lab responsibilities; and appoint a school-site coordinator to monitor and promote computer-education activities.

In summary, the principal is a key school-change agent. The principal must communicate the importance of the computer-education program and must actively promote it. All change requires broad-based support, and the principal must ensure that this support is provided.

DEFINING THE ROLES OF THE SCHOOL-SITE AND DISTRICT-LEVEL COORDINATORS

Most school districts separate responsibility for district- and building-level computer activities. The building-level, or school-site, coordinator is responsible for developing the school's computer-education program and facilitating its implementation. Moursund (1985) has summarized this individual's specific duties:

☐ working with the district-level coordinator;
☐ working with teachers in developing building-level plans;
☐ helping teachers develop classroom applications and lesson plans;
☐ conducting formal and informal workshops for teachers, administrators, aides, volunteers, and student assistants;
☐ coordinating lab maintenance and purchases;
☐ keeping current with hardware and software developments by reading journals and attending conferences;
☐ assisting students who have special needs; and
☐ developing evaluation procedures for assessing the program's effectiveness.

To carry out these duties, the school-site coordinator ideally should serve full-time. However, because many school systems establishing computer-education programs cannot afford immediately a new position, the school-site computer coordinator may be a teacher given a significant amount of release time from classroom duties. Along with this release time, the school-site coordinator will need a clear description of his or her facilitating and monitoring duties, and the full support of the principal and other key school administrators.

The primary function of the district-level coordinator is to give continuing support to school-site coordinators and to teachers throughout the system. Among the qualifications for this position included in a recent school-district job listing were:

☐ background in all areas of computer programs, K–12;
☐ ability to provide technical leadership and assistance to classroom teachers in the operation of computer-assisted and computer-managed instruction (CAI and CMI);
☐ coordination of the production of all computer programs originating in the district;
☐ ability to plan, develop, and implement K–12 instructional computer programs;
☐ ability to organize, coordinate and evaluate in-service programs; and
☐ technical knowledge of computers in order to provide the assistance needed to solve user-related hardware problems.

Moursund (1985) adds that the district-level coordinator must be a true facilitator: someone who can relate well to school-site personnel, focus on curriculum applications, and maintain a future perspective.

In addition to these responsibilities, the district coordinator might play a consultative role in planning building-level programs. Some states now require that each school district write an instructional computer plan and that each school site develop its own specific plan within this overall framework. The district coordinator, having an in-depth knowledge of this framework, can help school building staff develop such plans.

A word of warning: all too often the district coordinator spends most of his or her time repairing and maintaining hardware. Other critical duties, such as district-wide planning, curriculum integration, and in-service training, are neglected. If hardware maintenance becomes too time-consuming, the district should make a contractual arrangement with an outside vendor.

In summary, both the school-site and the district-level computer coordinators can facilitate the implementation of the computer-education program. The time and skills of these individuals should be used wisely. In particular, the school-site coordinator should not be overburdened with teaching responsibilities, nor the district coordinator with hardware maintenance.

FACILITATING EQUAL ACCESS

If students and teachers throughout the school are to use computers, they must have easy access to them. Placing all machines within one or two departments will inevitably discourage students and teachers outside of those departments from computer use.

According to a recent survey of 30 high schools (Cannings & Polin, 1985), the most frequent users of computer labs in secondary schools are math and business departments. Math departments use microcomputers to teach programming (mainly using BASIC), and business departments use them to teach accounting procedures and word processing skills. Most of the teachers and department heads interviewed recommended wider use of the computer by other departments.

Use that is restricted to selected departments or computer activities is problematic, in part because it raises important social issues. For example, advanced mathematics classes (where computers are most frequently used) and programming classes tend to be disproportionately dominated by white males. Business word-processing classes, on the other hand, are often overwhelmingly female. Intentional or not, these differences in allocating access and type of activity to gender and social groups only reinforce stereotypes that limit students' economic and intellectual opportunities.

To achieve a greater diversity of computer use across student groups, lab time for the following range of classes and activities should be considered:

- ☐ Math: programming, CAI;
- ☐ Business: accounting, word processing;
- ☐ English: word processing, CAI, accessing external databases (AEDs);
- ☐ Social Studies: CAI, word processing, accessing external databases (AEDs), database management, simulations, electronic spreadsheets; and
- ☐ Science: database management, CAI, word processing, accessing external databases (AEDs), simulations, telecommunications.

Rather than establishing a single lab of 30 microcomputers within one of the traditional departments, computer educators should consider alternative equipment allocations. Two options designed to facilitate equal access in secondary schools are suggested:

Option A:
- ☐ one lab of 15 microcomputers, accessible to the math and science department;
- ☐ three labs of five to eight microcomputers in the social studies, English, and science departments;
- ☐ six to eight microcomputers "floating" among different classrooms;
- ☐ five microcomputers located in the library.

Option B:
- ☐ labs of five to six machines in each subject area. As new computers are purchased, they can be allocated to subject areas that need them.

For elementary schools, three alternative allocations are posed:

Option A:
- ☐ one lab of 15 microcomputers, closely monitored to ensure use by a range of students and for a range of purposes.

Option B:
- ☐ machines placed in individual classrooms. This allocation offers a greater chance of access to each student but probably less time per student using the machine.

Option C:
- ☐ clusters of five microcomputers placed in strategic locations such as in a mini-lab, library, or central resource center, or in a space adjoining two classrooms.

Of course, once computers are placed in numerous locations, rather than within a single lab, control, maintenance, and security become more difficult. Some machines may be moved from student areas to staff offices; minor hardware problems may go unresolved until they become major ones; and parts may disappear. However, if accessibility is indeed a key issue, some loss of control may have to be tolerated.

MONITORING PROGRAM IMPLEMENTATION

Program monitoring never stops. It begins during the early planning stages and continues throughout the life of a program. In essence, monitoring activities are intended to answer the question, "How is the program progressing?" The monitoring process is a type of formative evaluation: it provides continual feedback to site administrators, planning committees, and teachers involved in program implementation, telling them where additional support and assistance are needed.

One common means of program monitoring is to document the progress of the program and then compare that progress to program plans. If a discrepancy is discovered, it is evaluated to determine if it indicates a problem in program operation or, alternatively, an improvement in operation not yet reflected in program plans. As computing technology is new to most educators, they may not know what constitutes optimal use. Therefore, they must tolerate a fair amount of deviation from program plans, in the form of experimentation with alternative teaching strategies and organizations. When such experimentation leads to improvements, program plans should be updated to reflect these developments, so that plans are in line with program functioning.

These monitoring concepts can be illustrated within the context of using the computer as a tool to achieve traditional curricular goals. When used as a tool, the computer becomes a device for accessing, manipulating, and analyzing information at all grade levels and across all subject areas. The computer performs these information-handling tasks through such applications as word processing, database management, and electronic spreadsheet programs, and programming languages.

Figure 9–2 presents an instrument for monitoring this type of program: this survey should be used periodically, perhaps once a month. Included in the instrument are sections for monitoring computer use at the elementary and secondary levels, and the portion devoted to elementary level monitoring is further divided into laboratory- and classroom-based computer activities. Analysis of the results of the instrument should help identify:

- ☐ hardware maintenance problems;
- ☐ software availability problems;
- ☐ problems of student access, including the types of classes, subject areas, and grade levels using computers, and the types and primary emphasis of computing activities; and
- ☐ the need for additional staff development and support.

FIGURE 9–2 Monitoring a computer education program

Elementary School Usage

Laboratory Set-Up

A. Is the lab being used?

    1. By whom?

	Boys	Girls
	Number of times per week	
Pre-school		
Kindergarten		
1st grade		
2nd grade		
3rd grade		
4th grade		
5th grade		
6th grade		

    2. How often?

	Hours per week
Pre-school	
Kindergarten	
1st grade	
2nd grade	
3rd grade	
4th grade	
5th grade	
6th grade	

    3. For what purpose?

	Minutes/hours per week or number of students							
	Pre	K	1	2	3	4	5	6
Word processing								
CAI								
Keyboard skills								
Graphics								
Database mgmt.								
AEDs								
Telecommunications								
Spreadsheets								
Math calcs								
Art								
Logo								
BASIC								
Other								

FIGURE 9–2 Continued

Individual Class Use

A. Are the micros being used?
   1. By whom?

	Boys	Girls
	Number per week	

   2. How often?

	Hours per week
Micro #1	
Micro #2	
Micro #3	
Micro #4	

   3. For what purpose?

	Grade/Class			
	Micro			
	#1	#2	#3	#4
Word processing				
CAI				
Keyboard skills				
Graphics				
Database mgmt.				
AEDs				
Telecommunications				
Spreadsheets				
Math calcs				
Art				
Logo				
BASIC				
Other				

B. Is the hardware maintained?

	Microcomputer	
	# down per semester	# repaired per semester
CPU		
Monitors		
Disk drives		
Other peripherals		

FIGURE 9–2 Continued

C. Is software available?

	# per semester
Program disks permanently damaged Data disks permanently damaged Program disks lost Program disks misplaced/misfiled Documentation missing	

High School/Junior High Usage

A. Is the lab being used?

1. By whom?

	Males	Females
	Number of times per week	
English Math Business Social studies Science Remedial Computer literacy requirements Other		

2. How often?

	# of hours per week
English Math Business Social studies Science Remedial Computer literacy requirements Other	

FIGURE 9–2 Continued

3. For what purpose?

	Sessions per week							
	Eng.	Math	Bus.	S. Stud.	Sci.	Rem.	Comp Lit.	Other
Programming								
Word processing								
CAI								
AEDs								
Telecommunications								
Keyboard skills								
Graphics								
Database mgmt.								
Spreadsheets								
Math calcs								
Art								
Other								

B. Do students with special needs have access?
   1. Special-education students

	Hours per week			
Access Location	1–2	3–4	5–6	7–8
School lab				
Own department				
Individual micros				

   2. Remedial students

	Hours per week			
Access Location	1–2	3–4	5–6	7–8
School lab				
Own department				
Individual micros				

C. Is the hardware maintained?

	Microcomputers	
	# down per semester	# repaired per semester
CPU		
Monitors		
Disk drives		
Other peripherals		

D. Is software available?

	# per semester
Program disks permanently damaged	
Data disks permanently damaged	
Program disks lost	
Program disks misplaced/misfiled	
Documentation missing	

Specific actions can be taken once areas requiring improvement have been identified; problems may arise with hardware, software, accessibility, and staff development and support.

Hardware Problems

The monitoring instrument relays information about the condition of hardware; for example, the assessment may indicate that a substantial number of microcomputers break down during the semester. In such a case, the specific types of problems should be determined. For instance, if disk-drive doors are breaking off, students might be asked to open and close doors with greater care.

Power surges, and other electrical conditions, also can affect computer functioning. If the survey suggests a possible power problem, the advice of a qualified technician should be sought to ascertain the source and commonality of the problem. A separate power line, not shared with other equipment, and a surge protector may be needed (see Chapter 5, on establishing the computer center, for more information).

Software Problems

If the survey shows that software items are damaged or missing, coordinators should check:

- ☐ software security procedures;
- ☐ software distribution and return procedures; and
- ☐ the handling of software by students.

Problems in software security are frequently the cause of missing program disks. If a locked storeroom is available adjacent to the lab, only lab assistants or the teacher should be allowed into the area. At other times, the room should be locked to prevent unauthorized entry. If a closet or cupboard is available within the room, the lab assistant or the teacher using the lab must control access to it.

Missing program disks also may be the result of poorly organized distribution procedures. The distribution of software to individual students can be handled by a lab assistant or teacher. Students should exchange their ID card, or some other identification, for a program disk. When the disk is returned, so is the identification. For group lessons in which all students use copies of the same program, the teacher should ask all students to be seated, then distribute one program disk to the student(s) at each machine. Before the period ends, he or she should collect the disks.

Damage to software can be minimized by following two rules:

1   Only back-up program disks should be used by students. In this way any program disks that are damaged easily can be replaced with new back-up copies.

2 Students should be given responsibility for their own data disks, thus permitting lab staff to focus on the protection and care of program disks.

If these guidelines are followed, the need to replace damaged program disks will be reduced.

Accessibility

The monitoring instrument also assesses the type of use that students from different groups are making of computers. Among the computer activities sampled are programming, CAI, and the use of application packages. Accessibility of the machines is indicated for students from different subject areas and grade levels, for males and females, and for pupils in special education and remedial programs. Other groups, such as various ethnic minorities, can be added and assessed easily as to their use of computers.

The monitoring survey can also record the amount of time different students are spending on various computing activities. For example, it should be possible to determine from the survey whether females get less access or a different type of access than males. If less access, or a different type of access, is found, administrators must explore the reasons for that condition and institute strategies for encouraging equal treatment.

Depending on the situation, the following strategies might be considered:

☐ eliminating advanced prerequisites (e.g., high-level mathematics courses) for computer use. Such prerequisites prevent low-achieving students from participating in computer-education activities.

☐ discouraging the use of arcade-type, shoot-'em-up games in computer club and free-time lab activities. These games are often of greatest interest to males, and the widespread use of these games may discourage females from joining in club and lab activities.

☐ encouraging meaningful uses of computers in a variety of courses. In this way, all students have a chance to engage in computing activities.

Staff Development and Support

The monitoring instrument can provide information relevant to staff development and support by identifying the extent to which various teachers are using computers and the ways in which they are using them. If monitoring indicates minimal or restricted use among some teachers or groups of teachers, the problem may be either a lack of knowledge or a lack of time. Teachers may not know how to apply the computer to classroom activities; this problem can be addressed through a series of training sessions focused on using the computer in specific subject areas. In conjunction with these sessions, a resource teacher might be assigned to support teachers in each curricular area.

Besides having limited understanding, some teachers may lack the time to design computer applications. Research suggests that this lack of time is a significant problem in implementing computer-education programs (Cline, Bennett, Kershaw, Schneiderman, Stecher, & Wilson, 1986). Besides the time needed to learn hardware and software, teachers need time to develop lesson plans, student exercises, and any necessary data files (e.g., for database management exercises). If a lack of time is posing a problem, teachers should be granted release time to allow them to work out ideas, make lesson plans, construct exercises and develop other necessary procedures and materials. If release time for a large number of teachers is not within district resources, whatever time is available might be given to a master teacher to begin designing curricular materials for use by others.

SUMMARY

Systematic efforts to facilitate and monitor computer-education programs must be made if these innovative programs are to succeed. Six questions should be repeatedly asked as part of the facilitating and monitoring process:

1　Is a school-site perspective being promoted in planning, implementing, and evaluating the program?
2　Are the right people involved in the process: teachers, building and district administrators, students, and parents? Is the best use being made of local human resources in developing and implementing the program?
3　Does the principal actively and visibly support the computer-education program? Has this individual been directly involved in its development and implementation?
4　What roles are the school-site and district-level computer coordinators playing in program development and implementation?
5　Do all student groups have access to the computers and to similar types of computing activities?
6　Is the operation of the program routinely and systematically monitored?

By asking these questions and acting upon the answers, administrators, coordinators, and teachers should greatly enhance the process of implementing a computer-education program.

REFERENCES

Bentzen, M. M. (1972). *Changing schools: The magic feather principle*. New York: McGraw-Hill.
Berman, P., & McLaughlin, M. W. (1977). *Federal programs supporting educational change: Factors affecting implementation and continuation* (Vol. VIII). Santa Monica, CA: Rand Corporation.

Cannings, T. R., & Polin, L. (1985). *The instructional use of computers at thirty high schools in Southern California.* Unpublished manuscript, Pepperdine University.

Cline, H. F., Bennett, R. E., Kershaw, R. C., Schneiderman, M. B., Stecher, B., & Wilson, S. (1986). *The electronic schoolhouse.* Hillsdale, NJ: Lawrence Erlbaum Associates.

Corporate cultures. (1984, May 14). *Businessweek,* p. 130.

Deal, T. (1982). *Corporate cultures.* Reading, MA: Addison-Wesley.

Goodlad, J. I. (1975). *The dynamics of educational change.* New York: McGraw-Hill.

Goodlad, J. I. (1984). *A place called school.* New York: McGraw-Hill.

Hall, G. E., & Loucks, S. F. (1978). Teacher concerns as a basis for facilitating staff development. In A. Lieberman & L. Miller (Eds.), *Staff development: New demands, new realities, new perspectives.* New York: Teachers College Press.

Heckman, P. E., Oakes, J., & Sirotnik, K. A. (1983, April). Expanding the concepts of school renewal and change. *Educational Leadership,* pp. 26–32.

Lieberman, A., & Miller, L. (1984). *Teachers, their world, and their work.* Alexandria, VA: Association for Supervision and Curriculum Development.

Loucks, S. F., & Hall, G. E. (1979). *Implementing innovation in schools: A concerns-based approach.* Austin, TX: Research and Development Center for Teacher Education, The University of Texas.

Loucks-Horsley, S., & Hergert, L. F. (1985). *An action guide to school improvement.* Alexandria, VA: Association for Supervision and Curriculum Development.

Moursund, D. (1985). *The computer coordinator.* Eugene, OR: International Council for Computers in Education.

Peters, T. J., & Waterman, R. H., Jr. (1982). *In search of excellence.* New York: Harper and Row.

Sarason, S. (1982). *The culture of the school and the problem of change.* Boston, MA: Allyn and Bacon.

10

Evaluating the Outcomes of Computer Education Programs

Brian Stecher

WHY EVALUATE COMPUTER EDUCATION?

Many experienced educators cringe when they learn that their program is going to be evaluated. They have learned, through frustrating experience, that evaluation can be a tedious, time-consuming task that intrudes upon the instructional program and provides few benefits or rewards. Because this viewpoint is so prevalent, it seems appropriate to begin this chapter by explaining what evaluation means and why a concerned computer educator might want to engage in such an activity. For those who have been fortunate enough to have been involved in useful, responsive evaluations this section will be a brief reminder of the rationale for these endeavors.

√ Evaluation is the process of gathering and reporting information to answer questions of interest. What kinds of information? This depends upon the questions that are asked. The information might include such things as students' feelings about using computers, changes in achievement or performance associated with the use of computers, or different kinds of problem-solving behaviors that emerge in students' use of computers. What kinds of questions? Whatever the people who commission or organize the evaluation would like to know: has students' writing improved as a result of the use of word processing software? What impact has computer-based drill and practice had upon the achievment of remedial students? How have student interaction and collaboration been affected by peer tutors who answer questions in the computer laboratory?

Why might educators feel negative about an activity directed toward producing such useful information? For one thing, evaluations do not always realize their potential benefits. Answering questions can be much more difficult than asking them. In addition, the people who carry out evaluations are not always as knowledgeable, concerned, or sensitive as one might like.

But a more important reason for educators' dislike of evaluation is that most of the evaluations that have been conducted in education have been of limited use to them. Mandated by funding agencies or governmental authorities as broad monitoring tools to maintain global program responsibility, such evaluations usually followed guidelines set by other authorities and resulted in reports that conveyed information up the chain of command. They were not initiated by people directly involved in program development or instruction. Evaluations whose primary purpose is compliance or reporting to funding agencies often are not very useful to those responsible for carrying out programs.

In contrast to such "compliance-oriented" evaluation, this chapter focuses on "user-oriented" evaluation. This phrase embodies an important perspective, emphasizing the importance of framing the evaluation in terms that are relevant to the primary users: the computer coordinator, the principal or other administrator, the staff, and the program participants. The type of evaluation to be discussed here is one that serves the needs and interests of these client groups; this perspective increases the likelihood that the information produced will be meaningful and will be used for program improvement (Patton, 1978).

Using Evaluative Information

Knowing how well a program is functioning and what results are being achieved can help computer educators improve the project and make it as effective as possible. Computers, a relatively new technology for education, are being used for many different purposes: some of these purposes may prove worthwhile; others may not. The only way to determine which innovations should be retained, which require modification, and which should be discarded is to obtain accurate information about their impact on students and staff.

Such information can be used in two ways. First, it can be used to make immediate program changes. If on Thursday teachers discover that a particular piece of software confuses students about an arithmetic procedure, they can change the lesson involving the software by Friday. This type of evaluative procedure is called formative evaluation—providing data for immediate program enhancement.

The other broad use for evaluation information is to judge the overall effectiveness of an educational approach or program. For example, one school may implement a computer-managed reading program with the expectation that students will learn to read more efficiently over the course of a year than they would have using the regular, basal, reading series alone. Information on students' reading ability at the beginning and end of the school year would help in judging the success of the program. Collecting such information would be part of a summative evaluation—gathering data to judge the overall impact of a program. Computer educators should be interested in both formative and summative evaluation.

Moreover, different kinds of information are likely to be of interest at different stages of a computer-education program (Stecher, 1985). Table 10–1 illustrates one view of the stages of development of a computer project and the different activities that typify each stage.

The first stage is called exploration. When a school first obtains computers the staff often begins a variety of exploratory activities. A school in an exploratory phase needs a particular type of information. Computer coordinators and administrators will want to know about options, staff expertise, equipment availability, etc.

At a certain point a school may begin to implement a well-defined "program," and its information needs will change. Instead of asking what is possible and how various approaches compare, the staff will be interested in monitoring the implementation of the approach they have chosen, making quick improvements and ensuring that the program functions smoothly.

Finally, when a program is mature, the staff's attention may shift to measuring outcomes and doing fine-tuning. These different questions and information needs are illustrated in Table 10–2.

The point of this introduction is that evaluation can play a meaningful role in computer education. Sensitivity to the needs of administrators and staff will permit evaluators to target in their evaluation the questions of inter-

TABLE 10–1 Stages of computer-based education

Stage	Typical Activities
1 Exploration	acquiring computers exploring uses taking stock of existing resources planning programs
2 New Program	implementing programs monitoring revising
3 Mature Program	measuring impact fine tuning

TABLE 10–2 Educational concerns in computer-based programs

Stage	Activity	Questions & Concerns
1 Exploration	acquiring computers	What hardware/software should be purchased? At what cost? Where should machines be located? What plans should be made for security?
	exploring uses	What activities should be tried: BASIC programming, Logo, CAI? How much time should be devoted to computers? What are other schools doing?
	taking stock	What exists: facilities, staff expertise, student knowledge, parent/community resources?
	planning	What are the goals and objectives? Which activities should be conducted at which grades? What materials are needed? How should training and support be provided? How much will this cost?
2 New programs	implementing	Are required equipment and materials available? Do teachers have time, motivation and training to carry out duties? What are the start-up costs?
	monitoring	How many children are being served? Are students/teachers responding well? Is there enough time? Are resources adequate? Do problems exist?
	revising	Do schedules need changing? Is additional equipment necessary? Do staff need more training? What problems still exist?
3 Mature program	determining impact	What did students learn? Were goals achieved? Were there unanticipated outcomes? Did results justify costs? Was one approach better than another?
	fine tuning	Are there any continuing problems? Which students are benefiting least? Which topics are most difficult for students/teachers?

est at any stage in the development of a computer-education program, and the best way to determine what these important questions are is to involve program staff in the evaluation process. This perspective underlies the guidelines presented in the following sections.

THE RELATIONSHIP BETWEEN PROGRAM ACTIVITIES AND OUTCOMES

The results of a project are measured in order to determine if program activities are having beneficial effects. Clearly such measurement presumes that there is a strong causal relationship between what goes on in the classroom or laboratory and what is learned by students—that school practices result in student outcomes. Few educators would question the existence of this link between instructional variables and learning. As a consequence, in an evaluation one typically examines the results—the outcomes—to determine the effectiveness of a program. (Classroom variables are not, of course, the only ones that affect learning; each student is also affected by innumerable factors outside of school, factors such as the home environment, the community, and so on.)

Evaluators must keep in mind that the program side of the relationship—the school's practices—is just as important as the outcome side; it is as important to know causes as it is to know impacts. If the results are judged to be good, then administrators might want to expand the program; if they are judged to be poor, then elements of the program will need to be changed. Yet, neither expansion nor modification is possible unless evaluators provide a clear picture of the program itself. What really took place? Why did students in one classroom "love" their time on the computer, while students in another found it "boring"? Understanding what happened—the nature of the program—is just as important to meaningful decision making as knowing the results.

Consequently, both program components and outcomes will be discussed in this section. First we will clarify *what* should be measured in a computer-education evaluation, and then we will discuss *how* to go about measuring it.

A Model of a Computer-Education Program

A computer-education program (or any education program) consists of three basic components: inputs (or resources), procedures (or activities), and outcomes (including knowledge, attitudes, and so on). Figure 10–1 illustrates their causal relationship: the outcomes are a result of the input and the procedures.

FIGURE 10–1   A simple model for a computer-education program

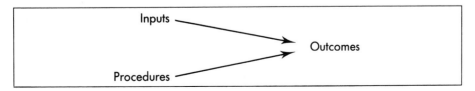

Inputs.   In a computer-education program the inputs usually include these elements:

- ☐ Personnel: Many people may be involved in a computer-education program, including teachers, computer coordinators, classroom aides, laboratory technicians, student aides, peer tutors, consultants, administrators, parents, community members, district resource personnel, and staff from other schools.
- ☐ Hardware: Computer hardware includes microcomputers, disk drives, monitors, minicomputers with terminals, printers, large-screen projection systems, modems, light pens, graphics tablets, and other peripheral devices.
- ☐ Software: This category includes all programs that control what the computer does: simulations, computer-assisted instruction, tutorials, programming languages, and productivity tools such as word processors, spreadsheets, grade books, classroom management software, and database managers.
- ☐ Curriculum: This label refers to the lessons and assignments that go into the program, the scope and sequence of instruction, and the specific textbooks and workbooks that are used to organize a course of study. The curriculum is directly related to the manner in which the computer is integrated into the educational process—as a supplement to achieve traditional curricular goals or as an object of instruction itself.
- ☐ Materials and Supplies: This category refers specifically to supplemental materials such as blank disks, ribbons, special paper and other program-specific supplies.
- ☐ Other resources: A computer-education program also requires buildings and other facilities, furniture, electricity, maintenance services, security, and community support.

The length of this list may be surprising; people tend to focus on the microcomputer as the basic unit of computer education. However, all the resources on this list are required in bringing computers into the educational process. Discussion of all of these elements, as well as the outcomes, should be part of any dialogue about the effectiveness of computer education. As educators share evaluative information about programs, they should also share information about the basic resources that go into these programs.

Procedures.   After inputs, the next component of computer education, as illustrated in Figure 10–1, is the activities that actually take place. What is done with the resources that have been gathered to facilitate the program? How are they used by staff and students? These are questions about program procedures and program implementation. Computer-education programs typically include these types of activities:

☐ Human-Human Interactions: This category includes a wide variety of instructional activities, such as large and small group lessons, tutoring by classroom aides, peer tutoring, and computer demonstration lessons.

☐ Human-Computer Interactions: This category includes computer-assisted instruction (as with drill-and-practice software), problem-solving lessons, simulations, individual assignments using productivity tools, programming, and other ways in which students use computers.

☐ Individual Work: Frequently, students work alone on assignments as part of their computer-education activities. Individual lessons include activities from workbooks or textbooks, papers or reports, problem sets, and progamming tasks.

This list mentions only a few broad types of instructional activities illustrating the variety of methods that various computer-education programs use. If, as we noted above, it is important to know what resources went into a program in order to make sense of the outcomes, then it is certainly necessary to know how those resources were used. In many cases, it may be as important to examine the inputs and procedures as it is to measure the results. One way to do this is through implementation evaluation, which examines the extent to which a "program" really exists; that is, the extent to which activities are taking place as planned, materials are available as needed, and the instructional practices being used in one room or laboratory are similar to those being used in another.

Another way to examine these procedural issues is to consider discrepancies and issues of tension or conflict. By exploring specifically what is missing, what training may be lacking, what materials may not be available on time, and where teachers and students are feeling stress, educators can learn things about their program which will help explain the information they obtain about its results.

Outcomes.   The outcomes—the results of participation in the program—are the final category in Figure 10–1's simplified model of a computer-education program. Although most discussions of program effectiveness stress student outcomes, teachers, community members, and others may change too as a result of the program. Outcomes can be grouped into three broad categories:

☐ Knowledge: This includes all the facts and information gained as a result of the program, such things as the names of the various components of a computer system, situations in which different kinds of computerized devices are used, or the effect of home computers on careers, as well as knowledge in traditional classroom subjects such as reading and mathematics.

☐ Skills and Abilities: These labels refer to behaviors and the capacity to perform them, that is, to actions. For example, teachers may be able to type more rapidly as a result of using a word processor to prepare classroom examinations; students may improve their thinking and problem-solving skills by learning to program a computer; etc.

☐ Attitudes and Feelings: The previous two categories represented cognitive attributes. However, computer education also may have an affective or emotional effect. Because attitudes can be an important part of education, educators should not overlook the fact that a computer-education program may affect students' and teachers' motivation, self-concepts, and attitudes toward school. In fact, such affective outcomes are among the primary objectives of many computer-education programs.

These three components of a computer-education program—inputs, procedures, and outcomes—and the elements of each component are summarized in Table 10–3.

Table 10–3 may be useful in planning an evaluation of a computer-education program, although not every evaluation must examine every one of these conditions. Each program has a distinct focus and uses a certain set of components; a computer-literacy program will be very different from an Advanced Placement class in computer science or a computer-assisted instruction program in mathematics. In each case certain elements from Table 10–3 will receive more attention than others, and elements not included in the list also may come into play.

MEASURING THE OUTCOMES OF COMPUTER EDUCATION

Once its planners have <u>specified the elements o</u>f a computer-education program, they can turn their attention to the issue of measuring its out-

TABLE 10–3 Components of computer-education programs

Inputs	Procedures	Outcomes
Personnel	Human-human interactions	Knowledge
Hardware	Human-computer interactions	Skills and abilities
Software	Individual work	Attitudes and feelings
Curriculum		
Materials and supplies		
Other resources		

comes. How can the existence of particular attributes be quantified? How can knowledge, skills and abilities, or attitudes and feelings be measured?

Five basic techniques are commonly used for gathering information about the impact of an educational program: tests, questionnaires, interviews, observations, and document analysis. Some of these techniques can be used as well for measuring inputs and procedures.

Tests.   Most educators know a great deal about tests, even though they may never have received formal training in test design or development. A test consists of a series of questions and problems with correct or preferred answers. The most familiar tests are standardized achievement tests; these tests present a series of questions written to determine if the test taker knows a particular fact, can apply a principle or rule in a given situation, can analyze a statement or situation to identify the component parts, and so on. These are examples of cognitive processes, and most tests that are used in school—and the type that might be most useful in evaluating computer education—focus on the cognitive domain.

When to use a test.   A test can be a very useful tool for measuring certain outcomes, particularly knowledge and skills, that are typical of computer-education programs. If one of the goals of the program is to improve achievement—in reading, mathematics, computer programming, computer literacy, etc.—then an achievement test may be a good device for measuring growth.

The usefulness of a test for measuring knowledge depends upon two factors: the precision of the test (its reliability), and the match between the content of the test and the goals of the program (its validity). Whether a new test is developed specifically for this application or an existing test is used, these two features are critical. A test that is unreliable—confusing, inconsistent, ambiguous, or awkwardly written—will not provide any useful information. Similarly, a test that purports to measure a topic (for example, "algebra,") but does not measure the specific skills being addressed in the program under study (or does so at a reading level that is too difficult for the students to understand), will give a false and misleading impression of the program's effectiveness. The content specifications and the actual test items must show a logical correspondence between the subject of the test and the content of the program. Test content should be reviewed in detail to verify this match with curriculum.

Many tests are available in traditional subjects such as reading and mathematics, but the dearth of standardized tests in the areas of computer literacy, computer science, and computer applications may make it necessary for teachers to develop new tests to evaluate particular outcomes. These locally developed tests may be the most efficient way to measure the knowledge relevant to a specific program. Trained evaluators can assist with test development or test selection (as well as the design, management, and analysis of any computer-education evaluation); too, a number of new computer-related tests are being developed. For example, the Northwest Regional Educational Laboratory recently released a series of tests of computer literacy, and Appendix A presents a sample of questions from the seventh-grade test. Any program with a matching definition of computer literacy might find these tests useful. Appendix B presents another example of a computer-literacy test, developed by Billings and Moursund (1979).

Questionnaires.   Questionnaires are designed to gather information about a topic, soliciting facts (do you have a computer at home?), opinions (which word processor do you think will be easiest for our students to use?), and feelings (how much did you like learning about fractions in the computer lab?). There are no right or wrong answers on a questionnaire; this is what distinguishes it from a test.

Common types of questionnaires include checklists, rating scales, inventories, indexes, and grids. These labels overlap somewhat, and different types of questionnaires can be distinguished most easily on the basis of the type of response that must be given. Responses can be either open (the respondent is free to indicate anything he or she might want to say) or closed (the respondent must choose from alternatives specified by the person who developed the questionnaire). In a closed question, both the number of response alternatives and the kinds of responses can vary.

When to use a questionnaire.   Because they are so flexible, questionnaires are useful for gathering many different kinds of data: facts, opinions, and feelings. Questionnaires are particularly useful for gathering information about affective outcomes, such as attitudes toward computers or feelings about learning fractions; they also have been used successfully for gathering descriptive information about program resources and procedures. The choice of questionnaire format depends upon the type of information to be gathered, the knowledge and sophistication of the people who will be queried, the amount of time that is available, and the need to be able to analyze and summarize the results.

For example, a good way to determine whether a new adult computer-education program had raised community awareness about the school's computer facilities is to put together a questionnaire for parents and community members. Lockheed, Hunter, Anderson, Beazley, and Esty (1983) provide an excellent source of questionnaire items of this type. (This volume was commissioned by the National Center for Education Statistics and contains over 300 survey items about computer education designed for superintendents, principals, teachers, and students.)

Evaluators should exercise care when using a questionnaire to solicit opinions, attitudes and feelings. Respondents may hide their true feelings when the questions concern sensitive, emotionally charged, or private topics. For example, teachers may be reluctant to comment candidly about the manner in which the computer-education program was planned or implemented. Similarly, students may be very guarded with their opinions about other students, teachers, or administrators involved in the computer-education effort.

Respondents' desire to give "right" answers also can color their responses to certain types of questions. For example, teachers may say they encourage girls and minority students to participate in computer-education activities when, in fact, they do not; they respond positively because they know that support for equal access to computer education is the "socially desirable" response.

Interviews.   An interview can be an effective tool for gathering information from administrators, teachers, and students. The conversational format permits detailed probing about issues, and the personal nature of a face-to-face interview can yield insights that would be difficult to obtain in any other manner. The forms of interviews range from casual conversations to carefully structured question-and-answer sessions. At the former extreme the interviewer is free to follow up on ideas expressed by the respondent and explore each individual's perceptions about the program. At the latter extreme the process resembles an oral questionnaire; questions are standardized and comparable data are gathered from all respondents.

Because interviewing is a time-consuming way to gather information, it is not used as often as the other methods described here. In addition, effective, data-gathering interviews are not easy to conduct. Interviewers need careful training and practice before they can obtain valid data that is free from bias. For these reasons, we will discuss interviewing only briefly.

When to use an interview.   The main advantage of interviews over questionnaires is their ability to provide personal information and insights into the perceptions of individuals. Interviewers can probe more deeply into contextual elements and interpersonal variables that may affect program operations. In this regard interviews are good exploratory tools to help the evaluator identify issues and concerns that may be worthy of further investigation.

Observations.   For most teachers, observations are the primary source of information about students; observational techniques can be used to gather valuable information about computer-education programs as well. Just as teachers use both formal methods and informal observational techniques in class, evaluators may want to incorporate both strategies in an evaluation.

Most of the observational information teachers acquire is informal. For example, if a student is working diligently on a programming assignment when the teacher walks past, the teacher may form a positive impression. On the other hand, if another student asks for help with a simple problem, such as how to make the program flow jump from one place to another, the teacher may lower his or her estimate of that student's ability. Consciously or subconsciously, teachers use such information to build impressions about students' knowledge, skills, and personality; administrators form similar judgments about teachers from informal observation.

Teachers also engage in more systematic observation. For example, a teacher may ask each student to complete a review lesson on the classroom microcomputer and afterwards may "observe" the computer's record of each student's complete interaction. Similarly, a teacher may circulate around the computer laboratory while students are working on an assignment that involves the use of a computerized database and carefully note each student's progress. In both cases the observation is more systematic than in the earlier examples: the teacher follows or initiates a routine in order to gather information that can be compared.

When to use observation. Observations, useful for answering questions about skills and abilities, are a particularly good tool for measuring behaviors and for answering questions about interactions. Formal observation is a very good way to examine pupil-computer interactions, pupil-pupil sharing and problem-solving behaviors. For example, a concern about whether boys get more hands-on time on the computer when working in pairs with girls might be explored through systematic observations.

In addition, informal observation can be used to develop impressions about the program that can help to identify issues for further study. Watching students interact with computers may suggest questions to be explored. For example, are word processors more effective for students with advanced reading skills than for students with reading problems? Questions such as this might arise from informal observations of programs.

To be a good evaluation tool, observation must provide information uncontaminated by the influences of irrelevant factors. Unfortunately, the biggest source of irrelevant influences are the observers themselves. Observers have the same biases and inconsistencies as other people do; as observers, they can be influenced by such factors as boredom, fatigue, hunger, and likes and dislikes.

To minimize the effect of these external factors and make the procedure as valid as possible, a detailed recording procedure, like some form of checklist, should be used to record the observations. Secondly, actions should be described in very specific terms; the observer should not need to make complex judgments about what he or she is seeing. The sample observer's checklist in Figure 10–2 will help clarify some of these points.

This checklist was designed to gather information about one of the questions asked above: do boys dominate or control the activities when they are

FIGURE 10–2 Observational coding sheet

Find a place to sit where you can observe the assigned pair of students and see the computer keyboard clearly. Note the time at which the students begin their assignment. Start your stopwatch and record the behavior of each student at 30-second intervals. Once you start your watch do not stop it until the class is over. Make one observation at each full minute and one at each half-minute (30 seconds).

Record observations by placing a tally mark in the appropriate box.

Behavior Type	Student A M or F (circle)	Student B M or F (circle)
Watching computer screen		
Giving directions		
Using the keyboard		
Listening to peer		
Note taking/recording		
Neutral activity		
Off-task		

paired with girls at the computer? If they do, then the computer-education program is not providing an equal learning opportunity for students of both genders. If girls actually have fewer opportunities for "hands-on" learning and less real instruction because of an administrative decision to have mixed-sex pairs work together, then that decision should be changed. Such a possibility warrants further examination, and an observational checklist would be one effective way to find out.

The rows of the checklist shown in Figure 10–2 each designate a different type of behavior that students might exhibit during the computer session. Seven types of behaviors have been specified: using the keyboard to enter information, watching the computer screen, telling the other person what should be done, listening to the other person's ideas, taking notes or recording results, performing neutral actions, and being actively off-task. The behavior of each person in the work pair is recorded separately.

The observers should be given very specific instructions and training in using the observational checklist. In this case, the observers are supposed to make one observation every 30 seconds, starting at a randomly designated time. At each 30-second point they observe exactly what each member of the pair is doing and mark a tally in the appropriate section of the recording sheet. After 30 minutes, each member of the pair will have been observed 60 times (30 minutes × 2 observations per minute = 60 observations). Comparing information from the observation of boy-boy pairs, boy-girl pairs, and girl-girl pairs on similar tasks will provide data to help answer the question of gender dominance. This comparison may be the basis for recommending changes in the program.

Document analysis.   Evaluators often overlook one of the richest sources of information about program accomplishments—existing records and documents. Homework and class assignments can provide very clear indications of knowledge and skill levels. The teacher's written comments and corrections may also be useful measures. Other documents that can contain valuable information are sign-in sheets or logs from the computer laboratory, lesson plans, requisition and supply order forms, diskette sales records from the school store, and library loan records (both books and software). In some cases, the evaluator may want to create new reporting forms to gather information during the year. For example, consider a school with a computer laboratory in the library which is available on a drop-in basis. One concern with such labs is that a few students (from the classrooms of a few teachers) may use the machines to the exclusion of others. Teachers could be asked to fill out weekly summaries of the names of students who were sent to the library computer lab so the administrator could determine if many students were being denied access to the computers by a few "regulars."

The key to using documentary evidence as part of an evaluation is developing a procedure to summarize and/or quantify the information. Some records—like the sales of blank disks—are easily tabulated and compared. Others, like student homework or classwork, are not so easily quantified and incorporated into an evaluation.

Content analysis is a process for reviewing documents and extracting specific kinds of information; the many approaches to content analysis share certain features. To reduce subjectivity, evaluators must specify in advance what elements are being sought, in what form they might appear, and how they are to be tallied. The procedure is similar to that employed when grading an essay examination with analytic scoring. For example, the quality of written expression may be judged by the desired characteristics of grammar, punctuation, expressing main ideas, and paragraph structure, with specific examples and descriptions provided to explain how scores are to be assigned for each characteristic. The essays are read and assigned scores in each analytic category, according to models prepared in advance.

In computer education, this type of procedure might be employed to examine the improvement in programming technique exhibited by students in a BASIC programming course. Programming homework assignments from the beginning, middle, and end of the year might be compared on a number of variables including, but not limited to, successful solution of the problem. Other variables might be: frequency of use of unconditional branches (GOTO) compared with conditional branching strategies (DO WHILE) and evidence of top-down, hierarchical structure using GOSUBs. Counting the occurrence of these variables will provide information about the course's impact on developing good programming habits.

When to use document analysis.   Document analysis makes the most sense when documentation of accomplishment is already part of the program's operational routine or is easily inserted into it. If the records or other products typically produced by the program are relevant to the evaluation questions being investigated, then they should be used. For example, students enrolled in computing classes may routinely produce program listings or database files, products that are likely to be relevant to an evaluation of program accomplishment. If the products are not relevant, it may be possible to institute new documentation for staff or students to complete. Those staffing the school store, for example might be asked to begin keeping records of who buys floppy disks so that an analysis can be made of whether sales increases are attributable to students in computing classes or, alternatively, to other students buying discounted supplies for their parents' home computers. The success of new documentation requirements will depend very much on how cumbersome the requirements are and on how much they interfere with staff and student routines. In general, the simpler and the more concise the documentation requirements, the greater the likelihood of gathering complete information.

Unanticipated outcomes.   One potential negative side-effect of focusing on measurement techniques is to narrow the reader's attention to specified program goals and objectives. While program goals and objectives are a natural starting place for organizing an evaluation, they are by no means the only questions worthy of attention nor the only variables worth measuring.

One of the most valuable results of an evaluation can be the discovery of the unanticipated consequences—both positive and negative—of a program. For example, students often have to share computers because schools have limited resources. However, this sharing may lead to better communication and to cooperative learning. Similarly, an unanticipated side effect of installing a CAI laboratory may be that regular lessons improve because teachers have more planning time while their students are in the lab.

It is good not to be too limited by rigid statements of goals and objectives. Informal observation and conversations with students, teachers, and administrators can be very productive. An observer not directly involved in the daily operation of the program can be an important source of insight into program operations and outcomes.

DESIGNING AN OUTCOME EVALUATION

The final step in preparing to evaluate the outcomes of a computer-education program is to identify an appropriate evaluation design, a strategy for gathering information on program participants and non-participants so that dependable conclusions can be drawn about program effectiveness. An evaluation design almost always involves comparisons of participants with students who are not participating in the computer-education program, so that the impact of the program can be judged. The purpose of the design is to make certain that the differences uncovered by the outcome evaluation are the result of the computer-education program rather than other, spurious causes. An evaluation design "isolates" the results of the program from the effects of other activities.

An example will illustrate the type of problem that is solved by using an adequate evaluation design. A district wishes to evaluate the effectiveness of two different textbooks for teaching computer programming. School A has been using textbook A, and school B, which is beginning its first computer programming course, is asked to use textbook B. At the end of the year the two programming teachers agree to give the same final examination. The students in school B do much better on the final examination than those in school A, and the district concludes that B is the better book. The problem with this conclusion is that it ignores other possible explanations for the results. Students at school B might have done better in the course because their teacher was more effective than the teacher at school A. The students in school B might have had better preparation in mathematics and higher aptitude for computers when they started the course than the students in school A. Students in school B might have had greater access to computers for hands-on work. Any of these reasons might have accounted for the difference in final examination scores.

None of these alternative explanations contradicts the fact that the scores in school B were higher than the scores in school A. However, the possibility of other influences raises serious doubts about the interpretation that these differences were caused solely by the different textbooks. Evaluation designs consist of procedures to ensure that the inferences drawn from the data are not subject to such doubts and alternative explanations. These procedures are described in the next section.

What is an Evaluation Design?

An evaluation design is an organizational structure that specifies how data collection will be carried out; its purpose is to organize the data collection and analysis process to rule out logically as many alternative explanations of the results as possible. The basic method for accomplishing this goal is to compare another non-participating group of students with the program group. If the two groups can be matched on every characteristic except participation in the computer-education program, then the inferences drawn about that program will be valid.

In the example above, if two classes of identical students were taught and tested by the same teacher under similar conditions differing only in the choice of books, evaluators could be confident that the differences in performance at the end of the evaluation were due to the different books. Of course, this ideal situation is difficult to achieve. The purpose of an experimental design is to approximate these conditions as closely as possible. If an acceptable match cannot be achieved, evaluators must try to quantify the differences between groups, so that less certain, but probable, inferences still can be made.

The basic tools of experimental design are control groups, comparison groups and longitudinal data collection. The most powerful tool for ruling out extraneous influences is to match another group of students and teachers with the program group in every way except for their participation in the program. Comparing the outcomes of these two groups provides a measure of the impact of the program. To the extent that all other factors are the same, the only cause for differences in the performance of the groups is the program itself.

Unfortunately, two groups will never match on every relevant characteristic. Yet, evaluators can rule out extraneous influences by assuring that each member of the relevant student population has an equally likely chance of being in either group. If this is done, then differences at the end of the program will not be related to any special characteristic of one group or the other. This goal is accomplished by randomly assigning students (and teachers, if their assignment is relevant) to program and non-program groups for comparison purposes. If the assignment is truly random then there will be no systematic variation between the groups. When participants are assigned randomly to groups, the group that does not participate in the program is called a control group; using a control group is the strongest action evaluators can take to ensure the validity of their conclusions. Designs that use randomly assigned control groups are called true experimental designs.

Unfortunately, students cannot always be assigned randomly to groups in the school setting. Most programs are delivered to existing classes by existing teachers, and rearranging these for evaluation purposes would be disruptive. When random assignment cannot be used, it is still useful to compare participants to an outside group that resembles them as closely as possible. Such a group is called a comparison group.

Because systematic differences might exist between the program participants and a comparison group, evaluators should measure as many of the important confounding variables as possible. For example, in the programming textbook example discussed above, it would have been useful to know the mathematics background of the two groups as well as their scores on any relevant aptitude measures. If the two groups turned out to have similar aptitudes and experiences, the argument that the textbooks caused the differences in final examination results would have greater credibility. When control groups cannot be established, evaluators should use similar groups as comparison groups and document as much about their similarities and differences as possible. These designs, using non-random comparison groups, are called quasi-experimental designs.

Under certain circumstances it may be impossible to find either a control group or a comparison group: for instance, if every student in the school participates in the program under study. If every student learns word processing as part of a program to improve written composition skills, no one is left to serve in a comparison group. In this case it may be possible to have the students serve as their own controls: charting their past, present, and future behavior may reveal if the project has changed their pattern of growth and achievement. Such procedures are called time-series or longitudinal designs. By collecting information about relevant outcomes over a lengthy period, evaluators may see changes in growth patterns at the time when the new computer-education program was initiated. Of course, they must have enough data points to establish clearly the pattern of growth before and after the intervention, and they must strive to rule out other possible causes.

These strategies—control groups, comparison groups, and longitudinal data collection—are the basis for many different experimental designs, quasi-experimental designs, and time-series designs. The next section presents a few of the more useful designs for computer education; Fitz-Gibbon and Morris (1978) also provide a good practical discussion of evaluation design.

Useful Evaluation Designs for Computer Education

The four evaluation designs described in this section exhibit the different characteristics of designs. Their names are cumbersome, but quite descriptive; they usually contain all the elements that have been incorporated into the design. The four examples described are summarized in Table 10–4. Many variations on these models are possible. An evaluator can help program administrators select an appropriate evaluation design before the program begins.

Post–test only control group design.   The most basic design, this serves as a building block for many more complex approaches. In this design a control group is used for comparison purposes, and outcomes are measured only at the conclusion of the program: students are randomly assigned to treatment or control groups (and teachers are randomly assigned, too, if they are a significant part of the program). The use of these controls ensures that all other factors are equally likely to appear in either group and, therefore, all extraneous influences balance out between the two groups. Comparing scores on the post-test yields a valid measure of the results of the program.

☐ *Example:* Jefferson Elementary School desires to evaluate two pieces of software designed to teach "keyboarding" skills. They want to choose the most effective program to use with all upper-grade students. Typing speed at the end of five weeks is the outcome they are interested in measuring.

A post-test only control group design is appropriate for this purpose. Students are randomly assigned to two groups, and each group works with a different piece of software for five weeks. (Since the learning is completely individualized, there are no administrative problems with random assignment.) At the conclusion of the five weeks the students' typing skills are measured, and the means and standard deviations (statistics summarizing performance) for each group are computed. These numbers provide a direct measure of the effectiveness of the two pieces of software for students at Jefferson.

Pre-test post-test control group design.   This design is similar to the post-test only control group design, but an additional administration of the test is given at the beginning of the evaluation. Having both pre-test and post-test scores allows the evaluator to calculate the amount of growth achieved by students during the program. Program effectiveness is determined by comparing the growth scores of the two groups. The pre-test post-test control group design is popular with educators because growth scores (and other measures derived from the two performance scores) are commonly used indices of program accomplishment.

☐ *Example:* The Katherine Jay Junior High School mathematics department staff want to evaluate the effectiveness of a microcomputer-based mathematics program that is being used on an experimental basis.

Since the school is departmentalized it is not too difficult to assign students to the microcomputer program or the regular program on a random basis. Students in the two groups are tested at the beginning and the end of the term. One way to compare the groups is to calculate each student's growth from pre-test to post-test and compare the average growth across groups. This provides a measure of the relative effectiveness of the two alternatives.

Pre-test post-test quasi-experimental design.   This is a "quasi-experimental" design because it lacks the random assignment needed to ensure that the two groups are equivalent in all non-program aspects. It is a popular design because circumstances in schools sometimes make it impossible to assign participants at random. In such instances the pre-test takes on added importance: it helps to establish the comparability of the two groups. In addition, evaluators should try to measure any other variables that might be relevant to student performance in the program. Statistical methods can be used to adjust for some factors that cannot be controlled by random assignment.

☐ *Example:* The English department of Eastpark High School embarks on a composition program involving word processing. Since the school has only one room of computers it is not possible for every student to work on the computers for an extended period of time. Consequently, the principal decides that three classes will participate in the program, one each from the ninth, tenth, and eleventh grades. All other students continue to receive their regular instruction in composition. A pre-test post-test quasi-experimental design is appropriate under these circumstances, with all the non-computer users serving as the comparison group.

All students are asked to write essays on the same topic at the beginning of the year and again at the end of the year. Composition skills will be measured by scoring these written assignments using an analytic content-analysis scheme. In addition, all students take a general aptitude test. Both aptitude scores and the beginning English composition scores are used to determine the comparability of the two groups. Growth scores and other statistics are used to determine the effectiveness of the program. The results are interpreted in light of the known differences between participants and non-participants.

Time-series design.   A time-series design is one in which a series of observations establishes expectations for student achievement; these expectations are compared with actual achievement after the introduction of a new program. This design is used when appropriate comparison groups cannot be found; for example, when all students participate in the program. The effectiveness of the program is judged by deviations from the expected pattern of growth after the introduction of the new activity.

☐ *Example:* Casey School inaugurates a computer-literacy program for all students. One goal of the program is to improve school morale by giving all students experience with computers. Under these circumstances a longitudinal design could be used to structure the evaluation.

Morale is a difficult concept to assess, but some outward signs that can be measured are the incidence of vandalism, the amount of trash left on school grounds, the rate of absenteeism, the rate of attendance at school events, and the sales of clothing and other items bearing the school insignia; these particular variables are selected because Casey School's principal has been keeping records of them for two years before computer-literacy classes began. These data will serve as a baseline for evaluating the effect on morale of the computer-literacy program. By continuing to collect data during the year following the initiation of the new program, the principal may detect a change coincident with the introduction of the computer classes. To eliminate possible competing causes for the observed changes in the morale indicators, the principal will need additional data about other changes that occurred at the same time.

These four examples—the post-test only control group design, the pre-test post-test control group design, the pre-test post-test quasi-experimental design, and the time-series design—are only some of the ways designs can be used in evaluating computer-education programs. Other designs are frequently used in education, and combinations of designs are often utilized to yield additional information and add certainty to evaluators' conclusions.

An Evaluation Management Plan

Once administrators choose a design, they should develop a detailed evaluation plan around it. The plan should specify when the desired information is to be gathered, from whom, and in what manner. It should outline the procedures to be used for selecting students to be assessed or observed, collecting information, analyzing the data and reporting the results to interested parties. Such a plan serves as a management tool to ensure that the evaluation is carried out efficiently. The *Program Evaluation Kit* (Morris,

TABLE 10-4 Examples of questions, measures, and designs

Question	Measurement	Design
Is one piece of keyboarding software more effective than another?	Typing test	Post-test only control group design.
Is a CAI mathematics program more effective than the regular program?	Mathematics test	Pre-test post-test control group design.
Does written expression improve through the use of word processors?	Document analysis of essays	Pre-test post-test quasi-experimental design.
Did the computer literacy program improve school morale?	Observation and document analysis	Time-series design.

1978), developed by the UCLA Center for the Study of Evaluation, is a good general guide to planning and conducting an evaluation.

USING EVALUATION RESULTS TO IMPROVE COMPUTER EDUCATION

Computer educators, in planning evaluations, must keep one goal in mind: evaluations should be designed to be useful. Unless the likelihood that the information will be used is strong, there is little point in conducting the evaluation. The goal of evaluation is to improve computer-education programs, and so the rationale for conducting an evaluation is to provide information that will help achieve this goal. It would be a shame if computer educators duplicated the past mistakes of their colleagues and expended large amounts of resources on evaluations that served very limited purposes, were directed to distant audiences, and were seldom used by the local program staff.

Research shows that much can be done to increase the likelihood that evaluation results will be used to improve computer education. The single most important factor in increasing the utilization of evaluation findings is the involvement, from the beginning of the process, of the people who are in a position to use the results: the computer coordinator, other administrators, key staff members, community members, and even students. Earlier, we called this a *user-oriented* evaluation.

One method that has been used to make evaluation more meaningful and increase its usefulness is to form an evaluation advisory team. A group of people representing all the important constituencies that are likely to make use of the information is brought together at the start of the proceedings. They help to frame the evaluation, to determine which questions are important, to identify which techniques are appropriate for gathering information, and to interpret what the information means. Their involvement is not token, and they are not merely a rubber stamp; the process becomes "their" evaluation. Whether a professional evaluator is also employed or not, the results of the evaluation are more likely to be used if the users are involved from the outset.

Another procedure that is useful is to consult other individuals who are involved in similar activities. Evaluators should seek out other computer educators and share their experiences with them. People all around the country can benefit from the information produced by the evaluation of a single program. Just as teachers of mathematics, reading, history, and art have formed associations, computer-using teachers have banded together to facilitate the sharing of information. Books, journals, and magazines are written for computer educators. For example, Cline, Bennett, Kershaw, Schneiderman, Stecher, and Wilson (1986) present a profile of the implementation of a large-scale computer-education program. Computer education lacks good evaluation data, and many computer educators are eager to learn about others' experiences. Better evaluations can be a tool for expanding the network of concerned computer educators.

SUMMARY

The purpose of this chapter was to show how techniques for evaluating program outcomes can be adapted to the needs of computer-using educators. The rationale for learning to apply these techniques to computer education is simple: research shows that evaluation can be a useful tool for program improvement if the process is responsive to the needs of concerned program staff. The approach described in this chapter was designed to accomplish this end.

The first step in planning for an evaluation is to clarify the elements that make up the program. Does the program have well-established goals and objectives or is it really just a collection of flexible explorations of approaches to using the computer? If a well-established program exists, then one can identify the main components of the program: the inputs, procedures and outcomes that might be investigated. The program must be described clearly before any evaluation of its impact can make sense.

Once the program is described, the evaluator's attention can shift to measuring outcomes. A variety of techniques presented for accomplishing this task included tests, questionnaires, interviews, observations, and document analysis. The evaluator uses these tools to measure outcomes that might be caused by the program. To determine if the outcomes were, in fact, the results of the computer-education activities and not due to other, extraneous factors, the evaluator relies upon the principles of evaluation design. Control groups, comparison groups and longitudinal data collection are the basic strategies that are used to ensure that differences in measured outcomes are due to the computer-education program and not to other factors.

By combining this knowledge of program components, measurement techniques and evaluation design principles, the concerned computer educator should be able to conduct a meaningful evaluation of a computer-education program. His or her final task is to share the results with other computer educators so all can benefit from the information derived.

REFERENCES

Billings, K., & Moursund, D. (1979). *Are you computer literate?* Beaverton, OR: Dilithium Press.

Cline, H. F., Bennett, R. E., Kershaw, R. C., Schneiderman, M. B., Stecher, B., & Wilson, S. (1986). *The electronic schoolhouse.* Hillsdale, N.J.: Lawrence Erlbaum Associates.

Fitz-Gibbon, C. T., & Morris, L. L. (1978) *How to design a program evaluation.* Beverly Hills: Sage Publications.

Lockheed, M. E., Hunter, B., Anderson, R. E., Beazley, R. M., & Esty, E. T. (1983). *Computer literacy: Definition and survey items for assessment in schools.* Washington, D.C.: National Center for Education Statistics.

Morris, L. L. (Ed.). (1978). *Program evaluation kit.* Beverly Hills, CA: Sage Publications.

Patton, M. Q. (1978). *Utilization-focused evaluation.* Beverly Hills, CA: Sage Productions.

Stecher, B. (1985). Using evaluation to improve computer-based education, *THE Journal, 13* (3) 94–97.

Appendix A   Selections from Grade 7 computer literacy examination

The chart below contains a plan for making a phone call. The first two questions ask about this chart.

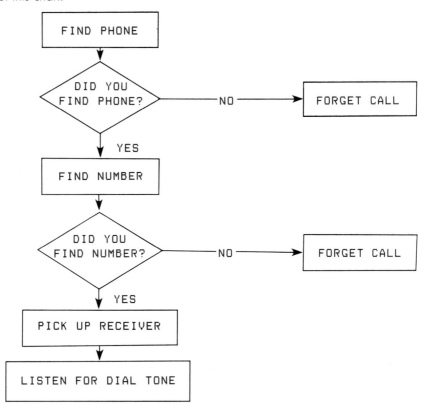

1. The rectangular shapes in the flowchart above mean
    A. Do something.
    B. Stop or start.
    C. Make a decision.
    D. Input or output.
2. The diamond shapes in the flowchart above mean
    A. Do something.
    B. Stop or start.
    C. Make a decision.
    D. Forget the call.

The next five questions ask you to think of the most logical way to solve a problem. Choose the response which best answers these questions.

3. Suppose you are going to the market and have about 30 items in your shopping basket. If you want to find out how much you are going to have to pay for them, what would you use?
   A. A microcomputer
   B. An adding machine
   C. A pencil and paper
   D. A hand-held calculator

4. Suppose you are an independent researcher who generally has about 40 cases of data and wants results immediately. What kind of computer would be best for you?
   A. Mainframe
   B. Microcomputer
   C. Minicomputer
   D. Maxicomputer

5. Suppose you are a mail carrier for the post office in your neighborhood. To help you to deliver the mail, how would you sort the mail first?
   A. By names alphabetically
   B. By street numbers/names
   C. By ZIP codes
   D. By the type of mail it is, like letters, bills, magazines

6. Suppose you worked in a large office and needed to store lots of information so that it could be found quickly. How would you store it?
   A. Alphabetically by general topics
   B. Numerically, giving each item a number
   C. By color coding
   D. Under symbols like *,%,&

7. Suppose you want to produce a set of single digit multiplication problems that you could practice with later. Which of the following instructions would you use?
   A. (1) print a number between 0 and 9
      (2) print "X"
      (3) print another number between 0 and 9
      (4) go back to (1)
   B. (1) print a number between 0 and 9
      (2) print "X"
      (3) go back to (1)
      (4) print answer
   C. (1) print a number between 0 and 9
      (2) print "X"
      (3) print another number between 0 and 9
      (4) print answer
   D. (1) print a number between 0 and 9
      (2) print another number between 0 and 9
      (3) print "X"
      (4) go back to (1)

The next three questions are about the BASIC programming language.

8. In BASIC programming you type in the line you want and then
   A. Type the line number.
   B. Press the RETURN key.
   C. Type RUN.
   D. Press the PRINT key.

9. In BASIC, a "string" contained within a PRINT statement is
   A. Enclosed by quotation marks.
   B. Enclosed by parentheses.
   C. Enclosed by commas.
   D. Enclosed by asterisks.

10. If the computer program says "GO TO 120," it will find step 120 and then
    A. Execute it and return to where it was.
    B. Execute it and stop.
    C. Execute it and continue.
    D. Execute it and wait.

Appendix B   Computer literacy final exam

Circle the *best* response of the four choices listed to complete each statement.

1. What is computer literacy? Is it:
   a. The ability to write computer programs?
   b. Knowing what a computer can and cannot do, how computers are used, and how they may change our lives?
   c. Knowing computer-related vocabulary, so you can read, write, and talk about computers?
   d. Understanding how to build a computer?
2. The first general purpose electronic digital computer became operational:
   a. Shortly after Ben Franklin performed his famous experiment using a kite and lightning.
   b. Shortly after the invention of the telephone.
   c. About the time the first television set was built.
   d. Shortly after the end of World War II.
3. A task quite suited to a computer is:
   a. To print out "personalized" form letters for advertising purposes.
   b. To take off, pilot, and land a small plane flying from San Francisco to Los Angeles.
   c. To analyze an X-ray and recommend a course of treatment for any diseases it detects.
   d. To take over most functions currently performed by teachers.
4. A good way to think about computers is:
   a. It is impossible for a computer to tell a lie.
   b. Computers are built and programmed by people and these people should be responsible for what computers do.
   c. Anything a human can do a computer can do better.
   d. Any problem that can be solved by a computer should be, since a computer cannot make a mistake.
5. A *good* definition of a computer is:
   a. An electronic automated device that can solve problems involving words and numbers.
   b. A superspeed pocket calculator.
   c. A machine that uses binary numbers to do math problems.
   d. Any machine that can add, subtract, multiply, and divide numbers.
6. When we say a computer "understands" an instruction we mean:
   a. The computer can execute (carry out) that instruction.
   b. The computer can explain the meaning of that instruction.
   c. The computer's keyboard has a key corresponding to the instruction.
   d. It can print out a definition of the instruction.
7. A magnetic disk pack:
   a. Is usually considered to be primary storage.
   b. Spins at 33⅓ revolutions per minute.
   c. Can store a very large number of characters in a relatively small space.
   d. Costs about the same as a magnetic tape cassette.

8. A modern large scale computer can perform about how many multiplications in one second?
   a. 100 to 1,000
   b. 10,000 to 100,000
   c. 1,000,000 to 10,000,000
   d. 100,000,000 to 1,000,000,000
9. The Jacquard loom is:
   a. A bird found in southern France and northern Italy.
   b. A weaving machine that uses punched cards to specify the raising and lowering of threads.
   c. The first computer-controlled loom, built in the early 1950s.
   d. A machine for automatically producing mathematics tables.
10. Herman Hollerith is best known for:
    a. Serving as president of IBM from 1902 to 1942.
    b. Building the first mechanical computer, called an analytical engine.
    c. Developing punched cards and data processing ideas used to process the U.S. Census data for 1890.
    d. Building the first relay computer in the 1930s.
11. The typical modern computer:
    a. Contains more than 10,000 vacuum tubes.
    b. Uses small magnetic cores for its secondary storage.
    c. Uses magnetic tape and/or disk for primary storage.
    d. Makes use of large scale integrated circuitry, called chips.
12. John von Neumann is well known for his contribution to:
    a. Design of computers.
    b. Help in developing game theory.
    c. Mathematics.
    d. All of the above.
13. If a computer program is quite short (less than 20 statements long) we can conclude:
    a. It will take less than one second to run on a computer.
    b. It is bug-free, since it is so short.
    c. It is not long enough to perform a useful task.
    d. None of the above.
14. Information to be processed by a computer is called:
    a. Records.
    b. Data.
    c. Intelligence.
    d. Files.
15. Most errors blamed on computers used in business are actually due to:
    a. Hardware problems.
    b. Programming errors.
    c. Data preparation and data entry errors.
    d. None of the above.

16. Key to tape and key to disk refer to:
    a. The locks found on most tape and disk cabinets.
    b. Indexes used in retrieving information from tape or disk.
    c. Data entry devices.
    d. Output devices.

17. A flowchart is best defined as:
    a. A chart or record showing weekly flow of programs through a computer.
    b. A diagram showing the flow of electricity through a computer memory.
    c. A two-dimensional picture, using boxes and connectors, showing a step-by-step set of directions.
    d. A computer-produced analysis of the steps needed to solve a problem.

18. BASIC is an example of:
    a. A language all computers understand.
    b. A language designed to be read and used by both people and computers.
    c. A natural language.
    d. A programming language most often used in business applications.

19. If a mail delivery robot working in an office building finds an obstacle in its path, it is most apt to:
    a. Blow a fuse.
    b. Signal for help.
    c. Remove the obstacle.
    d. Climb over the obstacle.

20. A thermostat is an example of:
    a. A microcomputer.
    b. An information retrieval machine.
    c. A process control device.
    d. Artificial intelligence.

21. A walking, talking robot is most likely to be found:
    a. Working in a modern factory.
    b. Teaching in a school or university.
    c. Working as a computer operator.
    d. In a science fiction movie.

22. Computer applications for information retrieval include:
    a. Supermarket checkout systems using UPC.
    b. Airline reservation systems.
    c. Computerized search of medical literature.
    d. All of the above.

23. Currently the people making the most use of full text searching are:
    a. Airline reservation clerks.
    b. Police.
    c. Lawyers.
    d. English teachers.

24. Data processing is:
    a. Any use of computers that produces data.
    b. The collection, storage, and processing of data to produce needed reports.
    c. The retrieval of data stored in a computerized data bank.
    d. All applications of computers outside the field of business.
25. A computer program for a mathematical model is called:
    a. A computer simulation.
    b. Artificial intelligence.
    c. A large scale integrated circuit.
    d. Computer graphics.
26. Word processing refers to the use of computers to:
    a. Alphabetize the words going into a new dictionary.
    b. Help automate a typewriter.
    c. Solve word puzzles.
    d. Try out various letter combinations in order to create new words.
27. Most things computers do:
    a. Can be done in other ways.
    b. Can only be done by computers.
    c. Can be done more cheaply if larger computers are used.
    d. Can be done more reliably by hand.
28. At the current time computers are:
    a. Able to take over most functions of a first grade teacher.
    b. Handling much of the administrative work in secondary schools.
    c. Becoming commonplace in medical education.
    d. Too expensive to use in schools.
29. With respect to computers and automation, it is correct to say:
    a. Computers are primarily responsible for our current levels of unemployment.
    b. Computers have helped wipe out many jobs but have helped create other jobs.
    c. That each computer displaces 15-20 workers.
    d. Computers are creating about two million jobs a year.
30. Large scale or national data banks are not a threat to privacy because:
    a. Truth cannot hurt people.
    b. They are prohibited by law.
    c. They are used only for our benefit.
    d. None of the above is correct.
31. The first step in using a computer library program to solve a problem is to:
    a. Gather all data and facts relevant to the problem.
    b. Find a computer library program designed to solve the problem.
    c. Understand the problem.
    d. Write the necessary program and place it in a computer library.

32. Computers can play checkers and chess fairly well, but currently they are not very good at:
    a. Language translation.
    b. Medical diagnostic work.
    c. Teaching students simple arithmetic.
    d. Storing and retrieving large amounts of information.
33. In solving a problem, a computer:
    a. Thinks much like a person.
    b. First has to understand the problem.
    c. Follows a program, written by people.
    d. Usually recalls the answer from memory.
34. Which of the following abbreviations is not commonly used in computer science?
    a. CRT
    b. IBM
    c. UPC
    d. ECT
35. A computer program:
    a. Lists instructions to the computer operator.
    b. Is about the same thing as a flowchart.
    c. Is a television program about computers.
    d. Contains exact instructions for each step needed to solve a certain type of problem.

Billings, K., and Moursund, D., 1979. *Are you computer literate?* Beaverton, OR: Dilithium Press. Used by permission.

11

Planning and Evaluation: A School Perspective

John F. McManus
Terence R. Cannings

This chapter describes how a high school in the Los Angeles area planned, implemented, and evaluated a microcomputer-based educational program and demonstrates in a practical manner how this school confronted the major issues surrounding such a significant undertaking. Because other schools certainly can benefit from this experience, both the successes achieved and problems encountered in carrying out the program are analyzed in this chapter.

The school, West High (not its real name), is a comprehensive public high school, located in a middle- to upper-middle-class neighborhood. A part of the Los Angeles Unified School District, West has nearly 2,800 students and a faculty of 125. Approximately 75 percent of the students pursue some form of higher education.

Computers have been a part of the school facility since 1978, when a TRS–80 laboratory was installed to support programming classes. West is extremely proud of its Advanced Placement program in computer science, since 83 percent of the students taking that class received college credit in 1984. The local community is noted for its strong support of educational programs at the school.

In 1983, West, along with 88 other secondary schools, was selected to participate in an $8 million program funded by IBM and administered by Educational Testing Service (Cline, Bennett, Kershaw, Schneiderman, Stecher, & Wilson, 1986). The IBM program offered four main components —hardware, software, teacher training, and support—and these components were integrated into a comprehensive program aimed at encouraging teachers to use computers as tools to achieve goals across the entire secondary curriculum.

Pepperdine University acted as one of twelve project Teacher Training Institutes (TTIs) located in California, New York, and Florida. Approximately 300 teachers from the 89 participating high schools were trained by staff from these TTIs during the summer of 1983. The staff of Pepperdine University trained 26 teachers from seven high schools, including those from West High.

During their training at Pepperdine, all teachers were encouraged to explore ways in which generic software, such as word processing, database, and spreadsheet programs, could be used to achieve traditional curricular goals. It was felt that this use of the computer would have the widest impact across subject and grade levels. Although teachers were not discouraged from other uses (e.g., teaching BASIC programming, using computer-assisted instruction packages), they were encouraged to explore the possibilities engendered through a broad-based focus on generic applications packages.

Information for this chapter was gathered from an intensive case study conducted from July 1983 through January 1985 by researchers at Pepperdine University. As part of the study, the researchers visited the school to observe classroom teaching, to interview participants and to meet with site administrators; they also examined school reports and project proposals and evaluated survey data gathered by ETS from the school site. They also made use of teachers' monthly reports for the first twelve months of the project, and conducted periodic interviews through the end of summer 1985, following the conclusion of the project.

The results of this research are described in terms of program organization and structure, the planning process, implementation, and evaluation. A final section identifies the critical success factors of this project.

PROGRAM ORGANIZATION AND STRUCTURE

As in most schools, West's principal assumed the major leadership role within the institution. This individual was instrumental in obtaining the support of district administrative staff as well as maintaining strong community support. A major indicator of this community support was an elaborate security system donated by two parents. Another indicator was the attendance of many parents at formal ribbon-cutting ceremonies recognizing the opening of the laboratory.

The vice principal was responsible for the overall operational administration of the program. It was her task to manage monies from a state grant designed to improve the quality of instruction through the support of teacher training. The grant provided approximately $12,000 per year for the three years, 1982–1985. In the 1983–84 school year, this money was used to support the IBM program: approximately 75 percent was targeted for release time to allow teachers to participate in training, and 25 percent was allocated to the purchase of hardware and software. The availability of this money and its allocation by the principal and vice principal to the IBM program contributed much to the project's success.

While the principal provided leadership and the vice principal overall direction, specific responsibility for program planning and operation was delegated to a committee. This committee was composed of four teachers trained at Pepperdine, each of whom was a department chair. As department chairs, each had administrative responsibility for an organizational unit of four to eleven teachers, and each reported directly to the principal. The committee structure exemplifes collaborative management: those responsible for carrying out decisions are involved actively in the decision-making process. Vesting a faculty committee with such authority and responsibility would pose a threat to many administrators but, to the credit of West's administrators, a committee of teachers was given these powers.

The committee was responsible for directing the planning, implementation, and evaluation of the IBM program. These tasks included setting up the laboratory, establishing security arrangements, developing policies and procedures for lab use, carrying out staff development, integrating the computer into the existing curriculum, scheduling the use of the lab, and recommending additional hardware and software purchases. Issues that could not be settled by the committee were referred to the vice principal for resolution.

In addition to these group tasks, each member of the committee had specific responsibilities. These included training his or her department faculty, as well as a portion of those teachers not in one of the four departments represented by the committee members. One teacher also oversaw operation of the IBM laboratory since her classes met in the TRS–80 lab next door.

THE PLANNING PROCESS

The initial planning of West's computer program took place at Pepperdine University during the 1983 summer training institute. During scheduled planning sessions, teachers developed three informal and tentative planning documents: a laboratory plan, a staff development plan, and a plan for developing and implementing instructional applications. To create the laboratory and staff development plans, West's teachers worked as a group. To complete the instructional applications plan, the teachers split up to work in subject-matter committees with colleagues from other schools.

At the end of the Pepperdine summer training session, a half-day was set aside for individual meetings between teachers and their administrators to allow the teachers to present their three plans for approval. To prepare for these meetings, teachers and their Pepperdine instructors talked about the nature of introducing change into an organization and developed an overall strategy for convincing administrators of the value of their plans. As a result of the meeting between West's teachers and administrators, all three plans were adopted.

IMPLEMENTATION

Project implementation tasks fell into six major categories: laboratory setup, software acquisition, hardware maintenance, staff development, instructional applications, and integration with school culture.

Laboratory Set-Up

The process of setting up the IBM computer laboratory involved site preparation, security, room and furniture design, and hardware and software installation. The lab equipment donated by IBM to each participating school consisted of 15 IBM PCs, each with 128K of main memory and a color monitor, and three IBM graphics printers. In addition, each school received several thousand dollars in software including Easywriter, pfs:FILE and pfs:REPORT, Multiplan, Delta Drawing, and selected computer-assisted instruction (CAI) programs. In return for this grant, each school had to commit funds to provide for the security and care of the equipment. Thus, the first step in implementing the program was site preparation.

Site preparation.   A classroom located on the second floor next to the TRS–80 lab was selected for the new IBM facility, because its location provided security, convenience, and easy manageability. The room was well ventilated and lighted; it offered ample space for the PCs and their peripherals, for a teacher's desk and for student work tables. Approximately 30 by 25 feet, the room had a large closet for storing software securely.

Security.   Since the room was on the second floor, the school district installed bars on the lab windows for added protection from outside penetration. Inside the building, the district made sure that all interior lab walls were made of concrete. Plates were placed around all door locks to prevent them from being picked, and the existing glass partition between the IBM and TRS–80 laboratories was replaced with unbreakable glass. In 1985, the standard hinges on all doors were replaced with special ones designed to prevent the doors from being removed.

Two parents donated additional protective devices, one a thin cable that connected each computer and its peripheral components to a metal plate in the floor, the other a motion-detection system that activated a loud siren. These two systems, combined with the window bars, the reinforced room construction, and the lab's second-floor location, made for a high level of security. To date, no hardware or software has been stolen.

Room and furniture design.   Four islands, each consisting of two rows of tables, were set up in the lab. The PCs were placed back to back on the tables so that students faced each other when seated. This arrangement, planners felt, would lead to more interaction and thus faster learning. The configuration was similar to that used during the Pepperdine summer training session.

The tables were approximately 26½ inches high, rather than the standard 29 inches characteristic of most secondary-school furniture. The school was able to acquire tables with adjustable legs that could be fixed to the most desirable height for computing, but returned to normal height if desired. Chairs also were adjustable and straight to provide maximum comfort and support. Finally, blackout curtains were hung in the windows to eliminate glare.

Though ordered early, a phone line was not installed in the lab until later in the school year. Several levels of district bureaucratic review delayed its installation.

Hardware and software installation.   Plans called for the hardware to be installed during the latter part of August, 1983, but because of a complex set of circumstances, the equipment did not arrive until mid-September. This delay required a significant adjustment in plans, especially for staff development. The original plan called for staff development to take place during the first week of September, when teachers were at school but did not have classes. These in-service sessions had to be cancelled and substituted with other activities. At several schools, this delay greatly damaged program credibility and diminished teacher interest.

Rather than offer staff development on alternative topics, West's committee demonstrated the new hardware and software using the three computers and the software distributed at summer training. This strategy paid off: the demonstrations piqued the interest of many teachers and heightened anticipation of the equipment's arrival. After these staff development sessions ended, the committee continued to create training materials and applications to prepare for the machines' arrival.

When the computers finally arrived, the committee was released from teaching for two days to set them up. Since the hardware had been tested by IBM before delivery, they encountered few problems in carrying out this task. More time-consuming was the organization of software. This job took two weeks: approximately 100 diskettes had to be inventoried, copied, and set up so that they could be loaded automatically when the machine was turned on. Once copied, all original diskettes were secured in a locked closet, to be used only if a back-up copy was destroyed.

Software Acquisition

West received approximately $12,000 in software through the IBM program. The initial packages distributed included DOS (disk operating system), BASIC, Easywriter, pfs:FILE; pfs:REPORT, Multiplan, Typing Tutor, The Instructor, Question, Computer Discovery, Free Enterprise, and Arithmetic Games. As part of two subsequent software deliveries, the school obtained Visicalc, Snooper Troops, UCSD Pascal, Logo, and other such titles. Given this substantial base, little interest in selecting new software appeared during the first 18 months of the project. The single major exception to this generalization concerned Easywriter; business and social-science department staff members wanted to purchase pfs:WRITE, a word processing program that teachers felt was easier to use. Funds for the purchase of pfs:WRITE came from a state grant.

Hardware Maintenance

All the equipment donated by IBM was delivered with a full 90-day warranty. As a part of the agreement to participate in the program, West had to provide maintenance for the remainder of the project year. The school decided to set aside money to support a drop-off program, whereby staff would bring any non-functioning components to the local IBM Product Center. The three malfunctions in the first year were a broken disk-drive door, CPU, and color monitor, and members of the committee delivered the damaged equipment to the Product Center.

Providing maintenance on an "as-needed" basis can be cost-effective if few problems occur. The committee explored two alternatives: a maintenance contract for parts and labor, and training staff to maintain equipment in-house. West chose to repair equipment as needed, an approach that seemed reasonable given their new and reliable machines. As they acquire more computers and peripherals, they will probably consider an in-house maintenance capability.

Staff Development

After the lab had been set up, security established, computers installed, and the software backed up, the focus of activity shifted to training the faculty in using the computers for instruction. During the first semester, every faculty member was enrolled in three two-hour training sessions. Easywriter and Visicalc were taught, along with the disk operating system (DOS) and IBM hardware components. Since committee members chaired the English, science, business, and mathematics departments, faculty from these units received additional training, three full-day sessions on software use. Other faculty desiring additional training scheduled individual sessions with committee members. All teachers were released from their regular duties during training sessions, with class supervision provided by substitute staff. Funds for this activity came from West's state grant.

The first software application introduced to teachers during training was word processing. This application was chosen for two reasons. First, the committee believed that the value of word processing for classroom administration and lesson planning would be immediately apparent. Second, the school's instructional computing plan called for using word processing in several subject areas; hence many teachers would need to master the application. Instruction in Visicalc, the other major application package taught, centered on developing personal budgets. This emphasis permitted teachers to learn software through an example familiar and relevant to them. Finally, DOS was taught because the committee felt that teachers should be able to carry out such important housekeeping functions as formatting and backing up diskettes.

Instructional Applications

During the first semester, student instruction focused on learning the hardware and becoming familiar with the word processing software. pfs:WRITE and the IBM PC replaced the typewriter in the business education classes. In the Advanced Placement computer science class, students compared pfs:WRITE and Easywriter and determined that, though easy to use, pfs:WRITE was not as powerful as Easywriter or sophisticated programs like WordStar. They, therefore, elected to use Easywriter until WordStar could be obtained. As of this writing, the school had not purchased WordStar due to budget constraints.

pfs:FILE became a popular piece of software in several classes. Students in the Advanced Placement computer science class used pfs:FILE to develop bibliographies for term papers they eventually wrote with Easywriter. Students developed 10 to 20 different file organizations and searching strategies to determine the fastest way to retrieve data from pfs:FILE; these included various orderings of elements in the database, as well as different combinations of retrieval tags. Students examined the impact of various retrieval protocols, such as value ranges and the *wildcard* and *not* commands.

In an English class, students used pfs:FILE to create a series of eight book reviews which they submitted to the teacher on diskette; no paper copy was used. In a science class, research information was stored in pfs:FILE. These files were subsequently printed, and served as input to the report writing process. Students wrote their reports with pfs:WRITE.

Teachers, too, took advantage of word processing and database management programs. They used Easywriter to create order forms for materials, letters to parents, and ditto masters; they used pfs:FILE to develop lesson plans and to implement the provisions of the Stull Bill, a state law requiring that instructional objectives be documented and that progress toward objectives be reported.

Integration with School Culture

Most of the first year was spent installing and checking the hardware and software, and conducting staff development. Much to the credit of the committee, members were able to develop several instructional applications for classroom use; however, few applications were developed by others. At the end of the first year, IBM support for the project was terminated, as planned. Program support, the development of instructional applications, and the purchase of additional hardware, software and supplies became the sole responsibility of the school.

There is no doubt that the infusion of hardware and software into West had a major positive impact. However, the program might have become integrated more quickly in the culture of the school given a longer period—say, three to five years—of external support. Such support is necessary to make the computer part of the instructional routine of the school: to develop applications, to become familiar with PC operations, and just to become comfortable with the idea of using computers in education.

Despite the termination of IBM support, the computer is being incorporated in the school's culture, as the pursuit and award of state, school district, and community funds attest.

State funds.   West applied for a second round of training funds from the state through Assembly Bill 551. The grant was awarded and, as of this writing, the school was in the first year of a new three-year funding cycle. Money will be used mainly to provide ongoing staff development for the school's educational computing program. Twenty-five percent of this money may be used for hardware and software.

In fall 1985 a series of training programs was initiated with this support. Groups of 16 teachers meet for two hours, one day a week for eight weeks, to receive training on the IBM PC on several topics: hardware, diskette care, DOS, and word processing, database management, and spreadsheet programs. The teachers who design and carry out the instruction receive compensation from the state funds.

A second state funding program permits teachers to apply for grants of up to $2000 for purchasing computer hardware and software. Groups of teachers from the same school are encouraged to create a mini-consortium designed to have a major impact on instruction. Seven teachers at West applied for and received the grant, and they requested Apple IIe computers and various types of instructional software for placement in individual classrooms. These machines are currently being used for a variety of instructional purposes, including CAI and generic applications.

A third program allows schools to apply for a grant of $12,000 for the purchase of computers to improve instruction. To apply for a grant, the district must have a strategic plan for the use of computers. As is true for the hardware grants program mentioned above, recommendations for funding are made by review boards of teachers and computer experts. The school received this grant and purchased an additional six Apple IIe microcomputers and software. These computers were placed in a laboratory to be used mainly by the math and science departments.

District funds.   West was selected to receive 30 Apple IIc microcomputers, with such software as Logo and AppleWorks (a word processor) for instructional use. This award was part of the $10,000,000 contract between the Los Angeles Unified School District and the Apple Computer Corporation. The 30 IIc's were set up in a room on the other side of the TRS–80 laboratory from the IBM lab, making for a comprehensive computing facility within the school. The award brings West's total number of microcomputers to more than 75 and increases the holdings of the already-extensive software library. The committee expects that their experience with the IBM project will assure that the planning and operation of the IIc program progresses smoothly.

Community funds.   In the evenings, the Regional Occupational Program (ROP) offers classes at West on a variety of topics. Through arrangement with the principal, a night class in computer applications was added to the ROP schedule. Members of the committee were offered first option to teach the class for additional compensation. In addition, the principal agreed that 25% of the gross revenues from the class could be used to purchase hardware and software for the school. This entrepreneurial approach has a motivating effect on teachers and provides for needed additions to the software library. The classes have been oversubscribed every semester.

The commitment of faculty and staff, and the enthusiasm of students, parents, and community members were major forces in obtaining West's broad-based—state, district, community—funding support. Along with increased expenditures on computer education, such commitment and enthusiasm are strong indicators that computers are beginning to permeate the culture of West High School.

EVALUATION

Evaluation was especially productive at West High; the committee used evaluation data as input to the needs analysis and background sections of proposals for the state grants they obtained. Their effective use of evaluation information supported bids for funding and resulted in the award of a total of $30,000 in hardware and software monies.

The evaluation information they collected included the following types of input and process data:

- [ ] a history of the use of computers for instruction at the school;
- [ ] the number of computers owned and their usage rates;
- [ ] the number of teachers involved in the program;
- [ ] examples of new instructional applications;
- [ ] the type of hardware and software required to implement new applications;
- [ ] how new hardware would be dispersed (i.e., laboratory, resource center or classroom), with a rationale for the distribution;
- [ ] the space available to house new hardware and software acquisitions; and
- [ ] the maintenance and expendable supplies support that would be provided by the school and the district.

Some specific data on these items underline the value of West's computer education efforts. Approximately 15 percent of the faculty became active users (i.e., used the computer as a part of their regular classroom instruction) in the first year of program operation. By the end of the second year, that number had increased to 50 percent. This latter figure is more than four times as high as the national average for high schools (Becker, 1985). By the end of school year 1985, a total of 76 microcomputers—Apples, IBMs, and TRS–80s—were owned by West. The computers were configured in three laboratories and four resource centers located in the science, English, business, math, and college advising departments. Funding requests emphasized the need for more resource centers to be used by subject-matter teachers. About half of the software budget requests were for CAI, with the rest for new and updated versions of generic software, such as word processing, database and spreadsheet programs. The school is considering acquiring its own in-house capability for repairing and maintaining the machines.

CRITICAL SUCCESS FACTORS

Seven critical success factors appear to have enabled West to reach its goals. If any one of these factors had been missing, the project's success likely would have been hampered.

1   *There was a critical mass of trained, dedicated teachers who planned and implemented the program.* A group of four teachers, all department chairs, were trained in an intensive four-week session to install

and operate a computer-education program. They designed their own plans and established their own policies and procedures for program operation. Without this group of hard-working teachers, there would have been no program. To a great extent, the four teachers added management of the program to their existing responsibilities. Thus, the choice of teachers willing to accept these added responsibilities was significant.

2 *There was a critical mass of hardware and software.* The amount of hardware and software donated was enough to encourage the rapid growth of computer education. The hardware and software was able to support a variety of instructional uses and to serve a significant number of students and teachers. Too, the size of the gift commanded the attention of the entire school community, lending an importance to the program that facilitated its operation.

3 *The administration gave support to the teachers and the program.* Several examples illustrate this support. Funds from a discretionary state grant were directed to the project to provide released time for staff development and to purchase hardware and software. The administration gave responsibility for planning and operating the program to the teachers. Because of the administration's attitude, the entire school understood that the program was a high-priority activity; consequently, teachers were encouraged to become involved in it. Finally, staff members were offered the opportunity to teach evening computer classes for extra compensation, and a certain proportion of revenue from these classes was set aside for the purchase of new software for the school.

4 *Staff development was provided for the entire faculty.* The involvement of the entire faculty is critical to any effort to use the computer meaningfully as a tool across curricular areas. More than 90 percent of the faculty were trained in the first year. Training sessions ranged from three hours to two days, and individual help was always available. In addition, the committee conducted fairs that permitted teachers to learn about the newest software in their fields.

5 *A majority of the computer applications were developed to support the existing curriculum.* Teachers generally have a substantial amount of work to complete: they must plan lessons, review and order materials, grade papers, construct tests, and perform supervisory duties, among other things. Adding to this load would be unacceptable. Therefore, the committee worked with teachers to design applications of generic software that would fit closely with the existing curriculum and ease—or at least not increase—job responsibilities.

6 *Sufficient time was allowed to develop the program and make it a part of the school culture.* The committee knew that establishing a computer-education program requires a multi-year effort, and the school administration supported their perspective. Now in its third year, the computer-

education program has become a part of the everyday lives of many students. New applications continue to be developed as teachers become more skilled in the preparation of computer-based lessons.

7   *The community provided substantial support to the activity.* This support came through the donations of parents and through community participation in school-sponsored computer-education activities. Parents' donation of security devices is one indication of parental and community interest, and oversubscribed enrollment in the evening school program is another. Community interest and support helped to create a positive attitude among students, teachers, and administrators that facilitated the success of the program.

SUMMARY

This chapter has provided a school-level perspective on planning, implementing, and evaluating a computer-education program. With respect to planning, teachers' creation of lab, staff development, and instructional applications plans were delineated. Program implementation activities discussed included lab set-up, software acquisition, hardware maintenance, staff development, instructional applications, and integration with school culture. Evaluation activities focused on the collection of input and process information which was used to support the bid for additional program funds. Finally, seven factors critical to the program's success were identified: a critical mass of trained, dedicated teachers; a critical mass of hardware and software; administrative support; staff development for the entire faculty; the creation of computer applications to support existing curricula; sufficient time to develop the program and integrate it with school culture; and community support.

REFERENCES

Becker, H. (1985, May). *Instructional uses of school computers: 1983 and 1985 national surveys.* Paper presented at Educational Testing Service, Princeton, NJ.

Cline, H. F., Bennett, R. E., Kershaw, R. C., Schneiderman, M. B., Stecher, B., & Wilson, S. (1986). *The electronic schoolhouse.* Hillsdale, NJ: Lawrence Erlbaum Associates.

12

Planning and Evaluation: A Districtwide Perspective

Robert J. Illback
John M. Hanna

In this chapter, a local district computer-education program, based on the extensive experience of the Fort Knox (KY) Community Schools, will be described. The Fort Knox Community Schools is a K–12 local education agency serving a population of approximately 3800 pupils in ten school buildings. Seven elementary schools, two middle schools, and a high school provide a full range of services to the district's students; the district enjoys a reputation within the state as progressive and well-staffed.

Particularly notable is the fact that the school system resides on the Fort Knox military installation (an Army post), and is funded by the Department of Defense. Only children whose families reside on the installation (by virtue of one parent being a military service member) are entitled to be served by the system. A large number of military families live off-post, and those children attend schools within the adjoining counties.

Though the district operates as any other school district in most respects, the system's association with the military has important implications. First, the student population is quite transient, with about one-third of the students turning over each year; this fact has been used to justify the need for a microcomputer project, as will be described. Too, funding sources and procurement procedures within the Department of Defense differ greatly from other schools, and this situation has both caused some interesting problems (e.g., waiving the need for a security clearance for computers) and created some unique possibilities for the microcomputer program.

Initially, to place the present program in focus, this chapter will review the history and organization of the Fort Knox program. Then, the district's response to a range of planning issues and problems within specific topical areas of microcomputer education will be described, including the overall philosophy of the program, operational goals, software selection guidelines and procedures, hardware selection guidelines and procedures, site preparation, and staff development. In the concluding section, a formative evaluation of the district's present status with respect to microcomputer education and a five-year plan for further development will be presented.

HISTORY AND ORGANIZATION OF THE MICROCOMPUTER PROGRAM

The earliest use of computers in the Fort Knox School System was at Fort Knox High School, where in 1976 the district acquired a DEC PDP 8e minicomputer for the mathematics department. Initially two, and eventually four, teletype terminals provided access to the minicomputer. Semester classes of beginning programming were offered at the outset (beginning programming has now been expanded to a two-semester sequence). The physics class also used the minicomputer, and in-service computer activities were offered to a small number of interested staff members.

In 1979, each of the two middle schools acquired a TRS–80 Model I microcomputer for their mathematics departments. The use of these machines was limited to enrichment activities for those students especially attracted to computers. In 1980, the high school installed a 16-unit TRS–80 Model I networked computer lab. The availability of this lab greatly increased computer use by instructional departments other than mathematics. At first, users primarily came from remedial mathematics, chemistry, physics, and English classes. Gradually, other applications were attempted, including word processing in the business department, publication of the school newspaper and literary magazine, and remedial activities in the special education department.

Seeking to provide direction for the growing computer project, the superintendent of schools reassigned the high school math/physics teacher to the position of microcomputer project coordinator beginning in the 1981–82 school year. The coordinator's initial task was to delineate a five-year plan for microcomputing. During 1981–82, the coordinator conducted various activities and fact-finding tasks, gave demonstration sessions in each of the district's ten school buildings to acquaint the school staff better with the computer's capabilities, and offered optional in-service activities, with many teachers and administrators participating in the "get-acquainted" and introductory programming activities.

The new computer coordinator also conducted demonstrations at parent-teacher meetings in order to kindle community interest in microcomputer education. These sessions were well attended and parents became enthusiastic about the need for their children to learn about and use computers in the classroom. In many of the schools, the coordinator worked closely with the program for gifted and talented students, giving advice about computers and beginning programming, demonstrating computer techniques in many classrooms.

During this year, the district planners identified and discussed many issues, often without consultation with experienced professionals since no schools in the region had significant microcomputer projects. Therefore, early in 1982, the assistant superintendent for instruction and the computer coordinator visited several school districts in Minnesota. Minnesota has a national reputation as a leader in microcomputer education, and the state's transition from time-sharing to microcomputers was at that time in its final stages. The districts visited were also in the early stages of deciding how they would configure their microcomputers. The fundamental issue was whether the Fort Knox district should utilize stand-alone units or network the microcomputers in laboratory settings.

After much discussion, and with the information gleaned from the trip to Minnesota, the district planners delineated five categories of planning decision:

☐ Hardware—microcomputers, support equipment, and supplies
☐ Software—instructional and application programs
☐ In-service—teacher preparation and program development
☐ Site preparation—building modifications and furnishings
☐ Service—maintenance and repair

With an eye toward maintaining the greatest programmatic flexibility, the planners decided to organize the microcomputer program using a dual configuration of hardware. They developed a five-year plan which called for installing microcomputer labs in each school building. Each lab could accommodate a class of thirty students with each student being able to operate a computer independently. In addition, at least one microcomputer would be acquired for each classroom or special area (e.g., the library, special education) where there was interest in its use. The two larger schools would contain two labs in order to accommodate all students.

Placing computers in a lab setting was an attractive idea because it provided the opportunity for all students to have meaningful access on a regular basis. The lab setting also allowed teachers to load software before students arrived, thereby maximizing computer access time. Also, the lab required fewer storage devices (disk drives) and printers since all the stations in a lab could access the centrally located disk drives and printer. Finally, the lab configuration allowed for increased individualization with respect to level and pace of the lesson, because a group of students could work on a range of different instructional activities. The teacher therefore had the option of either planning an integrated lesson in a particular instructional area for all students, or allowing students to work independently in various unrelated areas.

In addition to the lab-based machines, the planners recommended individual, movable units to accommodate the specific needs of classrooms and special areas, needs which might involve after-class activities, drill and practice, remediation, teachers' record keeping, or other specialized functions.

The initial proposal for the acquisitions related to this five-year plan was presented to the Board of Education in March 1982. The presentation emphasized the concept of computer-assisted instruction; part of the presentation involved showing a film on school computing, "Don't Bother Me, I'm Learning" (McGraw-Hill Publishing Company). The Board unanimously approved the plan.

Implementation of the plan proceeded rapidly, if not always smoothly. Due to unexpectedly increased budget allocations for 1982, one-half of the lab equipment, and about one-fourth of the individual classroom units, were acquired in the first year of the plan. Procurement problems, however, delayed delivery until November 1982, causing the start-up and initiation activities, including staff training, to be postponed until mid-year. The fact that each lab was now equipped with 16 computers caused a special problem in that two students were assigned to use each computer. Although this situation sometimes worked well in facilitating peer-mediated instruction, it also caused problems in sharing, with some students dominating access to the machines.

Thus, in spring 1983 the Board received and approved a proposal to purchase sufficient computers to allow for a configuration of 32 computers in each of the 12 labs and for an additional 80 stand-alone units. Twelve computer aides, one for each lab, were hired and trained during the 1982–83 school year. Finally, a comprehensive staff development program was implemented. During this start-up year the entire staff development program for the district centered on microcomputers: each staff member was required to complete three full days of in-service training, ranging from introductory workshops to sophisticated applications.

In fall 1983, the Board received a further proposal to complete the acquisitions as outlined in the original five-year plan. This proposal called for purchasing 100 more computers so that each classroom and special area would have at least one, and recommended that twelve additional units be purchased to support the school library programs, which had recently purchased software for an automated circulation system. Furniture to accompany these machines was also requested. This proposal met with considerable controversy among the Board of Education members and was not approved. Among other concerns, the Board felt that the staffing of the program needed to be re-evaluated, and they emphasized personnel training.

The net result of these discussions was that the coordinator, now the "director of computer media," shared responsibility with a centralized support staff for the project, including a computer specialist (responsible for teacher training and assistance), a computer programmer (responsible for developing software), a keyboarding specialist (responsible for developing a K–12 keyboarding skills program), and a centralized computer aide (responsible for cataloging, filing, copying, and distributing software).

PLANNING AND IMPLEMENTING THE MICROCOMPUTER PROGRAM

The following sections will describe in detail the issues, problems, decisions, and outcomes of the Fort Knox microcomputer project, focusing on the overall philosophy of the program, program goals, hardware and software selection considerations, site preparation, and staff development.

Program Philosophy

As computer-education efforts have flourished in the United States, educators have offered a range of justifications about how computers can be used to enhance learning. These justifications are not always well-articulated and often contain elements of more than one instructional philosophy. Confusion about the specific rationale(s) for a district's microcomputer program can cause difficulties in focusing the program and result in problems in resource allocation and program implementation.

The microcomputer program in the Fort Knox Community Schools has, almost from its inception, been built around the guiding principle of using the microcomputer as a form of instructional media. Specifically, the microcomputer has been described to staff and others (e.g., the Board of Education) as an alternative means by which instruction can be delivered. This philosophy can be seen as computer-based instruction: the computer is viewed as a useful adjunct to other means of instructional service delivery available to the teacher. Such an approach stands in sharp contrast to the "computer-literacy" philosophy, in which students focus on the computer itself through such activities as programming. At Fort Knox, the expectation is that a by-product of computer-based instruction will be greater student familiarity and facility with microcomputers. However, the focus is clearly upon using the technology for specific instructional purposes, rather than building a separate component of the curriculum around computer programming or some other salient feature of the technology.

Flowing from this philosophy of computer-based instruction has been Fort Knox's strong emphasis on using microcomputers in all instructional and related areas. A specific attempt has been made to purchase hardware and software useful in traditional academic areas such as reading, mathematics, and language, as well as in less central areas such as home economics, special education, gifted education, physical education, and extra curricular activities. No discipline or program was excluded from consideration so long as quality material was available to meet specific program needs. In this way, the microcomputer-education program at Fort Knox is meant to be broad based, versatile, and integrated.

This philosophy of computer-based instruction needs some clarification. In a strict sense, computer-based instruction implies the use of computer technology specifically to deliver instructional content. At Fort Knox, a range of special applications are seen as instructionally related and therefore as valid for inclusion within the project. Among these activities are using the computer to manage instruction, to construct and score tests, to keep class records, and to serve as prostheses for the physically handicapped. Essentially any classroom or special program application which supports the instructional process is viewed as appropriate for computer-based instruction.

Additionally, there is at least one important exception to the emphasis on computer-based instruction. Within the district's recently revised mathematics curriculum, a new strand focusing on computer literacy has been developed. As the idea for such a strand was being contemplated, a debate arose about the district's philosophy of microcomputer utilization, reflecting the national dilemma which has arisen around this issue. The group of teachers involved with the curriculum development project ultimately decided that features of the technology itself needed to receive some coverage within the curriculum, since mathematics and programming are so closely related. At the same time, the possible conceptual fallacy in tying computers so closely to mathematics was recognized, since in many ways they are more akin to language arts, relying as heavily as they do on language and logic. It is therefore important to note that this strand does not dominate the mathematics curriculum K–12, but rather is seen as one part of a multifaceted mathematics program. Accompanying this strand is an increased emphasis on programming at the middle- and high-school levels through specific course offerings.

Articulating a district philosophy about the relationship between microcomputers and the preexisting instructional program helped sort out various questions and issues as they arose. For example, a question raised in the early stages of the project was whether teachers should be trained in computer programming; many of the early college and university offerings in microcomputer education focused on computer literacy and programming. The district subsequently had to decide whether to follow this model in training staff members. Because of the district's clear emphasis on computer-based instruction, programming was deemphasized in favor of instructional software, generic applications packages (e.g., database management, word processing), authoring programs, and the like. In this context, programming was seen as a skill of limited utility, as most teachers were unlikely to obtain the sophistication required to write quality programs, and as most would not be teaching those skills to students. Training in programming has, however, been made available to interested staff members, and many have become proficient in at least the rudimentary aspects of programming for specific purposes. The vast majority have not found the development of these skills necessary and this lack of programming knowledge has not impeded any staff member's ability to contribute to the project.

The district philosophy toward computing has also resulted in a diverse and flexible in-service program. Teachers, not forced to learn about the microcomputer in a lock-step manner, can pursue professional development at their own pace. This flexibility has resulted in a continuum of users with various skills and abilities, and in an exceptionally diverse set of applications throughout the district. Generally speaking, this approach to involving staff has proven effective in that teachers have not been traumatized or overwhelmed by the introduction of new technology. However, in order to ensure full and appropriate utilization, the process has had to be managed carefully, with intervention in classrooms where the computers are not sufficiently used. Teachers in these classes are encouraged to become more involved through explicit goal-setting. Naturally, some teachers, despite these efforts, remain aloof from the project. These individuals are not forced to learn about microcomputers, but their students continue to participate in computer activities on a regular basis through the lab program.

Program Goals

Microcomputer acquisitions for schools are typically justified on the basis that the machines can revolutionize the teaching and learning process. Without disputing this claim, we can say that the specific outcomes that computers are expected to produce are rarely operationalized in the form of explicitly stated student and service delivery goals. School-district microcomputer goals are often global, and specific intentions can only be inferred from the activities which the district conducts. Although certain intentions were made clear in Fort Knox's articulation of its educational philosophy, the microcomputer program at Fort Knox has operated largely on implicit goals. As in any developing program, these implicit goals have changed and evolved over time.

First and foremost, the Fort Knox project has as its goal that student learning will be enhanced through the use of microcomputers. Five dominant themes have been emphasized: microcomputers can help to organize and deliver some forms of instruction; microcomputers can supplement the regular program of instruction through review, drill and practice, and related adjunctive activities within the regular class; microcomputers can increase individualization through better curriculum management and targeted instruction; microcomputers can improve instruction to special groups of children whose needs are not fully addressed by the regular program (e.g., gifted, handicapped); and microcomputers can be useful as a motivational device.

A second implicit goal for the microcomputer program has been improvement in instructional practice. By focusing on this new technology, staff members are forced to confront important decisions about the nature and scope of the instructional program itself, in the hope that a more coherent and integrated program will result. The task of integrating commercially available software with the district's already existing curricula has been a continuing challenge. Perhaps more than any other form of instructional media, the computer seems likely to cause educators to challenge their own practices. This re-examination may be an important by-product of microcomputer education that to date largely has been overlooked. To the extent that interest in the teaching and learning process can be rejuvenated, education seems likely to improve.

A third (and less well described) goal of the Fort Knox program has been to acquaint staff and students with the emerging technology of microcomputers, and to reduce any anxiety they may have about it. This particular goal has taken on added significance as educators have become concerned that microcomputers may further divide society along social class lines. In this context, students from homes where such technology is not likely to be found are probably at greater risk for low achievement in our "information age." Providing significant access to microcomputers in school may inoculate these "at-risk" students against such a problem. This exposure may be especially important for the transient Fort Knox student population.

As the project has evolved, new goals and activities have emerged; the most central of these has been the use of word processing for the teaching of reading and writing. An emerging goal in many classrooms is to teach reading through writing, an approach akin to the language experience approach to reading instruction, wherein the student's own vocabulary and language system serve as the foundation for daily lessons. The potential of the computer also seems likely to transform staff members' thinking about mathematics instruction. The important point is that unforeseen capabilities of the microcomputer have caused significant re-evaluation of fundamental aspects of the district's educational programs. As a result, new strategies and applications are emerging. In sum, Fort Knox has found it advantageous to be somewhat open with respect to goal-setting, clearly articulating some specific educational goals needed to drive the project, but leaving room for those goals to evolve and for new ones to emerge.

In retrospect, the project would have been enhanced by greater emphasis on communicating the underlying philosophy and goals of the program to staff members. The failure to communicate this critical information may have contributed to some of the initial implementation problems. To communicate this information to new teachers, a training package (possibly a videotaped presentation) is under consideration.

Software Selection

The philosophy and goals of a district's program should guide the selection of specific software. Because of Fort Knox's desire for a comprehensive and diverse microcomputer-education program, the district has made a concerted effort to obtain a broad base of quality software for all curricular and programmatic areas. This has been a considerable challenge, especially with respect to the more instructional specialized areas.

Another factor in Fort Knox's software selection is the district's belief that decisions about the purchase of software should precede hardware acquisition decisions. Though many hardware companies have been marketing software for education, only a few computers can support the quality and comprehensiveness dictated by the philosophy and goals of the Fort Knox project. Therefore, planners have chosen software first, then decided on the hardware to run it.

A third criterion for selection of software has been the need to support flexibly the multiple components of the project. Because the bulk of the computers were to be configured in building-based computer labs, specific "networkable" software (i.e., accessible to each of 32 microcomputer work stations through network controller equipment) had to be found. In both the building labs and the special applications areas, concern for ease of operation, relationship to the educational program's goals, and quality (e.g., attractiveness, instructional soundness, level of complexity) was paramount.

In the early stages of the microcomputer program at Fort Knox, software purchases were focused largely on programming tools, as for the DEC PDP 8e. Educationally relevant software for the TRS–80 Model I machines actually began the process of computer-based instruction in the district. The first large software acquisition came in 1982 when the district bought a comprehensive set of materials from the major vendors of that period: much of the software was purchased from the highly regarded Minnesota Educational Computing Consortium (MECC), of which the district became an institutional member. In large measure, the availability of quality MECC software dictated the decision to purchase Apple computers. Additionally, comprehensive software packages from Random House (for TRS–80 machines), Science Research Associates (SRA), Southwestern Publishing, and Encyclopedia Britannica were purchased and made available to all the schools.

Beyond these major software packages, the program explicitly attempted to procure whatever software was available across the various curricular and specialty areas. The rationale for seeking a comprehensive base of software was that, for the program to meet its goal of widespread computer-based instruction, all staff members must be included and the software must be infused into all curricular areas. This was a considerable challenge because microcomputer applications had not been extended to all areas and because much of the available material in some areas did not meet the district's standards for quality and instructional relevance. Reviews of software from various sources such as EPIE (Education Products Information Exchange) and *Consumer Reports* were available through the state educational television network. Though these were most often of minimal utility in choosing software, they did provide background information which at times was helpful in the selection process.

Before long, it became apparent that commercially available software, because of its lack of quality and relevance, would not satisfy all program needs. Teachers reported a desire for software that, although it might not be as sophisticated, more closely supported daily instructional activities. Often, commercially available software was found to be designed for single-lesson use, and did not support continuous, integrated educational activities. Therefore, in 1983 the program launched a software development project in which teachers collaborated with a programmer over the summer to develop "skeletal" software incorporating various game (e.g., Hangman) and presentation formats (e.g., completion, multiple choice, true/false), while at the same time allowing teachers to enter the instructional content related to their needs. These software packages have remained an important cornerstone of the project. Additionally, teachers have been encouraged to use "authoring" programs, which allow the development of more varied types of lesson.

To supplement the selection process still further, a software review program was begun in 1983. This program allowed teachers to receive in-service credit for explicitly reviewing software and writing evaluations in a pre-established format. These reviews have served as a database for decisions about further software acquisitions and are available to district teachers considering use of a particular software package. The review program has greatly increased information sharing among school buildings; out of this process has grown a district-wide software reference catalog, with annotations accompanying each software description.

At this time, the district's software holdings are quite extensive. The system by which software is procured has become less centralized, as buildings identify their own needs and circumstances; there is no longer a centralized budget process for software acquisition. However, the central staff still review software requests to avoid duplication and to assure compatibility. A continuing problem has been the identification of commercial software which is instructionally sound, as the market seems glutted with material that is less than adequate. Also, requests must be reviewed to assure that the software will in fact do what it is expected to do (e.g., run in a network setting). Finally, some movement toward integrated and generic forms of software is apparent as staff members become more confident of their abilities and clearer about their objectives.

Hardware Selection

To meet its goals, the district needed hardware that could function effectively in its lab configuration and that could accommodate the chosen software. At the time of program initiation, only a handful of microcomputers could meet these specifications, and following a bidding process through Army procurement, the district made a significant commitment to two types of machine.

For the labs, the TRS–80 Model III was selected for the initial acquisition, 16 computers per lab. In subsequent purchases, the compatible Model 4 was obtained, ultimately yielding 32 computers per lab. In the labs, these machines use a disk-sharing network system and are equipped with two primary host computer units. Each lab also has two printers: one dot-matrix and one daisy-wheel. The high school also has one four-unit lab in the journalism department (for use by journalism students and by the student newspaper staff), and one four-unit lab in the business department.

At the end of the 1983–84 school year, five-megabyte hard-disk drives were purchased for each of the primary host units to reduce the growing volume of floppy disks in use. In addition, the drives would increase the speed of access to, and the distribution of, programs. The connection of these five-megabyte drives to each lab primary host unit and the conversion of files from floppy-disk to hard-disk storage was accomplished during the first half of the 1984–85 school year.

The second major component of the initial (1982) hardware acquisition involved stand-alone, multi-purpose units. For these, Apple II computers were selected, initially Model II+ and then Model IIe. At present, the Fort Knox Schools have about 50 Apple II+ and about 80 Apple IIe units, for a total of about 130 stand-alone units with either one or two disk drives. These machines are served by about 50 printers. A range of peripheral devices also is distributed throughout the system.

The district has purchased some specialized hardware, including a plotter compatible with the TRS–80, a scanner for test scoring and data aggregation, and two Apple Macintosh systems (primarily for their graphics capabilities). Additionally, eight portable TRS–80 Model 4 computers have been purchased as replacement machines.

As hardware purchases were being contemplated, the acquisition of specialized furniture to house the units was planned. Because the district could not locate any commercial vendor whose product met the specifications for a lockable, movable (on rollers) cabinet for the stand-alone units, the district designed such a cabinet and contracted for its construction. One advantage of these units is that they do not need to be moved to a central location to be secured. Presently, each of the Apple computers is housed in one of these cabinets.

Site Preparation

Several site-preparation issues became apparent as the program was being planned. Because a computer lab was needed in each building, the hardest problem was locating space in already crowded buildings. To secure space, other programs had to be carefully consolidated or reorganized with the cooperation of staff members. Building principals played a key role in accomplishing this task. Sometimes, too, the identified room needed certain modifications, such as increased storage space or the removal of dividers.

The security of the equipment was a second crucial issue in site preparation. Initially, the Military Police (MP) indicated that the rooms housing the equipment would need to be drastically altered, with bars and heavy screens placed over the windows, and emergency exits modified. Additionally, a complicated alarm system linked to the MP station would need to be installed. These measures would have been prohibitively expensive, so a compromise was worked out; movement-activated devices that sounded only a local alarm were placed in each lab. Most other schools are concerned with purchasing insurance to protect further against theft, but the federal government is not insured against property loss; however, since such theft is a federal offense, the investigative arms of the federal government (e.g., the FBI) provide added protection. To date, only one incident of theft has occurred at Fort Knox, and in this instance the computer was eventually recovered.

A third potential problem with the lab sites concerned electrical requirements. Dedicated service was needed for each lab; no other electrical device could share the line. Electrical fluctuations or interrupted service caused by other devices (e.g., coffee pots) could in turn cause the computers to shut down unexpectedly, damaging both software and hardware. Also, the amount of power to the room had to meet the equipment manufacturer's specifications. A complicating factor in some buildings was termed "thin electricity": the total amount of power available to the building was limited, thus limiting the electrical modifications that could be made and the equipment that could be used. Many of the rooms were rewired, and the number of outlets in the designated rooms was increased and multiple power strips were installed to increase electrical flexibility. To prevent power interruptions, breaker boxes and other power sources were clearly labeled so that electricity would not be shut down unintentionally by lab or maintenance staff.

A final site-preparation consideration has been the need for individual work stations in the labs, necessary for privacy, to reduce distractions, and to provide ample storage space. Carrel-like enclosures that can be arranged in various lab configurations were purchased.

Special air conditioning was not purchased for the computer rooms, in part because a long-term project to air-condition all the schools was in process. Some of the computer repair problems may be attributable to high summer temperatures, as breakdowns often occur during fall start-up.

Staff Development

The original goal of the Fort Knox project had been to acquire most of the hardware and software during the summer of 1982 and to select building team leaders for computer education and provide them with five days of training prior to the school year, followed by three days of training for all staff. The training was to consist of an orientation to hardware and commercial software, and an introduction to computer concepts and applications in education (and perhaps some beginning programming); this training for all staff was to be led by the identified building leaders and certain vendors who, by virtue of their hardware/software contract, had agreed to provide instruction. However, due to procurement delays, the first computers did not arrive until November 1982. Thus, the original plan had to be scrapped in favor of a less structured in-service program delivered during the remainder of the school year, in which all teachers received three days of training. This approach was less than optimal because once the school year starts, it is difficult to pull staff together and focus them on training concerns. Training activities during 1982–83 included sessions on computer applications, the BASIC language, Logo, PILOT, authoring programs, word processing, and software review. Some vendors conducted these activities, but when planners realized that few vendors were capable of conducting educationally relevant in-service training, in-district and selected university trainers rapidly assumed control of training.

During the summer of 1983, a group of teachers with some computer knowledge was employed to develop "skeleton" software packages that individual teachers could use to develop custom courseware for their classes. This activity was expanded and repeated in the summer of 1984, and these programs have been used to develop custom materials which parallel each new text adopted by the district.

The results of a formal survey of staff development needs conducted during 1983–84 indicated strong interest in continuing and expanding the staff development program in computer education. Thus, in-service activities on microcomputer applications and new uses of microcomputers have been offered each year. The most widely attended offerings at present are word processing, beginning and intermediate programming, database management, authoring programs, and creative story building applications.

One aspect of the staff development plan which has yet to come to fruition was offering graduate credit for activities beyond required in-service. A district-financed graduate course designed around the curricular needs of the district would have given the district some degree of control over the quality and relevance of instruction, a desirable characteristic given the proliferation of low-quality university courses in this highly marketable area. Unfortunately, the district has not been able to identify a trainer and university to implement the plan.

The program does need an ongoing orientation for new teachers. At Fort Knox, there is a fairly high turnover of staff because of the transient nature of the military families from which the district draws teaching staff. Newly arrived staff members are often well behind their peers in computer competence because of the lack of computer in-service offerings in other school systems. This gap appears to be closing as the computer-education movement expands.

FUTURE PERSPECTIVES: THE FIVE-YEAR PLAN

Recently, a new five-year plan for computer education was submitted to and approved by the Board of Education. This plan calls for action in seven major areas: computer literacy, curricular integration, hardware, software, staff development, repair and maintenance, and program evaluation.

Computer Literacy

This goal represents a slight change in philosophy for the project: a formal, self-contained course of study at the elementary- and middle-school levels will be developed in order to provide students with knowledge about how computers work, with a familiarity with computer terminology, with information about computer applications and social implications, and with a sense of what the computer's capabilities and limitations are. At the high-school level, coursework in Pascal will be offered, eventually in the form of a two-semester course. Additionally, the creation of a computer-science department at the high school will be considered. A final part of the plan calls for the extension of the present keyboarding/touch-typing instructional program to grades K–2 (it presently covers grades 3–8).

Curricular Integration

Given the program's philosophy to support and strengthen curricular offerings, the five-year plan intends to integrate more fully microcomputer activities with the scope and sequence of the basic curriculum. As the practice in the district is to review and revise each curriculum area in a six-year rotating sequence, the director of computer media will work with each year's curriculum review committee to identify available software applications relevant to that particular area.

Hardware

For the computer labs, the projected goals in the five-year plan will speed up access time between the host and student units and increase the flexibility and capability of the available hardware so that a wider range of applications can be used. Technological developments will be closely monitored to identify new equipment that supports these goals.

At the high-school level, creating another lab with the capacity for both stand-alone and networked operation will be considered. This lab would allow students to use many business, finance, and management applications that do not presently run on a network configuration (e.g., spreadsheet programs, more powerful word processors, database managers, and integrated software packages).

Finally, the present configuration of stand-alone units, with computers typically shared between rooms, will be evaluated. Teachers will be asked to justify and document their usage levels. This evaluation may result in the allocation of more than one machine to some rooms and may make apparent the need for additional acquisitions to meet instructional goals.

Software

The program will institute procedures that ask teachers to specify what instructional objectives are being supported by particular software purchase requests. These procedures should encourage greater congruence between instructional objectives and activities. Although requests for software will come primarily from the buildings and will be paid for out of building budgets, a centralized software review and evaluation procedure will be implemented. The summer curriculum committees will continue to recommend specific software.

To fill the gap between commercially available software programs and specific curricular needs, the local software development project, composed of teachers and programmers, will continue.

Staff Development

Based on the results of a comprehensive assessment of staff and organizational "readiness" for microcomputers (see Illback & Hargan, 1984, for a discussion of the approach and instrument), a plan for further staff development wil be created and implemented. Various programs to accomplish staff development objectives will continue to be offered: on-site in-service sessions, flexible in-service opportunities, and after-school and summer workshops. The program will provide funding for staff to attend state, regional, and national conventions.

Hardware Repair and Maintenance

Repair and maintenance of computer equipment has been provided through both in-house and contracted services. The district director of computer media, the computer programmer, and the audio/video technician have all been trained to perform certain repairs, and the district maintains an inventory of parts for this purpose. The five-year plan calls for the computer program to receive additional training in this area. Also, a comprehensive preventive maintenance program has been proposed; all lab units will undergo diagnostic testing twice per year and other units once per year. To keep labs operating while computers are being repaired, replacement units will be purchased. The district staff will continue to send out equipment they cannot repair. Should this become too expensive, the program staff may receive upgraded repair training.

Evaluation

The director of computer media will conduct an annual evaluation of the five-year plan in each of the foregoing areas and will thus identify modifications to the present plan.

SUMMARY

In this chapter, one district's experiences with computer education have been described. The Fort Knox microcomputer effort has evolved over time, and as it has evolved, new issues and problems necessitating creative responses have come to light. No one approach to microcomputer education can address all the inherently complex issues that may be encountered. Therefore, a management-oriented planning strategy that allows a district to change with new technologies and applications is recommended.

REFERENCES

Illback, R. J., & Hargan, L. (1984). Assessing and facilitating school readiness for microcomputers. *Special Services in the Schools, 1,* 91–106.

13

Planning and Evaluation: A National Perspective

Stephen M. Shuller

In 1983, IBM established a secondary-school computer-education program, through which it donated hardware and software to 89 schools in three states and provided technical assistance and staff development through Educational Testing Service (ETS) and a network of twelve teacher training institutions.[1]

In 1984, IBM extended its Model School Computer Literacy Program to 140 additional schools in 26 states, the District of Columbia, and Puerto Rico. In this program, Bank Street College of Education (BSC) and the University of South Florida (USF) provided technical assistance and staff development to the participating schools and school districts through a network of Professional Development Centers (PDCs). This chapter describes the planning, implementation, and evaluation of the extended Model Schools Program from my point of view as the director of Bank Street's participation in the project.

The 1984 Model Schools program was planned jointly by IBM, BSC, and USF. Guided by the design and experience of the IBM/ETS program, IBM developed the framework of the program, thus providing a starting place and, in some cases, constraints from which BSC and USF developed pro-

[1]See Cline, Bennett, Kershaw, Schneiderman, Stecher & Wilson (1986); Bennett (1984, 1985); McManus, Cannings, & McCall (1985); Schneiderman (1984); and Stecher (1984) for further information about the IBM/ETS program.

*I would like to express my appreciation to Dana Brooks, Mark Gelber, Bob Granger, Kathy Rehfield, Ed Seidman, and Karen Warner for their thoughtful comments on an earlier draft of this chapter.

223

posals during the last few months of 1983. in January 1984, the three parties met and worked out a final plan for the project.

IBM's initial "givens" for the program included a focus and duration, a procedure for determining which school districts would be invited, and guidelines concerning participation, program activities, and donated hardware and software. The program was to focus on integrating computers into the curriculum, rather than on programming or computer science. The duration was limited to one year.

The procedure for selecting participating districts (see Table 13–1) was designed to include large, urban school districts while keeping the procedure as objective as possible. In general, the largest districts in the United States were invited to participate; however, only one district per state was invited, and the three states which had participated in the IBM/ETS program (California, Florida, and New York) were excluded.

Five schools were to participate from each local geographical area. In areas with substantial parochial school populations, one school was to be a parochial school. Local school officials were to choose the participating schools, in any combination of elementary, middle or junior high, and high schools. Each participating school was required to be eligible for Chapter 1 (formerly Title 1) funds and have a non-discriminatory admissions policy.

Each participating school district was to designate from each participating school five key teachers who would attend a four-week workshop during summer 1984 and monthly "network" meetings during the 1984–85 school year. The quota of five was chosen to provide in each school a "critical mass" of teachers interested in working with computers, without over-

TABLE 13–1   School districts participating in the Model School Computer Literacy Program, 1984

Bank Street College	University of South Florida
Baltimore, MD	Anoka-Hennepin, MN
Boston, MA	Albuquerque, NM
Burlington, VT	Charlotte-Mecklenberg, NC
Cleveland, OH	Chicago, IL
Detroit, MI	Clark County, NV
District of Columbia	Dekalb County, GA
Fairfax County, VA	Hawaii
Granite, UT	Houston, TX
Jefferson County, CO	Indianapolis, IN
Newark, NJ	Jefferson County, KY
Philadelphia, PA	Memphis, TN
Puerto Rico	Milwaukee, WI
St. Louis, MO	Mobile, AL
Tucson, AZ	New Orleans, LA

taxing the available equipment. A group of 25 local teachers, five in each of five participating local schools, was considered a reasonable size for the staff development activities of the program.

Each participating district was to select a local staff development institution to work with the 25 teachers in the program. This institution was to provide the four-week summer workshop and was to send two representatives to either BSC or USF for workshops during spring 1984. To compensate these institutions for their services, IBM would donate hardware and software and $10,000 to help cover expenses.

Each school in the program was to receive about 15 microcomputers, including one XT and a mixture of PCs and PCjrs. This configuration was designed to permit the schools to equip laboratories with one machine for every two students, assuming a maximum class size of 30 students. Each school was to receive a supply of software, selected from IBM-developed and IBM-distributed products. The participating school districts were to assume the other costs of running the program including site preparation, maintenance, staffing, supplies, and security. The donated computers were to be used only for educational purposes or by teachers for record keeping or for preparing instructional materials.

PLANNING

Developing a Planning Process

Within this framework, Bank Street and USF developed proposals for implementing the Model Schools program. At Bank Street, we approached this task by bringing together a committee representing a wide range of perspectives and expertise in education, technology, staff and curriculum development, research and evaluation, planning, and management of educational innovation projects.

Our previous experience with technology and education told us that each of these areas would be important as we planned and carried out the project. Furthermore, our involving key people from the beginning gave them a degree of ownership of the project, a sense which helped ensure their cooperation and support later on.

The committee began by considering three main questions:

1   What do we think is educationally valuable about using microcomputers?
2   How can microcomputers in general, and the Model Schools Program in particular, serve the needs of large, urban school districts?
3   What does Bank Street have to offer, and how can we deliver our services most effectively?

These questions were not easy to answer, and several rambling discussions took place before we achieved enough clarity to begin writing our proposal. Even though these discussions were sometimes frustrating, they were extremely valuable in giving the committee a common base of experience and in developing a common viewpoint that helped us work together during the course of the Model Schools program.

The committee intended to define project goals and objectives that would lead to the development of orderly plans for implementing and monitoring the project in accordance with accepted management procedures. In practice, however, there were too many unknowns for such a top-down approach to be effective. Instead, we evolved a more flexible management approach in which the director coordinated many semi-autonomous efforts and helped maintain a shared vision of the project. At the time, we felt somewhat uneasy about managing the project so intuitively; later, we discovered alternative management theories (Weick, 1982; Clark & McKibbin, 1982) which helped explain why traditional goal-based management approaches are probably not appropriate for many aspects of educational innovation projects.

The Educational Value of Computers

In considering the educational value of computers, we started with a common perspective: a student-centered model of education called the developmental-interaction or Bank Street approach. This approach has its roots in the educational philosophy of John Dewey (1902, 1938) and the progressive movement in American education. In this approach, teachers act as facilitators, engaging students in developmentally appropriate activities related to their experiences, interests, and goals. Teachers seek to empower students by helping them become independent learners.

In 1979–80, Bank Street had begun to explore educational uses for computers through research at our Center for Children and Technology (CCT) and School for Children, and through projects to develop software such as the *Bank Street Writer* and curriculum materials such as the *Voyage of the Mimi* (Newman, 1984). Based on our experience, we felt that computers could be viewed best as educational tools that might help teachers better serve the needs of their students.

Our discussion of the value of computers in education centered on two topics: computer literacy and integrating computers into the curriculum. Computer literacy became a topic for discussion because the program was called the "IBM Model School Computer Literacy Program." We were concerned about participating in a "computer-literacy" program, because we were not clear what computer literacy was, and did not agree with many of the approaches using that label.

We were skeptical about approaches to computer literacy that emphasized programming or learning technical information about computers. Computers are becoming pervasive in our society, but in the same manner that electric motors became pervasive (Kay, 1984; Weizenbaum, in Ebisch, 1984). Both are hidden inside appliances and machinery in ways which require of the users little or no technical knowledge. As Weizenbaum (in Ebisch, 1984) pointed out, lack of technical knowledge about computers "stops [people] from using a word processor in the same way that not knowing about satellites stops us from making long distance telephone calls."

Since most adults who use computers work with applications programs—word processors, spreadsheets, database managers and the like—teaching students how to use these programs seemed a good way to help prepare them for the world beyond school. Applications software also seemed likely to serve current educational needs because it is generic and, therefore, maximally flexible. For example, a word processor can be used as a tool for teaching writing, but it does not actually do the teaching or prescribe any particular teaching approach. Advocating the use of generic software rather than traditional computer-assisted instruction (CAI) assumes that teachers can be thoughtful, creative people who prefer flexibility to prescription. We wanted to make this assumption and to work with teachers to empower them along with their students.

Even though applications software requires very little technical expertise, we recognized that teachers and students would need a "demystifying experience" to help them feel in control of the machine. Traditionally, programming instruction has filled this need, but we felt that work on disk-operating systems (DOS) would be a useful substitute. We also recognized that well-constructed CAI software—particularly programs such as simulations and problem solving activities which create computer-based learning environments (Schwartz, Shuller, & Chernow, 1984)—could be valuable. At the beginning of 1984, however, such programs were in relatively short supply for the IBM PC. This practical constraint also helped us decide to focus on applications software in the Model Schools Program.

In addition to computer literacy, our discussions on the value of computers in education centered on curriculum integration. Our committee fully supported the program focus on integration, but we had several concerns. First, we were concerned that not enough was known about how to integrate computers into curriculum areas to provide appropriate guidance to teachers. Sometimes, in their enthusiasm about using computers, educators see applications almost everywhere, no matter how superficial or tenuous the need for a computer might be. As Mark Twain observed, "When the only tool you have is a hammer, everything looks like a nail."

A second danger was in supposing that teachers who learned how to use computers would find it easy to integrate them into the curriculum, without the array of supporting materials and other services which help them in other areas. The old adage that "teachers teach as they were taught" is generally true unless they are offered clear models showing them how to do otherwise. Without such models, it is tempting to speak glibly about integrating computers into the curriculum and send the teachers off to integrate them without really knowing just how this can be done.

We were also concerned that the available applications programs were not necessarily appropriate learning tools for students and teachers. For example, there are many useful curricular applications of database management (electronic filing) programs for information retrieval and hypothesis testing (Ross, 1984; Hunter, 1985), but the available software is better suited to managing business records than to comparing the voting patterns of presidential elections or classifying minerals. At Bank Street, we had been studying the features needed in applications software for educational uses (Kurland, 1983a, 1983b; Char, 1983; Sheingold, Hawkins, & Kurland, 1983; Freeman, Hawkins, & Char, 1984; Pea & Kurland, 1984; Pea, 1984) and had been designing software based on what we were learning. For the Model Schools program, we needed to select the most educationally valuable software available for the IBM PC family and find ways for teachers to use it in the curriculum.

A fourth issue in integrating computers into the curriculum was where the computers should be placed. The IBM/ETS program had recommended placement of computers in laboratories (Cline et al, 1986), citing research showing positive correlations between labs and desirable characteristics such as numbers and percent of student users, numbers of teachers using computers, breadth of use across applications, and computer time per student user (Center for Social Organization of Schools, 1983). On the other hand, a Bank Street study (Sheingold, Hawkins, & Char, 1984) found that classroom computer use encouraged collaborative learning and distributed expertise among students. The authors concluded that placing computers in labs might decrease their impact on the curriculum and on forms of classroom interaction.

Since we were interested in fostering collaborative learning and in maximizing the impact of computers on the curriculum, our committee wanted to encourage the participating schools to use computers in classrooms whenever possible. We realized, however, that concerns about the security of the equipment would make most schools opt immediately for laboratories. We decided to try to encourage flexibility—for example, placing some of the laboratory computers on movable carts so they could be wheeled into classrooms when needed.

Finally, we were concerned that the concept of integrating computers into the existing curriculum might preclude thinking about ways the curriculum should change. We wanted to make sure that teachers would be exposed to computer applications in ways that would raise questions about the adequacy of the present curriculum and suggest possibilities for improvement.

In summary, we wanted to use computers as tools to serve education, subordinating the technology to the educational needs of students and teachers. We felt that computers could help schools and school districts because of their value as tools, because they generate widespread interest among educators and students, and because discussions of how to use computers in education often lead to re-examination of fundamental educational issues (Cuffaro, 1984). At the same time, we felt that significant issues were unresolved, so we wanted to be somewhat cautious in our advocacy of computers in education, and work more as facilitators than as experts.

Serving the Needs of Large School Districts

The structure of the Model Schools Program seemed likely to benefit large school districts in several ways. Creating "model" schools would allow the districts to focus resources, to experiment, and to demonstrate approaches they would like to apply on a larger scale. In addition, being part of a national program would offer opportunities for "networking," and would give the districts' computer-education efforts enhanced visibility and prestige which might lead to additional support.

Most of the participating districts had in place three-, four-, or five-year plans for purchasing computers and implementing computer-related educational programs. Because the districts typically had hundreds of schools, these plans were massive in scale, calling for purchase and installation of thousands of computers and staff development for tens of thousands of teachers and administrators.

These large-scale efforts were necessary, by and large, to take advantage of current funding opportunities and to avoid inequitable treatment for any group of students. Unfortunately, in most cases, district computer coordinators and staff developers were swamped; since they had to provide breadth of services, they could not provide depth.

The Model Schools Program mandated some depth, by focusing services and attention on five schools. These schools could then become places at which the district could experiment with promising new approaches and demonstrate what might be possible eventually for the district as a whole. We felt that creating models was an important strategy for educational improvement in large school districts, and hoped that the Model Schools Program would be a model in this sense as well.

Aside from its structure, the national scope of the program seemed likely to benefit the participating districts. At a time when the prestige and morale of large, urban school districts was at a low point, participation in an upbeat program, sponsored by a prestigious corporation, was bound to generate enthusiasm which could be channeled toward improving education. The program also could provide an opportunity for districts with similar problems to work together, to share information and ideas, and possibly to influence policy in areas of common interest.

Bank Street's Contribution

Our concerns about integrating computers into the curriculum led us to advocate an experiential approach to implementing the Model Schools program. We felt that the program could be most effective by involving local teachers in experimenting with computers in their classrooms, learning from these experiences, and then disseminating what they learned to all the local school districts in the program. In this sort of program, staff development would necessarily precede curriculum development, because the teachers would need to learn about computers and computer applications in education before they could implement the classroom experiments on which curriculum development could be based (Shuller, 1984).

Although teacher-centered curriculum development is not currently the usual practice in American school systems, it has been used widely as an approach for involving teachers in educational improvement. For example, the Denver Plan of the 1930s successfully revitalized teaching in several school districts by involving teachers in curriculum development, thereby giving them a degree of control and ownership over significant aspects of their work (Cremin, 1961). We felt that the Model Schools program might provide an opportunity to demonstrate the value of this approach for educational innovation in large, urban school districts.

Looking at each local component of the Model Schools program as an educational innovation project helped us in two ways. Conceptually, it helped keep the focus of the program on educational improvement rather than on technology per se. Practically, the wealth of information available about planning, implementing, and institutionalizing educational innovation projects (Berman & McLaughlin, 1978; Hord & Loucks, 1980; Loucks-Horsley & Cox, 1984; Lieberman & Miller, 1984; Payne, 1984; Loucks-Horsley & Hergert, 1985) helped us plan our overall framework for the program and, in addition, provided a focus for our work with those responsible for implementing each local program.

The literature about educational innovation clearly shows that outside consultants are not effective in directly managing local change projects. Effective implementation strategies include staff development extended over time, classroom assistance from project or district staff, regular project meetings focused on practical problems, and local materials development (Berman & McLaughlin, 1978), all of which require ongoing local support. Successful projects are generally based on local needs (Loucks-Horsley &

Cox, 1984) and develop out of a process of the mutual adaptation of an overall plan for the project and local conditions (Berman & McLaughlin, 1978; Huberman, 1982).

The success of a large, national project relies on a hierarchical model of support. The organizations running the national project must work with key local people who will carry out the day-to-day functions cited above. For the project to respond appropriately to local needs, the hierarchy must be facilitative rather than directive. We wanted to work as facilitators to the local program coordinators, and we wanted to encourage them to develop a similar relationship to the local participating teachers. We knew that the bureaucracies of local school systems were usually more directive than facilitative, so we wanted to find ways to establish helping relationships and to demonstrate their efficacy to the local school districts.

In addition to a facilitative support structure, broad-based administrative support is critical to successful school improvement (Loucks-Horsley & Cox, 1984). We knew that we would have to find effective ways to involve key central office staff and building principals in the program, and that this might be difficult because the program originated with outsiders. To get key local people to take responsibility for the program, they would need to establish a degree of ownership.

Based on our understanding of the educational innovation implementation process, we felt very strongly that whenever possible the local program coordinators should be employees of the school system. District employees would be likely to know how to work within the system, and they would likely have more time for the ongoing contact with the teachers necessary for successful implementation. They would also make the program easier to institutionalize since they likely would be with the local school district on a long-term basis.

Third, we felt strongly that our involvement in the program should be longer than one year. Educational innovation projects typically take three to five years for successful implementation and institutionalization (Loucks-Horsley & Cox, 1984; Miles, 1982), so we were concerned that one year would not be enough time to ensure that the participating school districts would be able to continue on their own.

To summarize, we felt that our role in the IBM Model Schools Program would be to facilitate and coordinate a somewhat diverse set of local educational innovation projects with the common theme of using applications software to integrate computers into the curriculum. We expected to work mainly through a group of local project coordinators, helping them to act as facilitators with the local participating teachers, to guide local experimentation with educational uses of computers, and to institutionalize the successful aspects of the project within the local district.

Program Goals

Our goals for the Model Schools Program were:[2]

☐ to demonstrate effective ways to integrate computers into the curriculum through the use of generic applications software;
☐ to use technology as a catalyst for renewal in education;
☐ to enhance cooperation and information sharing about technology in education among 28 of the nation's largest school districts;
☐ to demonstrate an approach to staff and curriculum development in which teachers would play a central role and in which supervising specialists would act as facilitators; and
☐ to demonstrate the value of "model" schools, in which resources could be concentrated to permit experimentation and development of model programs for the school system.

We realized that we would not have much direct impact on the local teachers; even our contact with the local project coordinators would be too limited to attempt large-scale change in the teaching-learning process. We decided that our strategy would be to model our teaching and facilitative approaches whenever possible, and to work with each site individually to develop and implement a local project appropriate to its needs and available resources.

The Bank Street Proposal

The proposal Bank Street submitted to IBM in December 1983 described staff development for the local project coordinators, follow-up support for the local programs during the 1984–85 school year, telecommunications, a follow-up conference, and procedures for documenting the activities of the program.

The spring 1984 staff development activities for local project coordinators were to consist of two workshops about a month apart. In the first workshop, the participants would learn how to use the hardware provided by IBM and become familiar with selected applications software. In addition, sessions were offered on school improvement, on leadership skills, and on how to help the local schools plan for their participation in the project. During the month between workshops, the participants would meet with the principals and teachers of the local participating schools to help them begin planning their involvement in the program and would practice using the hardware and software introduced in the first workshop. In the second workshop, the participants would develop their skills further, according to the needs they identified while practicing on their own. They would use the

---

[2]The term "goals" here reflects common usage rather than a top-down planning process. They can more accurately be described as "themes" or "symbols" (Weick, 1982).

information they had gathered during their meetings with local school staff to plan their summer training program for the local participating teachers. The second workshop would also include sessions on integrating computers into specific curriculum areas, planning and implementing school-level computer projects, and additional work on leadership and school improvement.

Support for the local programs over the summer and during the 1984–85 school year was to include provisions for regular contact between Bank Street staff and the local program coordinators, for staff and facilities for dissemination of information and materials, and for site visits as needed. We planned to assign a specific Bank Street staff member to each site (three staff members with four or five sites each) to assure continuity and an adequate level of support.

We proposed two means for facilitating ongoing communication and information-sharing among the local sites: a telecommunications network linking all the sites with Bank Street and USF, and a follow-up conference for representatives from all 28 school districts, USF, and Bank Street at the end of the 1984–85 school year.

Finally, we proposed to document the project by collecting baseline data about computer-related activities in the participating schools and school districts, by collecting similar data at the end of our involvement in the program, by maintaining an archive of written materials developed during the program, and by keeping notes on all contacts with the participating school districts.

Finalizing the Plans

On January 9, 1984, representatives from IBM, USF, and BSC met to finalize plans for the Model Schools program. At this meeting, we reviewed our separate proposals for implementing the program, combined them, and agreed on procedures for working cooperatively.

First, we divided the local districts so that 14 would work primarily with USF and the other 14 with BSC. We agreed that we would have a common framework for the program and would plan joint activities for all 28 local districts whenever possible.

Second, we agreed to encourage each district to serve as its own local staff development institution, which we called the Professional Development Center or PDC. Having school district personnel as local program coordinators would make follow-up and institutionalization easier, and locating the PDCs in the districts would ensure the continuing availability of a computer laboratory for staff development. As long as demand for computers exceeds the supply in school districts, superintendents will have a difficult time, politically, allocating machines for staff development rather than for direct use by children. In the case of the Model Schools Program, however, the superintendent could choose whether to have the machines for staff development or not have them at all, a restriction that almost every superintendent privately welcomed.

Third, we agreed that our spring workshops for the local staff developers (called the Professional Staff Development Team or PSDT) would last three weeks and would be divided into two sessions, as described in BSC's proposal to IBM. After the first session in late March 1984, IBM would send each PSDT member a microcomputer and the applications software introduced during the workshop so each could practice until the second session in May.

Finally, we agreed to start the Model Schools Program with a conference designed to involve the school district superintendents in the program and to secure their support. At this Superintendents' Conference, we planned to distribute and discuss requirements for participating schools, PDCs, and PSDT members, criteria for choosing them, and a checklist of program implementation steps that had to be monitored locally. IBM agreed to invite all the superintendents and to pay their expenses.

At our January 9 meeting, we also discussed extending the project for more than one year and bringing all the PSDT members together for a follow up conference at the end of the 1984–85 school year. USF and BSC concurred that one year of IBM support was too short to ensure successful implementation of the program, but IBM did not agree to extend its involvement. We were not able to secure IBM support for the follow-up conference at this time, but later in the program a national and four regional follow-up conferences were held with IBM support.

Table 13–2 shows the planned schedule of critical events for the Model Schools Program.

IMPLEMENTATION

Introducing the Program

Near the end of January 1984 IBM invited the superintendents of the 28 selected districts to join the Model Schools Program. In the invitation letter, IBM advised the superintendents that participating in the program would entail an obligation to carry through the focus and staff development activities of the program and to assume substantial costs for items such as site preparation, maintenance, supplies, and staffing. Despite these caveats, every district accepted.

Superintendents or assistant superintendents represented 26 of the 28 participating districts at the Superintendents' Conference, which took place on March 1–2 in Tampa. The attendees were enthusiastic about the Model Schools Program and quite willing to be supportive. Many saw the program

TABLE 13-2 Model Schools Program time line, 1984

March 1–2	Superintendents' Conference Tampa, Florida
	Selection of Professional Staff Development Teams (PSDTs) and local schools (5 per site)
March 26–30	PSDT Workshop I Bank Street College and University of South Florida
	Local planning with participating schools
	PSDT practice with IBM equipment and software
May 7–11 & May 14–18	PSDT Workshop II Bank Street College and University of South Florida
	Planning for local staff development workshops
	Preparation of local Professional Development Centers (PDCs)
	Setting up telecommunications network
July	Local staff development workshops 4 weeks, 25 participants (5 teachers from each of 5 participating schools)
August	Teachers take home computers to practice
	Planning for school year
	Completion of in-school computer facilities
December 3–7	Follow-up Conference Bank Street, USF, PSDTs from 28 sites
September 1984– June 1985	Implementation in local schools
	Follow-up workshops and monthly "network" meetings

as an opportunity to generate renewed interest in education among students and staff, and welcomed our focus on educational improvement.

At the conference, we presented our criteria for choosing schools, PDCs, and PSDT members, along with the requirements for the participating schools and a list of responsibilities for the local PDCs and PSDTs. BSC and USF had developed these documents jointly prior to the conference.

Our criteria for school selection included eligibility for Chapter I funds; a strong, stable administrative staff committed to innovation and improving education; and a teaching staff motivated to support educational innovations. We also advised the administrators to choose schools where the district could best support the physical and financial requirements of the program. We debated which schools should be chosen—schools with or without previous experience with computers—but decided that successful programs could develop in either case.

We advised the superintendents to focus on one or two school levels (elementary, middle or junior high, high school) because we felt that a wider range of teacher backgrounds would make conducting the summer staff development workshops more difficult. If they decided to include two levels, we asked them to choose contiguous levels and, whenever possible, choose lower-level schools which fed into the upper-level school(s) chosen, in order to concentrate the effect of the Model Schools Program on schools that could work together to develop a coordinated computer-education effort.

Many of the superintendents later told us that they had chosen their participating schools before attending the Superintendents' Conference. In most of the districts, internal constraints dictated which schools would participate; in some systems, the internal constraints operated to place the Model Schools Program in the weakest schools in the system. These schools would not have been chosen according to our criteria but, in retrospect, they were the schools most in need of the lift we hoped the program could provide. In at least some of these schools, the program appears to have improved dramatically both student attendance and morale among students and staff.

We presented the superintendents with two options for choosing a PDC —working with an existing local institution (such as a college or educational support center) or establishing a PDC with district facilities and personnel— and discussed the responsibilities of the PDCs and PSDT members. These responsibilities included attending the spring workshops at BSC or USF; planning and conducting summer workshops for teachers and administrators from the participating local schools; providing follow-up support during the 1984–85 school year; and facilitating communication among the program participants through "network" meetings and telecommunications. We advised the superintendents to have the districts serve as their own PDCs, and all but two districts chose this option.[3]

---

[3]The other two project sites—Burlington, Vt., and Tucson, Ariz.—were not single districts but clusters of schools from smaller districts near IBM facilities. In these cases, external PDCs were needed.

We asked the superintendents to look for PSDT members with proven ability to conduct staff development programs[4]; familiarity with microcomputers and facility in learning about them; and interest in a student-centered approach to education. In many ways, the PSDT members would be the most important factor in the success of the local program, and we emphasized to the superintendents the importance of choosing the very best people they had, feeling that technical skills were less fundamental (and easier to teach in a short time) than leadership or teaching skills. Even so, we hoped not to have technological neophytes because in such an intensive program otherwise excellent candidates might be overwhelmed by all there was to learn.

We asked the superintendents to identify their PSDT members as quickly as possible, and gave them a questionnaire for the PSDT members to fill out and return to us. This questionnaire enabled us to gather data, for planning our spring workshops, about the PSDT members' background, technical skills, and areas of educational expertise. The participating schools had to be identified by the time the PSDT members returned from the March workshop so they could begin planning activities with those schools as soon as possible.

Staff Development: The National Workshops

After the Superintendents' Conference, we began planning our spring workshops for the PSDT members. These workshops were an especially important component of the Model Schools program because they represented our main opportunity for extended interaction with those who would play the key roles in the local projects. Through the workshops, we wanted to provide the PSDT members with the information and skills they would need to implement the local projects, and with a general framework for the national program which the local projects could adapt as needed.

Our planning for the initial, one-week workshop in March first identified four strands or themes: "networking," hardware/software, planning, and leadership. Networking activities were designed to help the PSDT members get to know each other, the Bank Street project staff, and the other technology-related resources of Bank Street and to facilitate sharing of information and ideas, peer teaching, and group problem-solving. We felt that effective networking would be essential for mutual support, given an experiential approach to integrating computers into the curriculum.

---

[4]We further specified this characteristic to include ability to work well with staff members of the five participating schools, experience with students and teachers of the grade levels in question, ability to convey personal warmth and enthusiasm, and ability to present information clearly and facilitate learning.

The hardware/software strand included sessions for the PSDT members to learn how to use the computers, peripherals, disk-operating system (DOS), and some basic applications programs. The PSDT members came with a wide range of technical expertise, so we individualized our instruction as much as possible, and encouraged peer tutoring. Even though the focus of the program was on tool software, languages such as Logo, BASIC, and Pascal were available. We offered support to anyone who wanted to work on programming skills, but we did not emphasize development in this area because of time constraints and program priorities.

The planning strand included presentations on procedures for implementing school computer projects, and sessions on educational improvement. We developed and distributed a questionnaire for collecting data on technology-related activities in the schools, and asked the PSDTs to complete them by interviewing school staff members when they returned to their districts. We saw the questionnaire both as a way to collect baseline data for program documentation and as an instrument for getting the PSDT members into the schools and familiar with their facilities, programs, and staff.

We included the leadership strand and presentations on educational improvement because we felt the PSDT members would need skills and information in these areas to coordinate the local projects effectively. Presentations covered effective leadership styles, conflict resolution, and strategies for successful implementation of educational improvement projects. We asked the participants to apply what they were learning to their districts and to provide us with information about the structure of each district. In several cases this information subsequently proved valuable in identifying the right personnel to help correct problems.[5]

During the second workshop, which lasted for two weeks in May 1984, we continued the four basic strands and added sessions on integrating computers into the various subject areas. The focus of the workshop was preparing the PSDT members to run their local projects.

The planning strand centered on preparing PSDT members for the local summer workshops, preparing facilities in the schools, and planning follow-up activities during the 1984–85 school year. Since they had visited the schools and collected information about their computer-related activities and interests, they were well prepared to plan workshops tailored to local needs. We presented staff development models which had proven success-

---

[5]The positions of the PSDT members in the district hierarchies varied considerably. In general, higher positions made support services easier to maintain. The two districts which sent classroom teachers as PSDT members had the most difficulty getting district support. In one of these districts, however, we were able to help the PSDT members become part of the central district staff, with positive effects on both the Model Schools Program and the level of district support for computer-related programs.

ful in our own work with local school districts and provided time for individual team planning and consultation with Bank Street staff.

The sessions on integrating computers in the curriculum took two forms. One set of sessions dealt with particular types of applications programs—word processors, for example. In these sessions, we worked on how to teach students to use the program and on finding the kinds of educational activities for which this type of program would be suitable.

The other set of sessions dealt with specific subject areas. In these sessions, we presented a range of ways to use microcomputers in particular subject areas and developed criteria for their use. We collected and distributed resource materials about specific curricular applications. We also conducted some group brainstorming sessions and distributed notes from these sessions to all the participants.

During the workshop, participants had time for viewing software and for ordering IBM-distributed programs for the local summer workshops. There was not nearly enough time to see all that was available, so the participants pooled their efforts and shared their informal evaluations.

In all the workshop activities, we tried to model our approach as facilitator rather than expert. We provided frequent opportunities for interaction among the participants, and for feedback about the structure and content of the workshop. We tried to be responsive to suggestions for improvement, and always to treat the participants with courtesy and respect. We made sure that facilities, equipment, and materials were available when needed, and paid special attention to creature comforts; for example, by providing refreshments during breaks. Our experience in conducting staff development workshops had been that these procedures dramatically increase the effectiveness of the workshops, and we hoped to encourage the PSDT members to use a similar approach in conducting their own training sessions.

Software Selection

During March and April, Bank Street and USF received from IBM sample copies of most of their applications and educational software, which we reviewed as thoroughly as possible in the limited time available.[6] From our reviews and on recommendations from colleagues, we identified a standard initial set of software, some of which would be shipped to BSC and USF for the March workshops, and the rest sent directly to the PDCs. This initial set consisted of word processors, a filing system, spreadsheets, communications software, DOS, BASIC, Logo, an authoring system, and a few aids to learning how to use the computer.

---

[6]Because of time constraints, these reviews were very informal. At Bank Street, we divided the software among our staff members, who reviewed it and reported their opinions at a meeting. USF later set up a more formal evaluation procedure and reporting system.

During April, we drew up a list of IBM-distributed software from which the PSDT members could choose for use in their summer workshops; this list focused on applications programs, but included some educational software as well. The PDCs were to loan this software to the participating teachers for the remainder of the summer, after which it would belong to the schools. The PSDT members calculated these orders (up to $16,000 per district) as a spreadsheet activity during the May workshop.

The PSDT members were responsible for ordering additional software for the schools ($13,000 per school) during their summer workshops in July. By then, they would know the participating teachers and could decide how best to involve them in the software selection process.

The remainder of funds available for IBM-distributed software was retained until spring 1985; by this time, the participants had experienced almost a full school year of the program and knew what their software needs were. Also, they then could order software released during the 1984–85 school year.

Starting in March 1984, Bank Street and USF solicited software donations from independent software producers on behalf of the school districts, knowing that the PSDT members and our own staff would need to be familiar with the range of available software in order to help teachers integrate computers in the curriculum. Even though the main focus of the program was on using applications software, we did not want to exclude resources which some of the participating teachers might find valuable.

Scholastic, Inc., donated 1100 copies of the *Bank Street Writer,* so that each PDC and participating school could have several copies. Many other software producers donated sample copies of their programs to each PDC; others donated single copies to BSC and USF, or loaned copies to us for examination during the workshops.[7]

Staff Development: Local Workshops

Following the spring workshops, the PSDT members went home to continue planning their summer workshops and help the schools prepare for the arrival of the computers. We recommended that they hold the workshops as early in the summer as possible so the participants would have time between the end of the workshop and the beginning of the school year to practice and to plan activities for their students.

---

[7]The following companies donated software, peripherals, and/or print materials to Bank Street College and/or the PDCs: Addison-Wesley, Alpha Software, American Peripherals, Bourbaki, CBS College Publishing, Celebrations Learning Systems, Classroom Consortia Media, Computer Access, Cross Educational Software, Digital Research, Diversified Educational Enterprises, DLM, Educational Materials and Equipment, Individual Software, Infocom, Knoware, Koala Technologies, Lifetree Software, McGraw-Hill, Microlab, Reston Computer Group, Scarborough Systems, Scholastic, SRA, Softech Microsystems, Software Publishing, Sterling Swift, Stoneware, Street Electronics, Sunburst, West Publishing.

IBM shipped two of each school's computers to the summer workshop sites so the teachers could take them home at the end of the workshop. The teachers were unanimously enthusiastic about this plan, though in some cases we needed to negotiate with district administrators to get permission for the teachers to take the computers home. With about 700 computers in the teachers' possession, no thefts and virtually no damage occurred.

Most of the four-week workshops took place in July, though a few districts with earlier summer breaks started in June. Their schedules varied considerably; most of the workshops lasted four weeks, but some were split into two-week sessions with a break of a week or two, and others lasted two or three weeks during the summer, with the remainder of the workshop time reserved for follow-up sessions during the school year.

The workshops also varied in other respects. Some local districts required the principals of the participating schools to attend the entire four-week workshop. Others held one or two workshop sessions specifically for administrators, in some cases involving the participating teachers as well. The content, presentation order, and teaching style also varied among districts.

Bank Street staff visited almost all of the summer workshops to underscore the national scope of the program, to observe, and to help in whatever ways the PSDT members requested. We also met with administrators at the building and district level to brief them on the program and to establish lines of communication. These contacts proved extremely valuable in helping the PSDT members solve subsequent problems.

At the end of the summer, we asked the PSDT members to fill out a questionnaire about the spring workshop at Bank Street and the summer workshop they had just conducted. All but one of the 14 sites with which we worked reported their summer workshops to be successful or highly successful (Zimiles, 1985). Overwhelmingly, they reported adopting the major features of the Bank Street workshop, including scheduling and organization, goals, content, focus, and teaching strategy. They also almost unanimously rated key themes of the Bank Street workshop as influencing the way they conducted their own training sessions, including the themes of building trust and giving people a sense of self-worth, cultivating a sense of ease and comfort, creating a spirit of helpfulness, using computers in many subject areas, and treating software as an adjunct to curriculum rather than an end in itself.

The following conclusions are based on field observations and interviews with PSDT members and other district staff:

☐ Dividing the workshop into a shorter summer component with follow-up workshops during the year was most effective.
☐ Including administrators in the summer workshop seemed to improve communication and cooperation on issues such as scheduling of stu-

dents and teachers, funds for maintenance and supplies, and other areas of program support.

☐ Starting with a word processor or another relatively simple, immediately useful program seemed more effective in getting the participants relaxed and "into" computers than starting with DOS or another more technical topic.

☐ Teachers were better prepared to integrate computers in the curriculum when the workshop included explicit work on curricular applications rather than information on how to use the software.

☐ The facilitative, supportive approach modeled at Bank Street and adopted by the school districts was effective in motivating teachers to take initiative and work independently. Many summer workshop participants came early and stayed late. Several commented about how well they were treated and how "professional" the workshops were.

Preparing Computer Facilities

Facilities preparation was an ongoing concern of the program from February 1984, when the first computers were delivered to Bank Street and USF, through late in the fall when the last school laboratory was set up. Technically and logistically, this was the most complex and difficult part of the project. Some of the problems were unique to a program of this type and size, but most were quite typical of facilities preparation for school-based computer projects.

We knew from our experience in consulting with local school districts and from the IBM/ETS Program that facilities preparation was an important program component (Cline et al, 1986). Before the May PSDT workshop, one of our staff members visited several New York area schools in the IBM/ETS program, and compiled a report and planning materials based on that experience (Payne, 1984). From what we learned, we conducted a session on facilities preparation during the May workshop, and followed up with each PSDT individually.

During this session, we also stressed the importance of working with the school principals to plan an appropriate schedule for lab use, including preparation time for the five program teachers. We learned from our study of the New York IBM/ETS sites that scheduling must be done in the spring, because at this time schools typically schedule students, teachers, and facilities for the following academic year.

The main problems concerning facilities preparation involved order-processing and initial equipment setup, along with the preparation of the laboratory rooms themselves. Because of the complexity of the program and the structure of the IBM ordering system (which was not designed for programs of this nature), equipment and software did not always arrive together at a precisely scheduled time; this meant that the districts needed procedures for keeping track of partial shipments and for distributing them to the schools and PDCs.

Setting up the equipment—setting internal switches in the PCs, installing boards, cabling, and attaching peripherals—was not difficult, but was time consuming. Since electronic equipment usually fails right away or not at all, some immediate malfunctions needed to be reported and repaired, and these repair problems pointed up others, with communications and with mismatches between district and IBM procedures. For example, some districts engrave markings on all incoming equipment. IBM, however, deals with some types of equipment problems by replacement, and was understandably reluctant to exchange permanently marked units for new ones.

Getting laboratory facilities prepared with proper wiring, lighting, air conditioning, furniture, and security devices often involved a considerable amount of red tape within the district. Some maintenance staffs already had work backlogs several months long, so we needed to lobby intensively with district administrators to get the work done on time. In some districts, spending freezes or court-mandated asbestos removal programs caused delays we could not prevent.

Despite everyone's best efforts, very few of the laboratories were running on the first day of school. Nevertheless, with a great deal of persistence and hard work on the part of PSDT members and with occasional Bank Street lobbying, most of the delays were short. When there were longer delays, we paid special attention to bolstering the morale and enthusiasm of the teachers by arranging for them to keep some of the equipment at home, by setting up at least some of the equipment in the schools on a makeshift basis with surplus furniture and power strips, or by holding additional workshops or brainstorming sessions at the PDC.

Telecommunications

An initial objective for the Model Schools Program was to establish a telecommunications network linking BSC, USF, the 28 PDCs, and the 140 participating schools, to be used for discussions and information-sharing among teachers and staff members and for educational purposes among students.

During spring 1984, we explored available options in telecommunications services and software. In May, we reached an agreement with CompuServe to waive membership fees, to provide accounts at a reduced educators' rate through June 1985, and to establish a private, project teleconference (which CompuServe calls a forum). In June, BSC and USF distributed applications for CompuServe accounts to all the participants, followed in July by telecommunications software and manuals explaining how to use the forum.

Some of the PDCs first came "on line" in July, but most were too busy with their summer workshops to learn about telecommunications right away. Many PDCs and some schools joined the forum during the fall, usually after a hands-on telecommunications session with a Bank Street staff member on a site visit. After the Model Schools Program conference in November, the remaining PDCs and several more schools joined the forum, and the volume of messages picked up considerably (Newman & Rehfield, 1985).

The forum was successful as an electronic mail system for the PSDT members, Bank Street, and USF. However, few ongoing discussions took place, and very few teachers and students used the forum for educational purposes (Newman & Rehfield, 1985).

One reason for the limited success of telecommunications in the program was that this topic proved difficult for the participants to learn from written materials. Even relatively sophisticated computer users had trouble, perhaps because they did not have the same intuitive bases for understanding telecommunications that they had developed in other areas of computing. If we had been able to work out the arrangements with CompuServe prior to the spring PSDT workshops, we might have provided hands-on experience at that time, but the added burden of learning telecommunications would probably have overloaded most of the PSDT members at that point.

Another reason for our limited success with telecommunications was the structure of the CompuServe forum system, which made it quite difficult to sustain ongoing discussions. Only 300 messages are stored on the system at a time, so older messages "roll off" and become lost. In addition, the structure of the forum makes it difficult to follow the thread of a particular discussion, and it has no mechanism for filing messages for later reference. As a result, users tended to answer short, informational inquiries right away, but to lose complex or more philosophical messages.

There were also problems with billings and credit which could not be satisfactorily resolved. CompuServe, like most commercial information networks, is set up to bill customers through credit cards. Schools cannot operate this way; in fact, some systems are constrained by law to pay only invoices itemized in particular ways.

Finally, in some respects the schools were not ready for telecommunications. Some districts would not allocate funds to pay for the accounts because they were not convinced of the value of telecommunications. Others refused to order accounts or telephone lines for fear that unsupervised students would run up large bills.

Despite these difficulties, the PDCs and schools which used the forum derived considerable benefit from doing so. PSDT members exchanged information and ideas on a regular basis, and some teachers and students learned about telecommunications and interacted with electronic penpals. Some of the participants also accessed other CompuServe features, such as news and stock market reports, an on-line encyclopedia, and an on-line software selection guide. (For more detailed descriptions of innovative ways to use telecommunications with students and teachers, see Bennett, 1985, and Cohen and Miyake, 1985.)

In some of the districts, the PSDT members established, independently of CompuServe, a local bulletin board system (BBS) to provide very low-cost message sharing within the district. With a local BBS, it became possible to have a single account on a national system such as CompuServe and give indirect access to it by downloading forum messages to the BBS and uploading BBS messages to the forum. We believe that this approach can alleviate many of the logistical problems of school telecommunications (Newman, 1985).

Educational Support

During the 1984–85 school year, Bank Street supported the PSDTs in their work with the local teachers and schools. At the beginning of the school year, most of our help was in mobilizing local resources for setting up labs, tracking down missing hardware and software, and providing technical assistance. As the teachers began using the labs, our work in educational support increased. We conducted site visits as requested, helping the PSDT members with in-school teacher support, attending meetings of the teacher networks, helping to maintain local administrative support, and observing the progress of the local program. We also kept in weekly contact with each PSDT, either by telephone or through telecommunications.

The districts varied considerably in their support of the project teachers after the start of the 1984–85 school year. Some districts provided very little support, either because the PSDT members were classroom teachers with little available time or district computer coordinators with little time and inadequate support staff. The districts able to provide adequate support, including regular school visits, generally achieved better results in helping teachers integrate computers in the curriculum.

Follow-Up Conferences

During the course of the program, representatives from BSC, USF, and IBM met periodically to review progress and to coordinate common features of the project; USF and Bank Street lobbied for an end-of-the-year conference for all the PSDT members, and IBM agreed to host such a conference in Atlanta in November, the early date due to budgeting constraints within IBM.

During the fall, representatives from Bank Street, USF, and the IBM Atlanta office planned the conference. Because of limited planning time and logistical constraints, we structured the conference ourselves, but we encouraged the PSDT members to help determine the content and to conduct the majority of the sessions. The conference provided an opportunity for the PSDT members who had attended spring workshops at USF to meet those who had been at Bank Street; it also provided an opportunity to share some of the classroom applications which had been developed in the districts, to learn about new hardware and software developments, and to increase skills through hands-on workshops in areas such as telecommunications.

Another focus of the conference was developing strategies for institutionalizing the Model Schools Program in the local school districts. We presented information about institutionalizing educational improvement projects (Berman & McLaughlin, 1978; Loucks-Horsley & Cox, 1984; Huberman, 1983), and engaged the PSDT members in a problem-solving session which seemed quite productive.

The Atlanta conference fostered a substantial increase in interaction among PSDT members, through visits, mail, telephone conversations, and telecommunications. Discussions at the conference laid the groundwork for four regional conferences during May 1985 and for the development of a new organization, the Council for the Integration of Technology in Education (CITE), to carry forward cooperative aspects of the program beyond the period of IBM support.

The regional conferences represented the beginning of a transition from IBM to district support and from BSC/USF to PSDT direction. A steering committee of PSDT members met to plan the conferences. IBM provided travel support for a district administrator, two PSDT members, and two local teachers from each site, and the districts absorbed most of the remaining costs; this travel support equalized the costs for each district to send representatives to the conferences. Teachers were included to demonstrate our recognition of their central role in the program and to provide a year-end activity which would enable each district to recognize the teachers who had developed especially creative classroom computer applications.

EVALUATION

In the Model Schools Program, evaluation took several forms, including monitoring program implementation, documenting activities and outcomes, identifying issues and problems for future research, and determining effectiveness. We focused our evaluation efforts on documentation and on producing formative information, and avoided summative comparisons across sites and the measurement of achievement.

We avoided comparisons for two reasons. First, we did not want to encourage competition among the participating school districts, because a program goal was to promote inter-district cooperation and information-sharing. Second, we felt that formally collecting comparative data could cause the districts to see our role as judgmental rather than facilitative. If they perceived our role as judgmental, they might be reluctant to tell us about problems, making it more difficult for us to support them during the critical early phases when many problems occurred.

We did not attempt to measure the effects of the program on student achievement—and actively discouraged the districts from doing so as well—because the project did not last long enough to make such procedures meaningful. Educational innovations typically take three to five years to implement successfully (Loucks-Horsley & Cox, 1984). During the first few years, the most appropriate role for evaluation is monitoring implementation to provide information which can serve as a basis for adjustments and fine tuning. Once the program has been implemented as originally intended, its effects on achievement can be determined. If we had attempted to assess achievement after only one year, we would not have known whether the effects we observed were due to the program we intended or to incomplete or deviant implementations.

A final reason for avoiding summative evaluation procedures was the experimental nature of the Model Schools Program. One of our original goals for the program was to encourage the districts to experiment with new approaches to integrating computers into the curriculum and to provide staff development. Under the pressure of impending evaluation, the districts might have been less willing to undertake the risks that experimentation requires (Watt, 1984).

Documentation

Documenting the Model Schools Program was especially important because of its experimental nature. As we worked with the local school districts, they transformed and adapted our themes and procedures to meet 28 different sets of local need. The mix of program features common to all sites and those which varied from site to site (see Table 13–3) provided a rich array of experiences from which to learn about the problems and possibilities of using computers in large school systems.

Because we could not know in advance which aspects of the program would be most significant, we used a variety of data collection techniques to provide as complete a record as possible: taking extensive field notes about site visits and telephone conversations with local program participants; collecting locally generated workshop and classroom materials; administering surveys and questionnaires; conducting interviews with local program participants; and maintaining an archive of project documents, correspondence, and telecommunications messages. We used these data to monitor the ongoing progress of the program, to keep the program staff informed about program activities, to formulate issues and topics for discussion and study, and to study areas in which our data and experience seemed likely to yield conclusions of general interest.

Specific documentation and evaluation activities included evaluating the national telecommunications network (Newman & Rehfield, 1985) and the

TABLE 13–3   Features that varied from site to site

Levels of local schools selected for the program: high schools, middle or junior high schools, elementary schools.

Focus on particular curriculum areas.

Positions of key local staff development personnel in the local school district hierarchy.

Aspects of the initial staff development workshop for the local teachers:
   Content, sequence of activities, teaching strategies used in the workshop.
   Scheduling
   Degree of involvement of administrative staff.

Nature and extent of follow-up staff development activities with the core project teachers.

Allocation of equipment and software to labs, classrooms, resource rooms.

Scheduling of computers for teacher and student use.

In the local project schools, degree of involvement of teachers in addition to the original five.

Degree of integration of the Model Schools Program into the overall district-wide computer-education program; degree of influence of the model schools program on the district-wide program.

Extent and types of district support for the program in the 1984–85 school year and beyond.

---

spring 1984 national workshops which we had provided for the PSDT members (Zimiles, 1985), identifying and discussing issues in educational uses of computers raised by the program (Shuller, 1985), assessing the impact of the program on the schools, and conducting case studies of program implementation in a representative sample of districts.

We evaluated the telecommunications network by collecting and analyzing all the public messages on the network, by surveying the PSDT members, and by interviewing selected users of the system. We evaluated the spring workshops in two ways—through informal "feedback" sessions during the workshops and through a questionnaire administered at the end of the summer. A useful feature of the workshop evaluation was delaying the questionnaire until after the local summer workshops: since the spring workshops were supposed to prepare the PSDT members to conduct their local summer workshops, responses at the end of the summer could reflect the longer-term practical value of the spring workshops rather than their immediate appeal.

To identify issues, we reviewed the program documentation, including field notes and correspondence, and talked informally with several PSDT members. To assess the impact of the program on the participating schools, we compared data from pre- and post-surveys about hardware, software, computer use, and staffing patterns.

During spring and fall 1985, two independent consultants conducted case studies in eight of the 28 districts.[8] These case studies were based on two-day site visits, interviews with administrators, PSDT members, and teachers, and observations in some of the schools.

Outcomes

From these various evaluation activities and data sources, we can identify several effects of the Model Schools Program on the school districts. These effects seem to fulfill most of the goals set out at the inception of the program, including enhancing cooperation and information sharing among the districts, demonstrating facilitative approaches to staff development, demonstrating the value of "model" schools, and to some extent demonstrating effective ways to integrate computers into the curriculum and using technology as a catalyst for educational innovation.

Most of the districts have shifted the focus of their computer-education programs towards integrating computers in the curriculum and towards the use of applications software, while moving away from an emphasis on programming or on the use of CAI. We believe that this shift had begun before the start of the Model Schools Program, but that the program acted as a catalyst and provided guidance needed to make the transition smoother than it otherwise might have been.

The program has also influenced how several districts view staff development. It demonstrated the importance of experimental approaches, of staff and curriculum developers working as facilitators, and of "model school" programs with in-depth staff development and extensive ongoing support.

In addition, the program appears to have strengthened many district support structures for technology in education, by helping to develop the skills of the PSDT members and by helping them to achieve or maintain leadership positions in the local district hierarchies. Furthermore, it has generated among many teachers and students interest and enthusiasm, improving morale and attendance at some of the schools.

---

[8]Case studies of Anoka-Hennepin, Burlington, Charlotte-Mecklenberg, District of Columbia, Jefferson County, Ky., Mobile, New Orleans, and Puerto Rico were conducted by Dan and Mollie Watt.

Finally, the program has developed an inter-district network of technology specialists who most probably will continue to work together. This network may prove to be a valuable resource which can help districts improve their programs at very little cost.

Has the Model Schools Program enabled the schools to integrate computer applications in the curriculum? For reasons discussed above, it is really too soon to tell. The regional conference presentations and site visit observations clearly show that some teachers have managed to develop exciting and worthwhile computer applications. Nevertheless, some experts believe that, for most teachers, managing general-purpose applications software is too difficult and time-consuming (Brady & Levine, 1985). In the next few years, the experiences of the model schools may shed some light on this issue.

SUMMARY

In this chapter, we have explored some of the processes, issues, and problems involved in planning, implementing, and evaluating a large-scale, national computer-education program. Some of the features of the IBM Model Schools Program are specific to it, but many features would apply more generally to other national efforts and to district and local school programs as well.

The use of computers in education is relatively new, and much remains to be learned about how best to use these tools in our schools. Under these circumstances, it is important to be flexible, to design programs with the expectation that we will be learning and adapting as we go along. For planning, flexibility means avoiding rigid, top-down models, and including frequent opportunities for reassessment and revision. For implementation, it means creating facilitative support structures and developing networks for communication and mutual assistance. For evaluation, it means focusing on formative procedures, thinking of evaluation as an essential part of the planning process, and finding ways to assess without stifling experimentation.

If we focus on education rather than on technology, if we use what we know about implementing educational innovations to design programs that can work, then computers and computer-education programs may help us revitalize education and make our schools better places for children to learn and grow.

REFERENCES

Bennett, R. E. (1984, November 13). Teachers reach out and touch with PCs. *PC Magazine, 3*(2), 335–337.

Bennett, R. E. (1985). *Educational telecomputing: The new frontier?* Paper presented at the annual meeting of the American Educational Research Association, Chicago, IL.

Berman, P., & McLaughlin, M. W. (1978). *Federal programs supporting educational change (Vol. VIII): Implementing and sustaining innovations.* Santa Monica, CA: Rand.

Brady, H., & Levine, M. (1985, February). Is computer education off track? An interview with Judah Schwartz. *Classroom Computer News, 5*(6), 20–24.

Center for the Social Organization of Schools. (1984). *School uses of microcomputers: Reports from a national survey* (Issue No. 5). Baltimore, MD: Johns Hopkins University.

Char, C. A. (1983). *Research and design issues concerning the development of educational software for children* (Technical Report No. 14). New York: Bank Street College of Education.

Clark, D. L., & McGibbon, S. (1982). From orthodoxy to pluralism: new views of school administration. *Phi Delta Kappan, 63*(10), 669–672.

Cline, H. F., Bennett, R. E., Kershaw, R. C., Schneiderman, M. B., Stecher, B., & Wilson, S. (1986). *The electronic schoolhouse.* Hillsdale, NJ: Lawrence Erlbaum Associates.

Cohen, M., & Miyake, N. (1985). *A worldwide intercultural network: Exploring electronic messaging for instruction.* Paper presented at the annual meeting of the American Educational Research Association, Chicago, IL.

Cremin, L. A. (1961). *The transformation of the school.* New York: Knopf.

Cuffaro, H. K. (1984). Microcomputers in education: Why is earlier better? *Teachers College Record, 85*(4), 559–568.

Dewey, J. (1902). *The child and the curriculum.* Chicago: University of Chicago Press.

Dewey, J. (1938). *Experience and education.* New York: Collier Books.

Ebisch, B. (1984, October). Trying to predict the future. Interview with Terrel H. Bell, Patricia Graham, John G. Kemeny, Herbert R. Kohl, Frank Lautenberg, Andrew R. Molnar, Seymour Papert, Ann Piestrup, Patricia Sturdivant, Joseph Weizenbaum, and Timothy E. Wirth. *Popular Computing,* 30–32, 35–36, 38, 43–44.

Freeman, C., Hawkins, J., & Char, C. (1984). *Information management tools for classrooms: Exploring database management systems* (Technical Report No. 28). New York: Bank Street College of Education.

Hord, S. M., & Loucks, S. F. (1980). *A concerns-based model for the delivery of inservice.* Austin, TX: Research and Development Center for Teacher Education, University of Texas.

Huberman, A. M. (1982, November). School improvement strategies that work: Some scenarios. *Educational Leadership, 41*(3), 23–27.

Hunter, B. (1985, May). Problem solving with databases. *The Computing Teacher, 12*(8), 20–27.

Kay, A. (1984, September). Computer software. *Scientific American, 251*(3), 52–59.

Kurland, D. M. (1983a). *Educational software tools: Designing a text editor for children* (Technical Report No. 8). New York: Bank Street College of Education.

Kurland, D. M. (1983b). *Software in the classroom: Issues in the design of effective software tools* (Technical Report No. 15). New York: Bank Street College of Education.

Lieberman, A., & Miller, L. (1984). *Teachers, their world, and their work.* Alexandria, VA: Association for Supervision and Curriculum Development.

Loucks-Horsley, S., & Cox, P. L. (1984). *It's all in the doing: What recent research says about implementation.* Paper presented at the annual meeting of the American Educational Research Association, New Orleans, LA.

Loucks-Horsley, S., & Hergert, L. F. (1985). *An action guide to school improvement.* Alexandria, VA: Association for Supervision and Curriculum Development.

McManus, J., Cannings, T., & McCall, C. (1985). *Developing instructional applications at the secondary level: The computer as a tool.* Paper presented at the annual meeting of the American Educational Research Association, Chicago, IL.

Miles, M. B. (1982, November). Unraveling the mystery of institutionalization. *Educational Leadership, 41*(3), 14–19.

Newman, D. (1984). *Functional environment for microcomputers in education* (Technical Report No. 25). New York: Bank Street College of Education.

Newman, D. (1985). *Networking systems for teacher education: Design issues.* Paper presented at the annual meeting of the Northeastern Educational Research Association, Kerhonkson, NY.

Newman, D., & Rehfield, K. (1985). *Using a national network for professional development.* Paper presented at the annual meeting of the American Educational Research Association, Chicago, IL.

Payne, C. M. (1984a). *Getting what we ask for: The ambiguity of success and failure in urban education.* Westport, CT: Greenwood.

Payne, C. M. (1984b). *Setting up a computer lab: A report on the first year's experience in NYC.* Unpublished manuscript, Bank Street College of Education, New York.

Pea, R. D. (1984). *Prospects and challenges for using microcomputers in schools* (Technical Report No. 7). New York: Bank Street College of Education.

Pea, R. D., & Kurland, D. M. (1984). *Toward cognitive technologies for writing* (Technical Report No. 30). New York: Bank Street College of Education.

Ross, A. (1984). *Making connections.* London: Council for Educational Technology.

Schneiderman, M. (1984, October). Making the case for innovation. *Popular Computing,* 88–94.

Sheingold, K., Hawkins. J., & Char, C. (1984). "I'm the thinkist, you're the typist": The interaction of technology and the social life of classrooms. *Journal of Social Issues, 40*(3), 44–61.

Sheingold, K., Hawkins, J., & Kurland, D. M. (1983). *Classroom software for the information age* (Technical Report No. 23). New York: Bank Street College of Education.

Shuller, S. M. (1984). *Notes on staff development to support technology-related programs in urban school districts.* Unpublished manuscript, Bank Street College of Education, New York.

Shuller, S. M. (1985). Implementing an innovative computer-education program in large school districts. In K. Duncan & D. Harris (Eds.), *Computers in education: Proceedings of the Fourth World Conference on Computers in Education.* Amsterdam: Elsevier.

Stecher, B. (1984, Winter). Improving computer in-service training programs for teachers. *AEDS Journal,* 95–105.

Swartz, T. F., Shuller, S. M., & Chernow, F. B. (1984). *Educator's complete guide to computers.* West Nyack, NY: Parker.

Watt, D. (1984, July). Computer evaluation cometh. *Popular Computing, 3,* 91–92, 94.

Weick, K. E. (1982). Administering education in loosely coupled schools. *Phi Delta Kappan, 63*(10), 673–676.

Zimiles, H. (1985). *Staff development in the IBM Model Schools Program: Some formative evaluation findings.* Unpublished manuscript, Bank Street College of Education, New York.

Index

Access. *See* Equal access
American Chemical Society (ACS), 117
Anderson, R. E., 172
Apple Computer Corp., 129, 203

Baird, W. E., 104, 106
Bank Street Approach, 226
Bank Street College of Education, 223,
    225, 228, 230–31, 232, 233, 234,
    235, 237, 239, 240, 241, 242, 243,
    244, 245, 246
BASIC. *See* Computer languages
Beazley, R. M., 172
Bennett, R. E., 7, 109, 184
Berman, P., 147, 149
Bibliographic Retrieval Service, 32
Billings, K., 172
Bitter, G. G., 111, 136
BRS. *See* Bibliographic Retrieval Service
BSC. *See* Bank Street College of
    Education

Camuse, R. A., 136
Change, planned, 147
Cline, H. F., 184

Community involvement, 206. *See also*
    Curriculum; Computer center;
    Programs, Computer education
CompuServe, 32, 46, 73, 243–45
Computers
    uses and roles, 26–31, 44–45
    value, 226–29
Computer center
    classroom teacher's role, 66
    community involvement, 65
    definition, 63–64
    electrical wiring, 69, 70, 72–73, 218
    environmental conditions, 73–74, 219
    establishing, 64
    furniture, 71, 199
    human resources management, 65–67
    IBM Model Schools Program, 242–43
    integrating classroom activities, 66–67
    lab setting, 111, 209–10, 228
    location, 67, 198, 218
    organization, 67–70, 199
    physical resources management,
        67–77
    planning team, 64–65, 67
    scheduling, 77

Computer center, continued
  security, 67, 76–77, 159, 198–99, 218
  space requirements, 74–76
  staff responsibilities, 65–66
  work station design, 70–72, 218
Computer languages, 27
  BASIC, 27, 82
  Logo, 27, 82, 99–100, 114–15, 116
  Pascal, 27, 82
Computer literacy, 26, 212, 220, 226–27.
    See also Resources; Teacher
    inservice training
  course, 80
  software, 27
  test, 187–89, 190–94
Computer programming. See
    Programming
Computer purchases, 1
Computer science, 27–28
Concerns-based adoption model
    (CBAM), 147
CONDUIT, 35
Consumer Reports, 216
Consumers Union, 34
Corporate Cultures, 146
Cost, 2
  analysis, 127–28, 129–40
  annual, 131–32, 138–39
  centers, 132–33
  continuing, 132
  definition, 128–29
  examples, 133–39
  ingredients approach, 129–40
  initial, 132, 133–38
  meeting, 142–43, 202–3, 203–4
  opportunity, 129, 131–32
  using cost information, 140–41
  valuing resources, 130–32
Council for the Integration of Technology
    in Education, 246
Courses, computer, 80
The Culture of the School and the
    Problem of Change, 146
Curriculum
  change, 81
  community involvement, 82, 84–85
  English and language arts, 91

equity issues. See Equal access
  goals, 82
  infusion and integration, 80, 82, 83,
    111, 211–12, 215–16, 220, 224,
    226–28, 239, 249, 250
  mathematics, 85–91
  plan, 82
  planning committee, 82
  problem-solving, 92
  program success, 205
  science, 92
  scope and sequence, 79, 83
  social studies, 91
  software ethics, 84
  teacher training, 83, 84. See also
    Teacher inservice training

Deal, T., 146
DeVault, M. V., 115
Dewey, J., 226
Don't Bother Me, I'm Learning, 210

Education Products Information
    Exchange (EPIE), 32, 33, 34, 35, 36,
    216
Education Resources Information Center
    (ERIC), 36
The Educational Software Selector
    (TESS), 32
Educational Testing Service (ETS), 195,
    196, 223
Encyclopedia Britannica, 215
EPIE. See Education Products
    Information Exchange
Equal access, 20–21, 48, 83–84, 214.
    See also Facilitating and monitoring
Equity. See Equal access
ERIC. See Education Resources
    Information Center
Esty, E. T., 172
ETS. See Educational Testing Service
Evaluation. See also Teacher inservice
    training
  advisory team, 184
  control group, 179–80, 180–81
  control group design, 180–81
  definition, 2–3, 163

design, 177–84
document analysis, 176–77
formative evaluation, 164, 246–47
framework. *See* Planning and
    evaluation
hardware evaluation. *See* Hardware
IBM Model Schools Program, 247–50
interviews, 173
longitudinal data collection, 179–80,
    182
management, 183–84
measurement, 170–77
monitoring. *See* Facilitating and
    monitoring
observations, 173–76
outcomes, 167, 169–70, 177, 249–50
questionnaires, 172–73, 241
questions, 166, 183, 184
random assignment, 179–82
rationale, 163–66, 184, 246–47
relating activities and outcomes,
    167–70
relating questions, 183
software evaluation. *See* Software
    evaluation
summative, 164–65
tests, 171–72, 187–89, 190–94
time-series design, 182–83
unanticipated outcomes, 177
user-oriented, 4–5, 164, 184
using information, 184–85, 203–4
Evaluation of Educational Software, 35
The Evaluator's Guide, 34

Facilitating and monitoring
    activities, 145
    district coordinator, 151–52
    equal access, 152–53, 158, 160
    hardware problems, 151–52, 159
    implementation, facilitating, 145–53,
        158, 230–31
    implementation, monitoring, 154–57,
        158–61, 247
    instrument, 154–57
    principal's role, 149–50
    school culture, 145–46, 202–3, 205
    school-site coordinator, 151, 152
    staff support, 160–61
    software problems, 159–60
Fisher, G., 141
Fitzgibbon, C. T., 180
Fort Knox Community Schools, 207, 208,
    209, 211, 213, 214, 215, 217, 218,
    219, 220
Fiske, J. C., 115

Glassboro State College, 115, 117
Goals, 13–19, 213–15, 226, 232
    evaluation, 166, 167, 169–70, 172–73,
        177, 241, 249–50
    teaching, 8, 12, 13–19, 28–30
Gressard, C., 105

Hall, G. E., 147
Hardware
    acquisition, 210
    arrangement. *See* Computer center
    bids, 57–58
    comparing and rating hardware,
        49–53
    disk drives, 55
    installation, 70–72, 199, 218, 243
    local-area networks (LANs), 46–47
    maintenance, 66, 75, 200, 222
    minicomputers, 47
    peripherals, 54–56
    printers, 55–56, 72, 74
    problems, 243. *See also* Facilitating
        and monitoring
    security, 217–18. *See also* Computer
        Center
    selection, 45–53, 217–18
    software considerations, 45, 215
    stand-alone microcomputers, 46
    vendors, 56–58
    video display devices, 54
Harvey, J. G., 115
Heckman, P. E., 146
Heller, R. S., 115
Houston Independent School District
    (HISD), 107
Hrelja, V., 115
Hunter, B., 172

IBM Corp. 15, 115, 195, 198, 199, 200, 202, 223, 224, 225, 232, 233, 239, 241, 245, 246
IBM Model School Computer Literacy Program, 223, 225, 226, 227, 228, 229, 230, 231, 232, 233, 234, 236, 237, 243, 244, 246, 247, 249, 250. *See also* Evaluation; IBM Secondary School Program; Staff development
IBM Secondary School Program, 115, 142, 195–96, 223, 224, 228, 242
Implementation. *See* Facilitating and monitoring
Inservice training. *See* Teacher inservice training
In Search of Excellence, 146
International Council for Computers in Education, 34, 111, 143

Joint Committee on Standards for Educational Evaluation, 3

Kershaw, R. C., 184
Killian, J. E., 105

Levin, H. M., 140, 141
Lieberman, A., 150
Lockheed, M. E., 172
Logo. *See* Computer languages
Los Angeles Unified School District, 195, 203
Loucks, S. F., 147
Loyd, B. H., 105

McLaughlin, M. W., 147, 149
Maher, C. A., 7
Martin, C. D., 115
Massat, M. E., 115
MECC. *See* Minnesota Educational Computing Corp.
MicroCourseware PRO/FILES, 34
MicroSIFT Project, 33, 34, 35, 36, 37
Miller, L., 150
Minnesota Educational Computing Corp. (MECC), 117, 215
Moore, M. L., 104, 106
Morris, L. L., 180
Moursund, D., 172

National Assessment of Educational Progress (NAEP), 1, 14
National Center for Education Statistics (NCES), 172
National Council of Teachers of Mathematics (NCTM), 104
National Institute of Education (NIE), 136
National Science Foundation, 103
National Science Teachers Association Task Force, 35
New Jersey Department of Education, 114
North Carolina Department of Public Instruction, 35
Northwest Regional Educational Laboratory, 32, 34, 35, 172

Oakes, J., 146

Pascal. *See* Computer languages
Pepperdine University, 196, 197, 199
Personnel. *See* Facilitating and monitoring; Teacher inservice training; Teachers
Planning, 2
process, 197–98, 225–26
Planning and evaluation
characteristics, 3, 9–10
content, 11
framework, 9–11
process, 5–7, 9
school, 3–4
tasks, 5–7
Planning committee, 197, 225–26. *See also* Computer center; Curriculum; Evaluation, advisory team
Programming. *See also* Teacher inservice training
languages. *See* Computer languages
teaching, 16, 17, 18–19, 27
software, 27
Program Evaluation Kit, 183
Programs
approaches, 14–16, 17
building-site, 145–46
community involvement, 9–10, 65, 82, 84–85

components, 167–70
concerns, 166
definition, 7, 8
evaluation. *See* Evaluation
facilitating. *See* Facilitating and
    monitoring
goals, 13–19, 177, 213–15, 226, 232.
    See also Evaluation, outcomes;
    Evaluation, questions; Goals
implementation, 198–203, 211–20,
    234–46
inputs, 167–68
model, 167–70
monitoring. *See* Facilitating and
    monitoring
organization, 196–97
outcomes. *See* Evaluation
philosophy, 211–13, 226–29
procedures, 167, 168–69
purpose, 13, 19–22
rationales, 13, 14, 15, 16–19
stages, 165
success factors, 240–6
teaching about computers, 8, 16–19,
    26–28
teaching with computers, 8, 12, 13–16,
    28–30
vocational preparation, 27
Project Seraphim, 117
Puerto Rico, 223
Purpose, 13
    choice, 19–22
    community involvement, 20
    effect on cost, 21
    identifying, 20–22
    statement, 21–22

Random House, 215
Resources
    audiovisual, 101–2
    books, 95–97, 98–99
    computer literacy, 96–97, 98–99
    magazines, 97–98
    newsletters, 98, 100
    programming, 95–96, 99
    software, 99–100
Resources in Computer Education, 32

Scholastic, Inc., 240
School Science and Mathematics
    Association, 104
Schneiderman, M. B., 184
Schulman, E., 115
Science Research Associates (SRA), 215
Service delivery areas, 7, 9
SIFTnet evaluation network, 34
Sirotnik, K. A., 146
Software. *See also* Teacher inservice
    training
    acquisition, 200, 215–17
    applications programs, 14–16, 30,
        196, 201–2, 227–29, 249, 250
    computer-based, 14, 211–12
    drill and practice, 28
    ethics, 84
    evaluation, 33–38, 111–12, 216
    IBM Model Schools Program, 239–40
    installation, 199
    instructional management software,
        30–31
    licensing arrangements, 37
    management, 66, 75–76, 159–60
    problem-solving, 29
    problems. *See* Facilitating and
        monitoring
    quality, 45, 216
    selection, 31–38, 215, 221
    simulation, 29
    tutorial, 28–29
    vocational, 27
    word processing, 15, 45, 201, 214,
        242
The Source, 46, 73
Staff development, 199, 160–61, 200–1,
    205, 210, 219–20, 221, 232–33. *See
    also* Curriculum; Teacher inservice
    training; Teachers IBM Model
    Schools Program, 237–39, 240–42
Stecher, B., 140, 143, 184
Support, 66, 84, 105, 149–50, 205, 231,
    233, 245. *See also* Facilitating and
    monitoring

Teachers. *See also* Facilitating and
    monitoring; Resources; Teacher
    inservice training

Teachers, continued
  computer specialist, 107
  nonspecialist, 107–9
  observations, 173–76
Teacher inservice training. *See also*
    Curriculum; Facilitating and
    monitoring; Staff Development
  applications software, 112–13
  audience, 107–9
  audiovisual materials, 122–23
  books, 123
  college programs, 125–26
  computer competence, 104, 105–9,
    110–15
  computer literacy, 104
  conduct, 109–10, 147–49, 239
  content, 110–15, 237–39
  evaluation, 241–42, 248–49
  locations, 117–18
  magazines and journals, 124–25
  needs, 105, 160–61, 219
  NSF model, 103
  objectives, 110–15, 237–39
  packages, 122
  philosophy, 213
  Professional Development Centers
    (PDCs), 223, 233, 235–36, 239,
    240, 243
  Professional Staff Development Team
    (PSDT), 234, 235–36, 237, 238,
    240–41, 242, 243, 244, 245, 246,
    248, 249
  program samples, 108, 113, 114, 116,
    119

  programming, 112, 212–13
  providers, 115, 117, 149, 219–20
  resources, 122–26
  schedules, 117–18, 150, 237, 238, 241
  software, 126
Telecommunications, 73, 110, 243–45,
  248
TESS. *See* The Educational Software
  Selector
Texas Education Agency, 36
Texas Educational Computing
  Cooperative, 117
Texas Assessment of Basic Skills, 36
Tool, computer as, 79, 81, 140, 158,
  195–96, 229. *See also* Software,
  applications

UCLA Center for the Study of
  Evaluation, 184
University of South Florida, 223, 225,
  233, 234, 235, 239, 240, 242, 243,
  244, 245, 246

Vocational preparation, 27
Voyage of the Mimi, 226

Weizenbaum, 227
Wilson, S., 184
Wisconsin Dept. of Public Instruction,
  118

Zalewski, D. L., 104, 106